..J. HAYDEN, M.D., F.R.C.P.(C)
20671 Douglas Crescent,
Langley. B.C. V3A 4B7
(604) 530-7646

PREVENTING MENTAL HEALTH DISTURBANCES IN CHILDHOOD

PREVENTING MENTAL HEALTH DISTURBANCES IN CHILDHOOD

Edited by

Stephen E. Goldston, Ed.D., M.S.P.H.
Formerly Associate Director, UCLA Preventive Psychiatry Center
Neuropsychiatric Institute
University of California, Los Angeles

Joel Yager, M.D.
Professor of Psychiatry, Director of Residency Education
Department of Psychiatry and Biobehavioral Sciences
University of California, Los Angeles

Christoph M. Heinicke, Ph.D.
Professor, Department of Psychiatry and Biobehavioral Sciences
University of California, Los Angeles

Robert S. Pynoos, M.D., M.P.H.
Associate Professor, Director, Prevention Intervention Program
in Trauma, Violence and Sudden Bereavement
Department of Psychiatry and Biobehavioral Sciences
University of California, Los Angeles

American Psychiatric Press, Inc.

1400 K Street, N.W.
Washington, DC 20005

Copyright © 1990 American Psychiatric Press, Inc., with the exception of Chapter 8, Copyright © 1989, David Shaffer; and Chapter 9, Copyright © 1987, Judith S. Wallerstein.
ALL RIGHTS RESERVED
Manufactured in the United States of America
First Edition
93 92 91 90 4 3 2 1

The paper used in this publication meets the minimum requirements of the American National Standard for Information Sciences—Permanence of Paper for Printed Library Materials, ANSI Z39.48—1984.　　∞

Library of Congress Cataloging-in-Publication Data

Preventing mental health disturbances in childhood/edited by Stephen E.
　　Goldston ... [et al.].—1st ed.
　　　　p.　　cm.
　　　"Contains in revised and expanded form the papers initially presented at
　　the First Annual UCLA National Conference on Preventive Psychiatry that
　　was convened in Santa Monica, California, on October 9–11, 1987"—Pref.
　　　Sponsored by the UCLA Preventive Psychiatry Center, and by the Dept. of
　　Psychiatry and Biobehavioral Sciences and the Dept. of Pediatrics at the
　　UCLA School of Medicine.
　　　Includes bibliographical references.
　　　ISBN 0-88048-322-9 (alk. paper)
　　　1. Mental illness—Prevention—Congresses.　2. Preventive health
　　services for children—Congresses.　I. Goldston, Stephen E.
　　II. UCLA National Conference on Preventive Psychiatry (1st: 1987: Santa
　　Monica, Calif.)
　　RJ499.P712　1990
　　618.92'8905–dc20
　　DNLM/DLC
　　for Library of Congress　　　　　　　　　　　　　　　　　89-17974
　　　　　　　　　　　　　　　　　　　　　　　　　　　　　　　　CIP

To

Beth and Lisa
Jonathan and Alison
Charlotte Levy
Marion, Victoria, Sophie, and Kate

Contents

Section III
Preventive Interventions With Older Children

Contributors

Kathleen Bacon, Ph.D.
Research Assistant, Department of Psychiatry
Columbia University, New York

Lorian Baker, Ph.D.
Research Psycholinguist, Department of Psychiatry and Biobehavioral
Sciences, University of California, Los Angeles

Leila Beckwith, Ph.D.
Professor of Pediatrics, Department of Pediatrics
University of California, Los Angeles

Nancy Brill, M.D.
Assistant Clinical Professor of Pediatrics, Department of Pediatrics,
University of California, Los Angeles

Dennis P. Cantwell, M.D.
Joseph Campbell Professor of Child Psychiatry and Director of
Residency Training in Child Psychiatry, Department of Psychiatry and
Biobehavioral Sciences, University of California, Los Angeles

Elizabeth Carlin, Ph.D.
Research Associate, Department of Psychiatry and Biobehavioral
Sciences, University of California, Los Angeles

Sarale Cohen, Ph.D.
Associate Professor of Pediatrics, Department of Pediatrics
University of California, Los Angeles

Dennis Drotar, Ph.D.
Professor, Departments of Psychiatry and Pediatrics
Case Western Reserve University, Cleveland, Ohio

Mary Fauvre, Ph.D.
Formerly Administrative Director, Child Development Service,
Department of Pediatrics, University of California, Los Angeles

Prudence Fisher, M.S.
Research Assistant, Department of Psychiatry
Columbia University, New York

Ann Garland, M.A.
Research Assistant, Department of Psychiatry
Columbia University, New York

Stephen E. Goldston, Ed.D., M.S.P.H.
Formerly Associate Director, UCLA Preventive Psychiatry Center,
Neuropsychiatric Institute, University of California, Los Angeles

Christoph M. Heinicke, Ph.D.
Professor, Department of Psychiatry and Biobehavioral Sciences,
University of California, Los Angeles

Judy Howard, M.D.
Associate Professor of Pediatrics, Department of Pediatrics
University of California, Los Angeles

Vickie Kropenske, P.H.N.
Director, UCLA Infants and Family Services Program,
Department of Pediatrics, University of California, Los Angeles

Richard D. Krugman, M.D.
Professor and Vice Chairman, Department of Pediatrics, University of
Colorado; Director, C. Henry Kempe National Center for the
Prevention and Treatment of Child Abuse and Neglect, Denver

Kathi Nader, M.S.W.
Director of Evaluations, Prevention Intervention Program in Trauma,
Violence and Sudden Bereavement, Department of Psychiatry and
Biobehavioral Sciences, University of California, Los Angeles

Robert S. Pynoos, M.D., M.P.H.
Associate Professor and Director, Prevention Intervention Program in Trauma, Violence and Sudden Bereavement, Department of Psychiatry and Biobehavioral Sciences, University of California, Los Angeles

Michael B. Rothenberg, M.D.
Professor Emeritus of Psychiatry and Behavioral Sciences and Pediatrics, University of Washington School of Medicine, Seattle

David Shaffer, M.D.
Irving Philips Professor of Child Psychiatry and Director of the Division of Child Psychiatry, Department of Psychiatry, Columbia University, New York

Anne Thompson, Ph.D.
Research Associate, Department of Psychiatry and Biobehavioral Sciences, University of California, Los Angeles

Veronica Vieland, Ph.D.
Research Fellow, Department of Psychiatry Columbia University, New York

Judith S. Wallerstein, Ph.D.
Executive Director, Center for the Family in Transition, Corte Madera, California; Senior Lecturer, School of Social Welfare, University of California, Berkeley

Joel Yager, M.D.
Professor of Psychiatry and Director of Residency Education, Department of Psychiatry and Biobehavioral Sciences, University of California, Los Angeles

Foreword

Primary care physicians in family medicine, internal medicine, and pediatrics generally endorse the need for prevention. At least some of them expend considerable effort attempting to reduce morbidity through office-based clinical preventive interventions. Unfortunately, psychiatrists, psychologists, and other mental health professionals have lagged behind in thinking about and implementing preventive programs in their clinical practices. During the past decade the theoretical and empirical literature regarding potential preventive activities in psychiatric settings has grown considerably. Nevertheless, little of this material appears significantly to have influenced clinical practice.

This volume is based on a conference on clinical mental health prevention sponsored by the UCLA Preventive Psychiatry Center. Leading experts describe practical preventive interventions for use in clinical practice, together with the research findings on which these interventions are based. UCLA has attempted to exercise leadership in fostering greater interest in prevention, and new initiatives in research and training in preventive psychiatry as well. With the assistance of an NIMH training grant, and with the establishment in 1987 of the UCLA Preventive Psychiatry Center, these critical and frequently neglected aspects of care have been strengthened at UCLA. As in other areas, faculty leaders who are enthusiastic about their work, and who stimulate the thinking of students, have crucial roles in the University's progress. By their own examples and commitment, such faculty members encourage residents and fellows to value prevention-related activities. Together with many other nationally recognized experts, these UCLA faculty leaders are well represented in this volume.

Although this book deals mainly with interventions directed toward children, we recognize that preventive psychiatry is relevant throughout the life span. Preventive efforts directed toward the elderly, minority

populations, and others subjected to particularly stressful life circumstances also merit attention. It is our hope that further work at UCLA
and elsewhere will continue to build a body of practical preventive
interventions for these and other populations, and that these strategies
will be increasingly employed by clinicians in the future.

Louis Jolyon West, M.D.
Professor
Department of Psychiatry and Biobehavioral Sciences
University of California, Los Angeles

Preface

This volume contains in revised and expanded form the papers initially presented at the First Annual UCLA National Conference on Preventive Psychiatry that was convened in Santa Monica, California, on October 9–11, 1987. The conference theme was "The Prevention of Mental Health Disturbances in Childhood." To the best of our knowledge, this conference represented an innovative effort to bring mental health and pediatric professionals together to focus on issues concerned with the promotion of mental health and the prevention of mental disorders among children.

From a historical perspective, this conference had three distinctions:

1. This event was the first national conference on preventive psychiatry to be held since the Symposium on Preventive and Social Psychiatry convened at Walter Reed Army Medical Center in Washington, D.C., in April 1957.
2. This gathering was the first national mental health prevention conference ever held west of the Potomac River.
3. This conference represented the first such enterprise cosponsored by two departments in a medical school—the Department of Psychiatry and Biobehavioral Sciences and the Department of Pediatrics at the UCLA School of Medicine. The conference was an integral aspect of the community education and consultation program of the UCLA Preventive Psychiatry Center, which was established in February 1987. The organization and management of the conference was conducted by the Department of Continuing Education in Health Sciences, UCLA Extension.

The primary objective both in planning the conference and in preparing this volume was to provide mental health and pediatric professionals with knowledge and skills derived from clinical research that would enable them to promote healthy development and adjustment, and prevent mental, emotional, and psychophysiological disturbances. The various chapters focus on preventive clinical skills to facilitate management of persons at risk for harmful psychological outcomes, and techniques to assist families in facilitating optimal child development.

In preparing their material, contributors were asked to address the following factors: conceptualization of the person-environment system considered, research evidence supporting this conceptualization, points of access for clinical preventive intervention, prevention goals, and clinical approaches for goal attainment. Within this framework, the book has been organized into three sections.

Section I provides introductory material on the conceptual and research bases for primary prevention in mental health, and a chapter on prevention needs from a broad societal perspective. Section II describes clinical preventive interventions with infants and young children. The chapters that comprise Section III address preventive interventions in response to specific stressful situations faced by older children, e.g., suicide, marital disruption, disasters, and child abuse, and the prevention of the psychiatric sequelae associated with communication disorders. Each section begins with an introduction to and commentary on the chapters within that section.

Appreciation is extended to the Bureau of Maternal and Child Health and Resources Development, Health Resources and Services Administration, U.S. Public Health Service, for partial support of the conference; Michael Fishman, M.D., served as project officer and consultant. This conference was conducted as a related program activity under a clinical prevention research training grant (MH-18380) awarded by the National Institute of Mental Health to the Neuropsychiatric Institute, University of California, Los Angeles; Joel Yager, M.D., was the training program director.

Hopefully, this volume will heighten awareness among mental health and pediatric professionals about preventive strategies and thereby enhance these professionals' overall effectiveness in serving children and their families.

Stephen E. Goldston, Ed.D., M.S.P.H.

Contextual Framework
for
Preventive Interventions

Introduction

Christoph M. Heinicke, Ph.D.

The two chapters in this section provide a contextual framework for the preventive interventions described in the remainder of the volume. In the first chapter Goldston defines the basic prevention concepts and then outlines six different prevention strategies. Countering a frequently heard stereotype that "prevention is a promissory note that has no cash value," the author documents the effectiveness of programs exemplifying the various prevention approaches.

Whereas Goldston convinces through the application of concepts and outcome studies, Rothenberg, in the second chapter, shocks us into recognition of the need for prevention in relation to public systems that either harm our children or simply fail to meet their needs. He cites overwhelming statistics while demanding change in public policy. For example, although studies have demonstrated that watching television violence increases aggressive behavior in child and adolescent viewers, the average American child will have witnessed approximately 18,000 murders on television by the time he or she is age 18.

Both authors underline the magnitude of the problems requiring prevention: the vast unmet needs of our children and the impossibility of meeting their needs through treatment. It is reasoned that prevention must be a part of the delivery of mental health and other human services. Goldston illustrates active efforts linking the various forms of prevention (primary, secondary, and tertiary) in specific programs and emphasizes the importance of training mental health professionals in preventive as well as treatment approaches. Rothenberg urges that mental health workers advocate for children's needs by directly confronting and altering those public policies that continue to have damaging effects on "our most treasured possessions."

CHAPTER 1

Some Fundamental Concepts About The Prevention of Mental and Emotional Disorders

Stephen E. Goldston, Ed.D., M.S.P.H.

Three decades ago, at the beginning of the community mental health movement in the United States, an explicit set of guidelines for the control of mental disorders was proposed to health and mental health planners (Gruenberg 1957). Based on public health theory and practice, these guidelines affirmed that first priority should be given to preventing what is preventable, second priority to terminating or arresting what can be terminated or arrested, and third priority to reducing the disability from those disorders that have not been prevented, terminated, or arrested.

These guidelines reflected historical public health triumphs and achievements, many of which had been attained on the basis of simple empirical procedures, such as specifying key linkages in the pathogenesis of a disease or observing the relationship of a disease to a specific modifiable aspect of the environment.

Nonetheless, there is little evidence that these guidelines were followed by according prevention highest priority for fiscal and staff resource allocations, research emphases, or the provision of services. While significant advances were forthcoming in the treatment and rehabilitation areas, prevention was at best an afterthought, if considered at all. Neglect of prevention was not due to the absence of a research base or ideas for program actions, but due more to the imperfect merger between the mental health enterprises and public health enterprises, each with their own unique histories, values, priorities, administrative structures, and modes of operation.

Over the past 30 years the research and knowledge base about actions that can be taken to control mental disorders has increased significantly. However, much of what is known to reduce the burden and extent of mental disorders remains unused. An unmet challenge is to apply this knowledge and to expand the scientific bases of prevention. Developing preventive services based on what is known, within existing mental health services and other community agencies and facilities, requires new perspectives, new mechanisms, and new priorities.

CONCEPTS AND DEFINITIONS

The community mental health movement, with its emphasis on community-based services rather than state hospital services, incorporated and widely utilized several key public health concepts, e.g., epidemiological approaches, statistical formulae dealing with incidence and prevalence rates, ideas about populations at risk and catchment areas for service delivery, and constructs about primary, secondary, and tertiary prevention.

This three-fold conceptualization of prevention—primary, secondary, and tertiary—was developed in the late 1940s by two physicians on the faculties of schools of public health: Hugh Leavell, professor of public health practice at Harvard University, and E. Guerney Clark, professor of epidemiology at Columbia University (Leavell and Clark 1965). Their notions about prevention were formulated in response to emerging needs for the public health field to expand beyond traditional concerns (e.g., communicable disease control and environmental sanitation) into new areas such as the provision and financing of health care. A conceptual framework was required that was both solidly grounded in public health and broad enough to encompass more expansive areas focused on the public's health. Leavell and Clark met this need for a new conceptualization of public health that formulated prevention in the following terms:

1. **Primary prevention** embraced two areas: (a) *health promotion*, involving those nonspecific actions aimed at fostering general health and well-being, such as proper nutrition; health education; attention to personality development; provision of adequate housing, recreation, and suitable working conditions; marriage counseling and sex education; genetics; and periodic examinations; and (b) *specific protection*, involving "measures applicable to a particular disease or group of diseases in order to intercept the causes of disease before they involve man," including "use of specific immunizations, attention to personal hygiene, use of environmental sanitation, protection against occupational hazards, protection from accidents, use of specific nu-

trients, protection from carcinogens, and avoidance of allergens" (Leavell and Clark 1965, p. 20).

2. **Secondary prevention** pertained to early diagnosis and prompt and effective treatment in order to halt and reverse the progression of an existing disease or disorder.
3. **Tertiary prevention** involved efforts to maximize the capacities of persons with irreversible conditions in order to limit the extent of their disability.

Subsequently, Caplan (1964) translated these public health concepts into mental health terms (see also Caplan and Grunebaum 1967). However, this tripartite framework did not enter the professional vocabulary as prevention, treatment, and rehabilitation, each a distinct area of activity. Instead, an overarching concept of prevention was created—a concept so broad and extensive as to encompass virtually all aspects of mental health work. This expansive concept of prevention, accommodating an extended range of mental health activities, has made the term prevention a virtual semantic Tower of Babel within the mental health field.

In addition to the confusion generated by the term prevention, this expanded conceptualization has hampered the development of primary prevention activities. Indeed, many endeavors labeled as prevention are not preventive at all in the sense of forestalling the onset of a condition, but are treatment aimed at halting ("preventing") the progression of an already existing disorder.

A more limited, but precise, definition of prevention was offered by the National Mental Health Association's Commission on the Prevention of Mental-Emotional Disabilities (1986, p. 9):

> Prevention means literally to keep something from happening. Within the field of mental health, it means intervening in a deliberate and positive way to counteract harmful circumstances before they cause disorder or disability. Early identification and treatment are essential mental health services, but if treatment is needed, the disability has not been prevented.

Until the concepts of prevention, treatment, and rehabilitation are more widely accepted among mental health workers, the primary, secondary, and tertiary prevention classification will endure.

Accordingly, need exists to discriminate clearly between the three levels of prevention. The statistical concepts of incidence and prevalence provide some clarification. Primary prevention is concerned with reducing the incidence, that is, the number of *new* cases of a disease or disorder within a given time period among a specified population. Prevalence refers to the *total* number of cases of a disease or disorder (both new and existing) at a particular time among a specified population

(Wilner et al. 1978). The greater the incidence or the greater the duration of a disease or disorder, the higher the prevalence. Primary prevention programs reduce prevalence by reducing incidence, while secondary and tertiary prevention programs reduce prevalence by reducing the duration of a disease or disorder (Bloom 1984, p. 197).

Preventionists debate where the boundaries of primary prevention halt and secondary prevention begins. For example, some primary prevention advocates maintain that crisis intervention and telephone hotlines are secondary, not primary, prevention activities because the recipients of such services have manifested signs and symptoms of disorder. Other preventionists posit that persons seen in a crisis intervention service are experiencing a transition, not a psychiatric disorder, and that the intervention occurs prior to the onset of a diagnosable disorder.

Increasingly over the past decade, many activities have been labeled prevention, whereas only a fraction appear to merit being classified as *primary* prevention. Mislabeling projects and redefining prevention for political purposes serve to "trivialize the concept of prevention" (Goldston 1986). One consequence is that many mental health workers remain confused about prevention and assert that their treatment of patients during the acute phase of a diagnosed disorder "prevents" the onset of a chronic disturbance. Such distorted and misleading claims tend to subvert efforts to secure resources and legitimacy for primary prevention activities.

MAGNITUDE OF THE PROBLEM OF MENTAL DISORDERS

Data from the National Institute of Mental Health (NIMH) Epidemiologic Catchment Area Program reveal that "15.4% of the population 18 years of age and over fulfilled criteria for at least one alcohol, drug abuse, or other mental disorder during the period one month before interview," with the rates increasing to 19.1% for a 6-month prevalence, and to 32.2% for a lifetime prevalence (Regier et al. 1988). Thus, almost one-third of all Americans experience an acute mental illness at some point in their lives. Based on the 6-month prevalence figure and a national population of 245 million, it is estimated that about 47 million persons in the United States have a diagnosable mental disorder.

Albee (1987) has calculated that another 6–7 million persons are classified as mentally deficient or retarded, while countless millions have physical conditions resulting from stress, such as hypertension. In addition, many millions experience an acute emotional upset as a consequence of life crises, e.g., marital disruption (Bloom et al. 1978), bereavement (Osterweis et al. 1984), and involuntary unemployment

(Brenner 1977). Kramer, in pointing out "the pandemic of mental disorders" (1983, p. 13), stated that ". . . the number of cases of mental disorder will continue to increase until effective methods are discovered for preventing their occurrence and equally effective and practical methods are found for their [the methods'] application" (1981, p. 27).

Not even one person in eight who needs mental health treatment services is seen by a mental health professional (Albee 1987). In 1980 Kiesler estimated that there were about 45,000 psychiatrists and psychologists in clinical practice in the United States, and that the total time available for therapy yearly by all licensed or certified practitioners approximated 40 million hours. Using those personnel estimates, Albee (1987) calculated that if even 34 million persons were in therapy, each would be seen about 72 minutes a year!

Prevention, not treatment, would appear to be the only feasible alternative to reduce the extent of mental disorder.

PRIMARY INTERVENTION

SOME FUNDAMENTAL PREVENTION NOTIONS

Among the basic ideas that underlie the foundation of primary prevention are the following notions (Goldston 1987, pp. 5–6):

1. Stress-inducing factors in the social environment affect people's mental health status. From a public health perspective, stress, like other foci of infection, can be identified and either reduced or eliminated.
2. A community's mental health or ill-health is revealed in its institutions, and key community agents such as teachers, police, and clergy, among others, have major impacts on the mental health status of a community.
3. Increasing knowledge about stressful life events has resulted in a growing emphasis on precipitating factors (the here-and-now life stress situation faced by an individual) rather than a focus on predisposing (developmental) factors in psychopathology (Bloom 1985).
4. Crisis theory and crisis intervention approaches offer a basis for understanding and anticipating stress points, as well as a framework for developing preventive interventions.
5. Mental health clinicians have the potential to perform a variety of preventive functions, e.g., consultation, mental health education, community organization, training of key community agents and caregivers, and prevention policy development.

These basic ideas emerge out of a commonly shared ideology about community mental health that affirms the following (Goldston 1977b, p. 25):

1. A commitment to raising the level of mental health of the *entire* community, not just the psychiatric casualties who appear at the doors of mental health facilities seeking direct treatment services.
2. An involvement in community institutions and systems, with an awareness that the mental health enterprise is but one among many service agencies concerned with the community's mental health.
3. The relevance of such public health concepts and practices as populations at risk, incidence rates, and epidemiological techniques and analyses. Two other public health concepts are integral to this common ideology: (a) No condition has been controlled or prevented only by treating the victims; community-wide approaches are required to effect control. (b) Prevention efforts require identifying a community's strengths, not just its pathology.

INTERVENTION STRATEGIES

In practice, primary prevention involves developing and conducting interventions that are designed (a) to prevent the occurrence of otherwise probable negative psychological outcomes, and/or (b) to train skills and competencies that help to build psychological health and serve as inoculants against psychological dysfunction (Cowen 1985, 1987).

Primary preventive interventions have some common characteristics (Cowen 1982, 1987):

1. They deal with well people prior to the onset of maladjustment.
2. They are usually directed to groups, not individuals.
3. They use educational and building approaches, not healing or repairing modalities.
4. They have the quality of "intentionality," that is, a planful goal, based on theory or research, of promoting psychological health or preventing maladaptation.

Within this framework six preventive intervention strategies are presented below (Cowen 1986). These strategies are not mutually exclusive, and in practice, depending on program design and operation, two or more strategies may be used in a single program.

Mental Health Promotion

The first strategy, mental health promotion, has two major approaches. The first approach is *skill or competence acquisition*. Research evidence demonstrates that certain life skills or competencies relate to healthy adjustment. Indeed, findings that clinical and maladjusted groups have been shown consistently to be deficient in such abilities support the view that these skills somehow mediate adjustment. Examples of such skills include the abilities to resolve interpersonal problems, plan ahead and set realistic goals, take the role of the other, and assert oneself when appropriate. These skills are teachable, particularly to young children. Programs that convey such skills to relevant target groups have the ultimate goal of increasing autonomy and/or self-reliance, strengthening adjustment, and/or reducing the occurrence or impact of maladaptive conditions.

Researchers at Hahnemann University (Spivack et al. 1976) showed that clinical and maladjusted individuals, across age levels, sociodemographic strata, and settings, were deficient in an interrelated cluster of interpersonal cognitive problem-solving (ICPS) skills such as the ability to recognize feelings, to generate alternative solutions to interpersonal problems, to take the role of the other, to identify alternative consequences of behavior, and to specify means-ends relationships. These findings suggested that teaching these skills to young children might enhance their adjustment. Subsequently, relevant curricula were developed and taught to inner-city preschoolers (Spivack and Shure 1974).

The above findings indicated that (a) trained children significantly exceeded controls in acquiring the program's targeted skills; (b) the children's adjustment, especially among those with initial problems of inhibition and maladjustment, also improved significantly; and (c) direct associations were shown between the cognitive and adjustive gains (Shure and Spivack 1982).

From a primary prevention perspective, the importance of this research is that young children's psychological problems were reduced and their adjustment advanced, not by engaging problems after they occurred in individuals, but by implementing a proactive training program for all children, designed to impart developmentally relevant competencies.

Spivack and Shure (1985) have summarized the relevance of their research to mental health in the following terms:

> If educators and clinicians have assumed that relieving emotional tension paves the way for one to think straight, our research would test the reverse idea: that ability to think straight can pave the way for emotional relief. (p. 230)

The second approach in the mental health promotion strategy is *mental health education*. This approach covers a range of activities that seek to promote adjustment by helping people to acquire new knowledge, attitudes, and behavioral skills to optimize their psychological well-being. The rationale for mental health education is supported by "data showing linkages between lack of knowledge, misinformation, and inappropriate attitudes on the one hand, and negative adjustment outcomes on the other" (Cowen 1987, p. 34).

Muñoz and his colleagues (1982) used the mass media, namely, a series of 10 4-minute televised segments over the course of a 2-week period, in an effort to prevent depression. Viewers indicated they (a) took more time than nonviewers to relax, (b) thought fewer negative thoughts, and (c) thought more of specific ways to avoid getting depressed. Among respondents with initially high depression levels, viewers' depression scores dropped significantly more than did those of nonviewers after the television series.

Transitional Life Crises and/or Stressful Life Events

A second strategy is preventive programs for transitional life crises and/ or stressful life events. Clear associations have been shown between several environmental and life stresses and maladaptation. Stressors include death and bereavement, marital disruption, involuntary unemployment, natural disasters, and major transitions (e.g., starting school, transferring to a new school, and birth of a sibling). Preventive interventions provide information, coping skills, support, and resources to strengthen adaptation and to obviate maladaptive psychological outcomes (Cowen 1985).

Studies have demonstrated the effectiveness of preventive interventions directed toward (a) newly separated and divorcing adults (Bloom 1988; Bloom and Hodges 1988); (b) children in families undergoing divorce (Pedro-Carroll and Cowen 1985); (c) adults who have experienced two or more critical life events (Roskin 1982); (d) adolescents undergoing the transition from junior high to high school (Felner and Adan 1988); (e) young children facing unknown, anxiety-provoking medical, dental, and surgical procedures (Melamed and Bush 1986); and (f) newly bereaved women participating in widow-to-widow programs (Silverman 1988).

Support Systems

The third preventive strategy involves support systems. The existing knowledge base suggests that (a) the absence of significant psychological support is a factor that seems to differentiate well people from poorly adjusted people; (b) troubled people tend to use natural, accessible support sources much sooner and more often than they use formal professional helping outlets; and (c) in some sectors of society, natural support is de facto the only form of help available to people in distress (Cowen 1985). Early preventive interventions built on this knowledge base can be developed, as for example: (a) developing support groups designed to strengthen coping and adjustment, and to prevent problems in at-risk groups, such as people experiencing divorce or bereavement, school transfer, or moving to a new community; and (b) promoting the development of natural support and mutual help groups in neighborhoods characterized by isolation, fragmentation, and anomic reactions, in order to strengthen residents' resources, self-image, and functioning, and/or to reduce depression and feelings of isolation (Cowen 1987).

For example, the effectiveness of Silverman's (1988) widow-to-widow program has been evaluated (Vachon et al. 1980). This intervention involved trained widow helpers providing recently bereaved widows with support and assistance on such matters as finances, insurance, housing, and social services. Results showed that participants were better adjusted than controls at 24 months following the intervention.

Creation of Psychologically Healthy Settings

A fourth strategy involves creating psychologically healthy settings. Relationships have been demonstrated between attributes of the environment and psychological or adjustive outcomes. Consistent, strong associations have been shown between the lack of adequate living conditions, nourishment, education, and life opportunities, and indices of maladjustment (Cowen 1987). Preventive interventions have been designed to explore environmental qualities, structures, and routines in order to increase adjustment and reduce psychological problems.

Moos and his colleagues (Insel and Moos 1974; Moos 1984) have developed sensitive, reliable measures of nine different types of social environments, e.g., work settings, military units, class environments, and hospital wards. Their research has explored relationships between environmental qualities and inhabitants' behavior and adaptations. Interventions have engineered environments to foster positive interactions, interdependence, and prosocial behavior, based on the premise that the promotion of environments that enhance competence will also prevent the occurrence of problems.

Research has demonstrated the positive results from modifying pediatric hospital practices to make services more humane, to help staff be more responsive to patient needs, to encourage parental involvement with their hospitalized youngster, to establish open visiting hours, to abolish age restrictions for visitors, and to implement psychological preparation programs prior to hospital admission—all actions that contribute to making the hospital environment more psychologically healthy, with positive outcomes redounding to patients, parents, and staff, as well as to the institution (Shore and Goldston 1978).

Prevention of Maladaptive Outcomes in High-Risk Conditions

The fifth strategy calls for preventing maladaptive outcomes in high-risk conditions. The offspring in multirisk problem families are especially vulnerable to maladaptive outcomes (Greenspan 1981). Early interventions for at-risk groups (e.g., the infants of unmarried teenagers, and children in families with severe parental pathology) are designed to strengthen coping skills and adjustment and to obviate adverse psychological outcomes.

Preventive interventions have been designed and tested that address "families' survival needs, provide support and a trusting relationship, and offer family training and specific, individualized clinical services to help children master relevant cognitive, social, and sensorimotor tasks" (Cowen 1986, p. 16). Infant mental health/psychiatry programs to prevent parenting disorders have proliferated in the past decade (Greenspan 1982; Osofsky 1986).

Prevention of Specific Psychopathologies or Disorders

The sixth strategy may also be perceived as an objective, namely, preventing specific psychopathologies or disorders. The present knowledge base suggests that certain constitutional factors and environmental variables, including life conditions and circumstances, may be associated with adverse psychological outcomes. Preventive interventions are constructed on this knowledge base and then tested out with groups known epidemiologically to be at risk for negative outcomes.

The first *Diagnostic and Statistical Manual of Mental Disorders*, published in 1952 (American Psychiatric Association), listed 60 types and subtypes of mental illness. The third edition of this manual, published in 1980 (American Psychiatric Association), reported 230 separate conditions. As presently classified, some mental disorders are preventable.

Several preventive intervention research studies have focused on preventing depression (Muñoz 1987; Lewinsohn 1987). Tableman and her colleagues (Tableman 1987) conducted a life-coping skills program for women on public assistance, designed to increase self-esteem and teach life planning and stress management strategies. Ten weeks of training resulted in significant changes in scores on measures of depression, psychological distress, anxiety, inadequacy, ego strength, and self-confidence.

As this brief review of preventive intervention strategies demonstrates, a body of knowledge about tested, well-evaluated preventive interventions exists—interventions that are ready to be adapted, adopted, and replicated (Price et al. 1988; Cowen 1982).

COST-EFFECTIVENESS OF PREVENTIVE INTERVENTIONS

Few studies have been conducted on the cost-effectiveness of either preventive interventions or psychotherapy. Nonetheless, skeptics about prevention often demand that prevention be held to a higher standard of efficacy and proof than treatment (Albee 1986). Given that funds for preventive intervention research have always been in short supply, it is no wonder there has been a paucity of studies of the cost-effectiveness of prevention.

Two meta-analytic studies reveal that brief psychoeducational interventions may be cost-effective with medical and surgical patients because the length of hospital stay is reduced. Mumford et al. (1982) reported on 13 studies using hospital days postsurgery or postheart attack as outcome indicators; on the average, psychoeducational interventions reduced hospitalization by approximately 2 days. Interventions included educational methods to provide patients with information about their condition and its likely course, as well as "approaches intended to provide reassurance, to soften irrational beliefs, or in general to offer emotional support and relieve anxiety" (pp. 142–143). Devine and Cook (1983) reviewed 49 studies dealing with the relationships between brief psychoeducational interventions and the length of postsurgical hospitalization; findings revealed that interventions reduced hospital stay by about 1¼ days.

Detailed cost-benefit data from the High/Scope Perry Preschool Program demonstrate the long-term effectiveness of a preschool intervention for youngsters at risk of school failure 14 years after the children had completed the program (Schweinhart and Weikart 1988). For every dollar invested in a 1-year program, six dollars was returned; for the 2-year program the ratio was three dollars returned for every dollar invested. The investigators summarized their findings:

> The total benefits to taxpayers for the program . . . were about $28,000 per participant, about six times the size of the annual program operation cost of $5,000 per participant. For each program participant, taxpayers saved about $5,000 for special education programs, $3,000 for crime, and $16,000 for welfare assistance. . . . Because of increased lifetime earnings (predicted because of more years of school completed), the average participant was expected to pay $5,000 more in taxes. (Schweinhart and Weikart 1988, p. 2061)

ROLE OF THE CLINICIAN IN PREVENTION

Two major obstacles appear to stand in the way of advancing prevention programming in community mental health settings: (a) Most mental health workers lack formal training in prevention. (b) With few exceptions, prevention has not been integrally related to a mental health agency's clinical program. Typically, prevention, if it exists at all, has been appended or loosely grafted onto an agency's program. This need not be the case, as the following approaches to these obstacles indicate.

UCLA CLINICAL PREVENTION TRAINING PROGRAM

Identifying opportunities in clinical situations is a challenge. As Hollister (1977) has pointed out, clinical prevention activities that involve the prevention of specific behaviors, role failures, relationship breakdowns, overreactions, and disabilities, can be carried out by clinicians in their work with individuals and families either before (primary prevention) or after disability has occurred (seondary or tertiary prevention).

The Neuropsychiatric Institute at the University of California, Los Angeles (UCLA), focused on this issue during 1985–1988 in connection with an NIMH clinical prevention research training grant (Yager 1985). This grant program called for incorporating ongoing preventive intervention research findings and methods into the clinical education of psychiatric residents and fellows and psychology interns.

The themes emphasized in the clinical prevention training program included the following:

1. Identifying risk factors such as trauma, poor parenting, and developmental problems that may place a child or adolescent at risk for specific disturbances.
2. Providing early access to and intervention with children and adolescents who were exposed to trauma or are experiencing developmental problems.
3. Teaching techniques for working with traumatized or bereaved children and adolescents, including correction of cognitive confusions and affective constriction, and new coping skills.
4. Intervening with parents and family to enhance communication, recognize traumatic responses and grief reactions, and teach parenting skills.
5. Intervening with teachers, school health and mental health professionals, pediatricians, and others in the child's social and community environment.

With respect to attitudes, by the end of training, residents, fellows, and interns were expected to achieve the following:

1. Think preventively and be expected to anticipate opportunities for preventive intervention in all clinical encounters.
2. Realize that with proper assessment and preventive techniques, interventions at an early stage can provide acute relief rather than traumatization and/or psychopathology.
3. Appreciate that intervention should occur at various levels, namely, the child, family, school, job, medical network, and social network.

In developing a knowledge base, residents, fellows, and interns were exposed to the following subject areas:

1. Psychiatric epidemiology
2. Principles of primary, secondary, and tertiary prevention
3. Proximal and distal effects of psychic trauma
4. Preventive intervention for bereavement, trauma, and pathological grief reactions
5. Risk factors, including developmental factors, that are predictive of psychopathology
6. Problems of children with psychotic parents
7. Life events, coping, and psychiatric illness
8. The effects of divorce, joblessness, alcoholism, and drug abuse on family mental health

As for skills, by the end of training, psychiatric residents were able to conduct the following interventions:

1. Grief and bereavement interventions
2. Assessment and brief interventions with children, adolescents, and adults who have been victims of psychic trauma, violence, and/or sexual abuse
3. Psychoeducational interventions with families having a schizophrenic member

Widespread inclusion of such preventive content in psychiatric training and psychology internship training should serve to advance prevention while reducing general indifference and misinformation about prevention.

LINKING PRIMARY AND OTHER LEVELS OF PREVENTION

The second obstacle to prevention programs at the local level is the need to integrate prevention with the mental health agency's clinical programs.

Opportunities exist to develop preventive interventions that incorporate multiple levels of prevention—that is, various combinations of linking primary with secondary or tertiary prevention. Such linkages make sense from prevention and treatment perspectives, and they serve to integrate primary prevention concerns with the predominant clinical interests and priorities of mental health service agencies and their staffs. Moreover, multilevel prevention approaches demonstrate that primary prevention strategies can be a useful adjunct to clinical practice, thereby optimizing clinicians' overall effectiveness.

Examples of such linkages illustrate the point:

1. Psychoeducational interventions focused on families in which a young adult member has been hospitalized for mental illness (usually schizophrenia) provide an opportunity to inform and educate family members about the disorder and about their roles in reducing the level of expressed emotion (Leff and Vaughn 1985), and facilitating the patient's recovery. For the participating family members, such interventions reduce the stress (primary prevention), while for the patient such actions are part of the rehabilitative process (tertiary prevention).
2. New mothers and fathers who are being treated for existing mental and emotional disorders, and who lack the emotional and cognitive resources to conduct their parenting responsibilities effectively, can benefit from participating in parent education and relationship enhancement interventions (primary prevention) linked to their treatment regimen (secondary prevention).
3. Educational programs about contraceptives and family planning services (primary prevention) can be directed to both female inpatients of childbearing ages prior to hospital furloughs or discharge, and male patients as part of an overall treatment program (secondary and tertiary prevention) (Lieberman 1964; Abernethy and Grunebaum 1972).
4. Developing primary preventive interventions aimed at the children of severely mentally ill parents as an integral part of mental health treatment services for all affected family members offers another opportunity to implement appropriate levels of prevention (Goodman 1984).

CONCLUDING NOTE

A major unfinished task involves educating and informing mental health practitioners, faculty role models, and students in professional training programs about the growing knowledge base for prevention research and practice, as well as about opportunities to involve themselves in preventive interventions. This challenge was boldly set forth by Bloom (1986) in the following terms:

> I urge practitioners who are considering how to identify a mental disorder worthy of being prevented to adopt a general principle: If it is a condition that mental health professionals would treat, then it is a condition that we have an equal opportunity to prevent. (p. 9)

REFERENCES

Abernethy VD, Grunebaum H: Toward a family planning program in psychiatric hospitals. Am J Public Health 62:1638–1646, 1972

Albee GW: Advocates and adversaries of prevention, in A Decade of Progress in Primary Prevention. Edited by Kessler M, Goldston SE. Hanover, NH, University Press of New England, 1986, pp 309–332

Albee GW: The rationale and need for primary prevention, in Concepts of Primary Prevention: A Framework for Program Development. Edited by Goldston SE. Sacramento, CA, California Department of Mental Health, 1987, pp 7–19

American Psychiatric Association: Diagnostic and Statistical Manual of Mental Disorders. Washington, DC, American Psychiatric Association, 1952

American Psychiatric Association: Diagnostic and Statistical Manual of Mental Disorders, 3rd Edition. Washington, DC, American Psychiatric Association, 1980

Bloom BL: Community Mental Health: A General Introduction, 2nd Edition. Monterey, CA, Brooks/Cole, 1984

Bloom BL: Stressful life events theory and research: implications for primary prevention (DHHS Publ No ADM-85-1385). Washington, DC, U.S. Government Printing Office, 1985

Bloom BL: Primary prevention: an overview, in Primary Prevention in Psychiatry: State of the Art. Edited by Barter JT, Talbott SW. Washington, DC, American Psychiatric Press, 1986

Bloom BL: University of Colorado separation and divorce program: a program manual (DHHS Publ No ADM-88-1556). Washington, DC, U.S. Government Printing Office, 1988

Bloom BL, Hodges WF: The Colorado separation and divorce program: a preventive intervention program for newly separated persons, in Fourteen Ounces of Prevention: A Casebook for Practitioners. Edited by Price RH, Cowen EL, Lorion RP, et al. Washington, DC, American Psychological Association, 1988, pp 153–164

Bloom BL, Asher SJ, White SW: Marital disruption, a stressor: a review and analysis. Psychol Bull 85:867–894, 1978

Brenner MH: Personal stability and economic security. Soc Policy 8:2–4, 1977

Caplan G: Principles of Preventive Psychiatry. New York, Basic Books, 1964

Caplan G, Grunebaum H: Perspectives on primary prevention: a review. Arch Gen Psychiatry 17:331–346, 1967

Cowen EL: The special number: a compleat roadmap, in Research in Primary Prevention in Mental Health. Edited by Cowen EL. Am J Community Psychol 10:239–250, 1982

Cowen EL: Person-centered approaches to primary prevention in mental health: situation-focused and competence-enhancement. Am J Community Psychol 13:31–48, 1985

Cowen EL: Primary prevention in mental health: ten years of retrospect and ten years of prospect, in A Decade of Progress in Primary Prevention. Edited by Kessler M, Goldston SE. Hanover, NH, University Press of New England, 1986, pp 3–45

Cowen EL: Research on primary prevention interventions: programs and applications, in Concepts of Primary Prevention: A Framework for Program Development. Edited by Goldston SE. Sacramento, CA, California State Department of Mental Health, 1987, pp 33–50

Devine EC, Cook TD: A meta-analytic analysis of effects of psychoeducational interventions on length of postsurgical hospital stay. Nurs Res 32:267–274, 1983

Felner RD, Adan AM: The school transitional environmental project: an ecological intervention and evaluation, in Fourteen Ounces of Prevention: A Casebook for Practitioners. Edited by Price RH, Cowen EL, Lorion RP, et al. Washington, DC, American Psychological Association, 1988, pp 111–122

Goldston SE: Current state of the art in primary prevention: an overview. Paper presented at the Primary Prevention Working Conference, National Council of Community Health Centers, Tucson, AZ, October 1977a

Goldston SE: An overview of primary prevention programing, in Primary prevention: an idea whose time has come (DHEW Publ No ADM-77-447). Edited by Klein DC, Goldston SE. Washington, DC, U.S. Government Printing Office, 1977b, p 25

Goldston SE: Primary prevention: historical perspectives and a blueprint for action. Am Psychol 41:453–460, 1986

Goldston SE: Introductory remarks: some basic ideas, in Concepts of Primary Prevention: A Framework for Program Development. Edited by Goldston SE. Sacramento, CA, California Department of Mental Health, 1987, pp 1–6

Goodman SH: Children of disturbed parents: the interface between research and intervention. Am J Community Psychol 12:663–687, 1984

Greenspan SI: Psychopathology and Adaptation in Infancy and Early Childhood: Principles of Clinical Diagnosis and Preventive Intervention (Clinical Infant Report No 1). New York, International Universities Press, 1981

Greenspan SI: Developmental morbidity in infants in multi-risk-factor families. Public Health Rep 97:16–23, 1982

Gruenberg EM: Application of control methods to mental illness. Am J Public Health 47:944–952, 1957

Hollister WG: Basic strategies in designing primary prevention programs, in Primary prevention: an idea whose time has come (DHEW Publ No ADM-77-447). Edited by Klein DC, Goldston SE. Washington, DC, U.S. Government Printing Office, 1977

Insel PM, Moos RH: Psychosocial environments: expanding the scope of human ecology. Am Psychol 29:179–188, 1974

Kiesler CA: Mental health policy as a field of inquiry for psychologists. Am Psychol 35:1066–1080, 1980

Kramer M: The increasing prevalence of mental disorders. Implications for the future. Paper presented at the National Conference on the Elderly Deinstitutionalized Patient in the Community, National Institute of Mental Health, May 1981

Kramer M: The continuing challenge: the rising prevalence of mental disorders, associated chronic diseases and disabling conditions. Am J Soc Psychiatry 3:13–24, 1983

Leavell HR, Clark EG: Preventive Medicine for the Doctor in His Community, 3rd Edition. New York, McGraw-Hill, 1965

Leff J, Vaughn C: Expressed Emotion in Families: Its Significance for Mental Illness. New York, Guilford Press, 1985

Lewinsohn PM: The coping-with-depression course, in Depression Prevention: Research Directions. Edited by Muñoz RF. Washington, DC, Hemisphere, 1987, pp 159–170

Lieberman EJ: Preventive psychiatry and family planning. J Marriage Fam 26:471–477, 1964

Melamed BG, Bush JP: Parent-child influences during medical procedures, in Crisis Intervention With Children and Families. Edited by Auerbach SM, Stolberg AL. Washington, DC, Hemisphere, 1986, pp 123–146

Moos RH: Context and coping: toward a unifying conceptual framework. Am J Community Psychol 12:5–23, 1984

Mumford E, Schlesinger HJ, Glass GV: The effects of psychological intervention on recovery from surgery and heart attacks: an analysis of the literature. Am J Public Health 72:141–151, 1982

Muñoz RF: Depression Prevention: Research Directions. Washington, DC, Hemisphere, 1987

Muñoz RF, Glish M, Soo-Hoo T, et al: The San Francisco mood project: preliminary work toward the prevention of depression. Am J Community Psychol 10:317–329, 1982

National Mental Health Association, Commission on the Prevention of Mental-Emotional Disabilities: The Prevention of Mental-Emotional Disabilities. Alexandria, VA, National Mental Health Association, 1986

Osofsky J: Perspectives on infant mental health, in A Decade of Progress in Primary Prevention. Edited by Kessler M, Goldston SE. Hanover, NH, University Press of New England, 1986, pp 181–201

Osterweis M, Solomon F, Green M: Bereavement: Reactions, Consequences, and Care. Washington, DC, National Academy Press, 1984

Pedro-Carroll JL, Cowen EL: The children of divorce intervention project: an investigation of the efficacy of a school-based prevention program. J Consult Clin Psychol 53:603–611, 1985

Price RH, Cowen EL, Lorion RP, et al (eds): Fourteen Ounces of Prevention: A Casebook for Practitioners. Washington, DC, American Psychological Association, 1988

Regier DA, Boyd JH, Burke JD, et al: One-month prevalence of mental disorders in the United States: based on five epidemiologic catchment area sites. Arch Gen Psychiatry 45:977–986, 1988

Roskin M: Coping with life changes: a preventive social work approach. Am J Community Psychol 10:331–340, 1982

Schweinhart LJ, Weikart DB: The High/Scope Perry preschool program, in Fourteen Ounces of Prevention: A Casebook for Practitioners. Edited by Price RH, Cowen EL, Lorion RP, et al. Washington, DC, American Psychological Association, 1988, pp 53–65

Shore MF, Goldston SE: The mental health aspects of pediatric care: historical review and current status, in Psychological Management of Pediatric Problems. Edited by Magrab PR. Baltimore, MD, University Park Press, 1978, pp 15–31

Shure MB, Spivack G: Interpersonal problem-solving in young children: a cognitive approach to prevention. Am J Community Psychol 10:341–356, 1982

Silverman PR: Widow-to-widow: a mutual help program for the widowed, in Fourteen Ounces of Prevention: A Casebook for Practitioners. Edited by Price RH, Cowen EL, Lorion RP, et al. Washington, DC, American Psychological Association, 1988, pp 175–186

Spivack G, Shure MB: Social Adjustment of Young Children. San Francisco, CA, Jossey-Bass, 1974

Spivack G, Shure MB: ICPS and beyond: centripetal and centrifugal forces. Am J Community Psychol 13:226–243, 1985

Spivack G, Platt JJ, Shure MB: The Problem-Solving Approach to Adjustment. San Francisco, CA, Jossey-Bass, 1976

Tableman B: Stress management training: an approach to the prevention of depression in low-income populations, in Depression Prevention: Research Directions. Edited by Muñoz RF. Washington, DC, Hemisphere, 1987, pp 171–184

Vachon M, Lyall WA, Rogers J, et al: A controlled study of a self-help intervention for widows. Am J Psychiatry 137:1380–1384, 1980

Wilner DM, Walkley RP, O'Neill EJ: Introduction to Public Health, 7th Edition. New York, Macmillan, 1978

Yager J: NIMH clinical training/human resource development: R & D prevention research utilization grant application. UCLA Neuropsychiatric Institute, Los Angeles, CA, 1985

CHAPTER 2

Child Advocacy: Using Public Policy to Prevent Mental Illness

Michael B. Rothenberg, M.D.

We Americans idealize and romanticize our children as much as any other people on earth. Yet for over 200 years the child in America has been exploited mainly as a producer—first on the farm, then in our factories, and currently as a cognitive whiz.

I would like to share my thoughts about seven systems in our society, in each of which I am convinced the most basic needs of many of our children are unmet. My thesis is that our failure to meet those basic needs puts millions of youngsters in this country at very high risk for the development of every conceivable kind of emotional and mental disorder, and indeed produces emotional and mental disorder in thousands of children every year.

THE MASS MEDIA

The average American child will have witnessed approximately 18,000 murders on television by the time he or she has graduated from high school at age 18. That child will also have witnessed countless episodes of robbery, beating, arson, rape, and other violence. And during that time, that youngster will have been exposed to approximately 350,000 commercials on television alone—60% of those commercials being for edible

I gratefully acknowledge the superb editorial assistance of my wife, Jo Rothenberg, in preparing this manuscript from an audiotape transcription of an oral presentation entitled "Child Advocacy: Using Public Policy to Prevent Mental Illness," presented at the First Annual UCLA National Conference on Preventive Psychiatry on October 9, 1987.

materials, and 55% of those edible materials being heavily sugared sweet stuffs such as candy, cookies, cakes, and sweet drinks. In fact, that youngster will have spent 15,000 hours in front of the television set, compared to only 11,000 hours in school.

In 1972, after a long period of study, a U.S. Surgeon General's Scientific Advisory Committee issued a six-volume report on the effects of television violence on children and youth. The Committee concluded that watching television violence increased aggressive behavior in child and adolescent viewers; that child and adolescent viewers could and did learn and remember new forms of aggressive behavior; and, contrary to the hypothesized catharsis theory (i.e., if you were to watch enough of other people committing mayhem, you would not have to commit it yourself), that watching violence increased the desire for and perpetration of violence by the viewer. And finally, the Committee concluded that the major deterrent to a viewer becoming more aggressive—that is, seeing the bloody, painful, long-term aftermath of violence—was largely absent on American commercial television.

In 1982, a second U.S. Surgeon General's Scientific Advisory Committee published a follow-up study. By this time, studies on all kinds of effects of television on child, adolescent, and adult viewers had brought the number of articles in the scientific literature to upward of 5,000. The second Scientific Advisory Committee noted that the problems with television violence were unabated. They also noted that the violence issues had been exacerbated by a new wave of distorted sex and sexuality on commercial television, and most particularly on cable pay television. But the Committee expressed as its major concern the role models to which children and adolescents are exposed during those 15,000 hours of television viewing in the first 18 years of their lives. It was noted that every conceivable segment of American society is largely presented on commercial television in stereotypical and caricatured ways. The Committee focused on the serious negative effects of these unrealistic role models on impressionable child and adolescent viewers.

In the face of all this, the commercial television industry in the United States, represented by the three major networks, has steadfastly refused to respond to the many suggestions that both Scientific Advisory Committees have made. In fact, I think it is fair to say that the networks are still fighting the battle of whether or not watching television violence increases the amount of aggressivity in the viewer, even though that issue was settled by the scientists at least 10 years ago.

Most recently, we have some phenomena that suggest we are going backward rather than forward. A consortium of organizations concerned with the epidemic of teenage pregnancy and abortion in this country has prepared a series of television public service announcements (PSAs) aimed at helping teenagers avoid becoming pregnant and therefore avoid having abortions. It is important to note that the consortium includes groups representing every viewpoint on this issue, from those advocating celibacy until marriage to those advocating the use of the Pill.

When the consortium representatives went to all the major television stations in New York City and attempted to purchase time to broadcast their PSAs, they were turned down by every single station. The reasons varied from station to station. One station said that there was the whole issue of having a balanced message. They could not have one group give a message about a controversial subject and not have another group give another message, and they were not interested in the fact that the consortium already represented all points of view about the subject. Another station said that it thought these PSAs were in poor taste and might offend some of its viewers. And another station said that it was concerned that these PSAs might be offensive to the religious beliefs of some of its viewers.

When the consortium representatives pointed out that these same stations were already airing a series of PSAs about AIDS, the answer was, "Well, we have to do that, because there's an AIDS epidemic." There have been approximately 42,000 cases of AIDS reported in the entire United States so far. In New York State there were 150,000 abortions in 1986 alone. But this number of abortions was not considered an epidemic by the television station managers in New York City.

Five-year-old children are now learning about drinking alcohol from television, as well as from the at-home behavior of their parents, a recent study reports. Television, as we know it, depicts people who can swill down unbelievable amounts of liquor and gorge themselves on incredible amounts of the unhealthiest kinds of food. But on television, everyone is gorgeous and handsome, and these people never get sick or have heart attacks; in fact, they almost never become intoxicated, except just before they commit violence. Thirty percent of our 13-year-old boys and 22% of our 13-year-old girls currently drink beer regularly. And the most recent statistics show that youngsters in this age group are switching from beer to wine coolers, which have a much higher alcohol content.

In the face of all this, from 8:00 A.M. on Monday morning to 8:00 A.M. on Saturday morning, there is not a single, regularly scheduled hour of age-appropriate television programming designed for children on any of the three major networks in the United States.

THE EDUCATION SYSTEM

A President's Commission on Public Education in the United States was convened a few years ago, and in 1985 it delivered a report after 14 months of deliberation. In essence, the Commission concluded that what our public education system needed to correct its deficiencies was for the children to spend one more hour a day in school, to have one more month of school a year, and to have more homework. I take issue with the Commission's methods, conclusions, and recommendations.

In fact, if you look at the educational literature, you will find exactly two methodologically sound scientific studies that give some decent information on what it is that makes children learn. These two studies were done independently of each other in the United States. They both came to the same conclusion: The only correlation that has any scientific validity is between the IQ of the teacher and how well the children do, regardless of the subject and regardless of the age of the children.

I think this conclusion is particularly significant because in the last 5 years, the average take-home pay of the American public school teacher has decreased by 12% in real buying dollars. It is not surprising, then, that we have many teachers leaving the public education system; nor is it surprising that the teachers with the highest IQs would be the ones who would most quickly find another way to earn a living that might be creative and satisfying. And indeed, the ones with the highest IQs have left, to the detriment of our children's education.

A study published in September 1987 revealed that one in eight of every Americans over the age of 18 is functionally illiterate. These individuals cannot read the baseball scores, cannot fill out a job application, cannot read the warnings on a package of cigarettes, and, if these persons are parents, cannot read a note sent home with their child from the teacher at school.

In 1986 a study was done of 8,000 17-year-old individuals, all juniors in high schools across the United States. The study used very nice cross-sectional methodology. These students were given two multiple-choice tests—one in American history and another in literature. They scored an average of 55% in American history and 52% in literature, which means that their average grade was F. One-third of these youngsters were unable to identify the Declaration of Independence as the primary document by which the 13 colonies severed themselves from the British Crown. Fewer than half of these youngsters could place the American Civil War in the correct half-century.

Another set of findings in this same study speaks to another issue in our public education system. The researchers made a special point that 20% of the top 25% of these 8,000 students were youngsters from minority groups who were not even in the academic track in high school; they had been assigned to vocational tracks. These minority youngsters, who were not even being given the opportunity to study American history or literature, nevertheless managed to represent 20% of the top 25% of the entire 8,000. They must have been extremely bright kids.

This finding indicated to the researchers that whatever other problems our American public education system has, it also has produced a two-track, two-class system. One track is for advantaged children who are heading toward more education after high school. The other track is for disadvantaged children who are not going to get any farther in the educational system because they are not even being considered for a precollege track in the vast majority of our public schools. And this situation must have some very negative effects on the mental health of these youngsters.

Corporal punishment also negatively affects the mental health of our school children. The American public school system reported administering three million paddlings with wooden paddles in 1986. We do not know how many went unreported. I would ask you to consider the effect of this on our children by comparing it to the following scenario:

> You work in an office. You come in to work on a Monday morning and your boss says to you: "We've been thinking about your job, and we're going to ask you to make some changes in what you do." He or she spends an hour with you to explain the new routine, and then you go back to your desk and get to work. The next day your boss comes rushing over to your desk, pulls you out of your seat, and shouts: "You're doing it all wrong! What's the matter with you? I couldn't have explained it more simply. Now sit down and do it right!" And he or she gives you a whack on the rear end to be sure you understand.

Well, I would suggest that if you did not deck your boss on the spot, then you might consider bringing an assault and battery charge against him or her—and you would win your case 100% of the time. You do not have to spend too many hours in a public school classroom before you see a scenario that is entirely analogous, in my view, to the one just presented. Think of that scenario and think of what goes on in our public schools day after week after month—three million paddlings a year.

Another hour a day in school and another month a year and more homework are not going to correct these problems.

THE LAW AND JUSTICE SYSTEM

On any given day in the United States there are somewhere between 350,000 and 500,000 children in adult jails. I am not talking about juvenile detention homes, though in my experience most of these detention homes certainly could be classified as jails. The vast majority of these children have not been charged with any crime, are not represented by any legal counsel, and in fact have been put in jail with no sentence. In legal jargon and in functional effect, they have an indeterminate sentence.

Most of these children are in jail because their parents or other adult caretakers have hauled them into court, declaring them incorrigible. The declaration of incorrigibility can be made on the basis that the child ran away from home—once—and that the parent or other caretaker feels that there is no way to prevent it from happening again. Clearly, children in this country do not enjoy equal protection under the law.

In 1979 a case came before the United States Supreme Court that originated in the Baltimore, Maryland, public schools. The case dealt with a youngster who had received corporal punishment at the hands of his teacher in a Baltimore junior high school. (Like most states in our country, Maryland permits, by law, corporal punishment in the public schools.) The case was not brought on the basis of whether or not the corporal punishment could be administered. Instead, it was brought as a constitutional case with the following argument: This child received cruel and unusual punishment for the alleged infraction of the rules, and he ought to have been protected by the Eighth Amendment to the Constitution of the United States, which prohibits cruel and unusual punishment.

The Court heard the case and found for the defendants, that is, for the school system and the teacher who had hit the child with a wooden paddle. The reason the Supreme Court gave for its finding was that children are not entitled to protection under the Eighth Amendment. This is the same amendment that protects prisoners in our federal prison system from cruel and unusual punishment by their warders.

CHILD ABUSE AND NEGLECT

The United States has more child abuse and does less to prevent and treat it than any other Western industrialized democracy. When we talk about child abuse, when the newspapers report child abuse and neglect, and when we have conferences about this subject, we are invariably focused on an episode or category of abuse (sexual, physical, or emotional) involving a single child and that child's caretaker. That is one level of child abuse.

Two other levels of child abuse often do not get recognized. One is institutional child abuse, as described above in the educational system and in the law and justice system. This type of abuse even occurs in hospitals. For example, a tertiary-care children's medical center where I am on the attending staff currently has one master's-level social worker for every 60 to 80 beds, despite the fact that the American Hospital Association urgently recommends that there be at least one M.S.W.-level social worker for every 22 beds in a children's tertiary-care hospital. In my view, this situation is a form of institutional abuse and neglect.

The third level of abuse is child abuse as a matter of public policy. This is the abuse that is talked about least but does the most damage.

I want to comment on teenage pregnancy and abortion in this context. In the early 1980s the Alan Guttmacher Institute in New York City, which studies population, childbirth, pregnancy, and contraception issues, embarked on a 37-country study on the issue of teenage sexuality in all of its facets. The initial findings were surprising. The Institute representatives discovered that the United States had a higher teenage abortion rate, corrected for population, than the combined teenage pregnancy and abortion rates of any one of the other 36 countries. (Approximately 1.25 million teenage pregnancies occur each year in this country, and about 50% are terminated by abortion.)

Once these statistics were validated, the Institute researchers redesigned some of their methodology so that they could examine, in the remaining years of the study, some causes for this finding. When the study was completed in the spring of 1985, the Institute reported that in comparison to the other countries—particularly Holland, Sweden, France, England, and Wales, with whom the United States was closely compared—there were three major differences to account for the pregnancy and abortion rate statistics in the United States:

1. We have no public policy that differentiates between teenage sexual behavior and teenage pregnancy, and that explicitly discourages teenage pregnancy.
2. We have no universal, free, confidential contraceptive services for teenagers.
3. We have no sex and sexuality education built in as part of a much broader health education program in all of our public schools from grades K through 12.

These three conditions that we do *not* have are the very policies and programs that the countries with much lower teenage pregnancy and abortion rates *do* have.

How are these findings related to child abuse and neglect? In this country approximately half a million babies are born to teenagers every year. In most cases, these babies are born unplanned, unwanted, unwelcomed, and underprivileged. Many are abused, and many grow up to become abusers of their own children. This is child abuse and neglect—to the teenagers and their babies—resulting directly from the absence of sound public policy and programs.

CHILD CARE

Fifty-nine percent of married women in America work outside the home, most of them as a matter of economic necessity. By 1990, 80% of women with children under the age of 1 year will be working outside of their homes. Keeping these numbers in mind, consider that there are approximately six million businesses of every size and type in the United States. A survey completed in 1987 revealed that of these six million businesses, fewer than 3,000 provided any kind of support for child care to any of their workers. Fewer than 1,000 of these six million businesses provided on-site child care for their workers.

If you look at support for teenage parents, there is almost no child care available. In most communities there is an average of five children waiting for every opening that occurs in any kind (irrespective of quality) of day care. Child-care workers in the United States earn, on average, about one-third the pay per hour of checkers in supermarkets. I do not begrudge supermarket checkers their wages, but this fact makes a statement about how we feel about our children.

In contrast to this dismal picture, Hungary provides up to 1 year of subsidy for any mother who chooses to stay home with her newborn, and guarantees that she will be able to return to her same job when she goes back to work. Sweden will provide up to 2 years of subsidy for a mother or father who wants to stay at home with a new baby. The fact is that the United States is one of only two Western industrialized nations without a federally mandated maternity leave law; the other country is the Republic of South Africa.

HEALTH CARE

Only two countries in the industrialized world do not have any universal health insurance program—the United States and the Republic of South Africa. Two-thirds of our children have no comprehensive health insurance coverage. A third of our children will reach age 18 without ever having seen a dentist. Our children and youth—nearly 30% of our population—receive approximately 5% of the nation's mental health budget.

We know that poverty causes an increase in the number of babies born with low birth weights, and we know that the sequelae of low birth weight are lifelong. A study about infant nutrition was done in the early 1980s at the Boston City Hospital. A population of infants were identified who were suffering from clear signs of protein malnutrition. This malnutrition was a direct result of the termination or severe cutback of their mothers' participation in the Supplemental Food Program for Women, Infants, and Children (WIC). Every major city in the United States has at least one inner-city section that has an infant mortality rate that is higher than the infant mortality rate of Malaysia.

Every year there are 23,000 deaths of children in this country due to unintentional injuries, i.e., excluding suicide and homicide. Fully a third of these deaths are preventable using current knowledge and technology. We are talking about saving the lives of 8,000 children in the United States every year. How? By implementing such measures as the use of smoke detectors, seat belts, bicycle helmets, and more school-crossing guards. In the face of this knowledge, in 1986 the National Institute for Child Health and Human Development awarded only one grant to researchers studying childhood injury prevention. Out of the Institute's total budget of $293 million that year, the grant was $150,000.

THE ECONOMY

In the United States we have toy, food, clothing, cosmetic, and music industries targeted solely at child and adolescent buyers, industries whose annual gross sales are in the billions of dollars. The toy industry reported sales of $12.6 billion between Halloween and Christmas in 1986, representing 60% of their total annual toy sales. These numbers remind me of the Code of Hammurabi, which in 2350 B.C. made selling something to a child, or buying something from a child without power of attorney, a crime punishable by death. Yet in 1987 A.D. our children are being exposed to 350,000 commercials on television alone that were created for them and that urge them to buy merchandise, most of which is potentially harmful to their health.

The United States is the only industrialized nation whose children make up its largest age group living in poverty. Twenty-three percent of our children—some 13 million—are poverty-stricken, and the number is increasing annually. Child and family programs make up approximately 10% of our federal budget, but these programs have absorbed almost 33% of the cuts in that budget since 1980. In the face of this poverty, we have to remind ourselves that poor children die at three times the rate of nonpoor children, and that there is six times as much poverty in households headed by females as there is in those headed by males. Finally, from the extrapolation of statistics put together by the State of Maine Department of Health, we have learned that in the United States every year, poverty is the ultimate cause of death for 11,000 children. That is, every five years we are killing more children by keeping them in poverty than all the young men and women we lost in the entire Vietnam conflict.

WHAT CAN BE DONE?

This litany of horrors amounts to child abuse and neglect as a matter of public policy in this country. But when we summarize the situation this way, I believe it points us to a solution: to organize ourselves in ways in which we can affect and change public policy. Instead of allowing children to be at risk for all kinds of mental and physical disorders, we can truly become involved in primary prevention. Children simply would not be at risk if their needs were to be met when they ought to be met.

Let me cite some specific examples of how this has worked. Norman Lear's spoof of soap operas, called "Mary Hartman, Mary Hartman!" dealt with all kinds of forbidden subjects. The program was independently produced by Mr. Lear and broadcast throughout the United States at 10:00 or 11:00 P.M., five nights a week.

In Seattle, Washington, the manager of the NBC-affiliated television station decided to air "Mary Hartman, Mary Hartman!" at 5:00 P.M. Five o'clock in the afternoon is prime television-viewing time for little children whose mothers or fathers are usually preparing dinner after working all day outside the home.

A mother in Bellevue, a community east of Seattle, was preparing dinner when she heard some horrible sounds coming out of the family room. She rushed in to find her three children watching an episode of "Mary Hartman, Mary Hartman!" in which a gentleman had just had a heart attack and was making a lot of loud noises in the process of drowning in his chicken soup. She said, "What in the world are you watching?" The children said, "Oh, Mom, get away from the front of the set. This is 'Mary Hartman, Mary Hartman!' Listen to the funny sounds that man is making in his soup."

Well, the mother turned off the set and discovered that her children had been watching this show every day for 2 weeks. She explained to them why they were not going to be watching it any more. And then she called up the television station and spoke to the manager. She said, "If you want to air that show, that's your business. I believe in the First Amendment. But why can't you put it on later in the evening so you don't have a lot of young children watching it? It's just totally inappropriate fare for them." The response she got was a lecture about the violence in Shakespeare.

When it became clear to her that the station manager was intransigent, she spoke to her husband and they changed their whole family schedule. For the next 2 weeks, he got home from work early and took care of the dinner duty, while she went upstairs to the small television in their bedroom and watched this show. Every time a commercial appeared—about every 8 or 10 minutes—she wrote down the name of the sponsor. After 2 weeks she put in a paid, person-to-person, long-distance phone call to the president of every company that had sponsored the show. She never got to speak to the presidents, but she did speak to persons in charge of consumer affairs. She introduced herself, told where she was calling from, and said she wondered if the consumer affairs representative knew what it was his or her company was sponsoring in the Seattle market at 5:00 P.M. Then she would always get the same patronizing lecture: "Well madam, we buy $26 million dollars of TV ads a year out of a company in Chicago. We don't know exactly what we're sponsoring in each city every day." And she would say, "I just wanted you to know that in this city, what you're sponsoring at five in the afternoon is 'Mary Hartman, Mary Hartman!' " And what she got at the other end was a loud gasp. In 3 months this woman removed 23 sponsors from that show in the Seattle market. One woman, no organization, using her own money.

Second example. In 1986, there was a particularly horrible child abuse case in Everett, Washington, in which a man ultimately murdered his 3-year-old son. It was widely reported because the Child Protective Services (CPS) did not remove the child from his home, despite repeated calls for intervention. So the Governor named a special commission, but nothing substantive happened. The apparent results were to include beefing up CPS a little and spreading a few more dollars around in the budget, and that was going to be the end of it as soon as the newspapers would let it go.

But some people did not want it to stop there. In January 1987 a group of businessmen in Spokane, Washington, decided to do something substantive on their own about child abuse prevention. They understood, as realistic businessmen, that the bureaucratic approach was not going to work. So among them they raised $100,000 to buy an old house, renovate it, and create a crisis respite center. Any parent who felt that he or she was about to lose control and hit or brutalize a child could call the center. The center took 200 children for respite care, at 3 days apiece, in its first 6 months of operation. While the children were at the center for those 3 days, the staff helped connect the family with a community agency that could provide ongoing treatment and support.

The Spokane program costs out to about $500 per child. It does not take much to figure out how much money you save if you fund programs like this one, compared to waiting until the children are already abused and then trying to put them back together again.

The savings resulting from prevention programs have been calculated by the Children's Defense Fund in Washington, D.C., and by many other organizations concerned with these prevention issues. In the most conservative approach, every dollar spent now for meaningful prevention programs means an average of seven dollars saved within the next 10 years. This applies to child abuse, teenage pregnancy, day care, health care, injury prevention, and every other area in which children are at risk.

A final example involves voting, which is one of the most important and least used ways of changing public policy. In the Seattle primary election in November 1987, only 12.9% of the registered eligible voters bothered to vote. If 50% of the eligible voters turn out for a national election, that makes headlines. In 1986, the balance of power in the United States Senate was changed by merely 56,000 votes in five closely contested districts all over the country.

Each individual vote *does* make a difference. And each time we write or call an elected representative, it makes a difference. It takes only a few minutes to say what the problem or unmet need is, how you think it ought to be solved, and what you want your representative to do about it. Children have neither money nor votes, and as such they are no politician's constituents. So if they are not going to be our constituency, then they will be no one's.

CONCLUSIONS

A newspaper reporter recently asked, "Tell me, Dr. Rothenberg, just what is it you think children are entitled to?" No one had ever put the question to me like that. I said, "I think every child is entitled to circumstances that will permit the fulfillment of the physical, intellectual, emotional, social, and spiritual potential with which he or she is born."

Enlightened self-interest, if nothing else, dictates that we help our children become our future producers and consumers, or they will surely become our future burden.

In the words of Rabbi Tarfan (Pirke Abot 1957), "We are not obligated to complete the task; but neither are we at liberty to abstain from it."

REFERENCES

Pirke Abot: The Wisdom of the Fathers. New York, New American Library, 1957

Children's Defense Fund Newsletter, 1986–1987

James H: Children in Trouble: A National Scandal. New York, David McKay, 1970

James H: The Little Victims: How America Treats Its Children. New York, David McKay, 1975

Rothenberg MB: The effect of television violence on children and youth. JAMA 234:1046–1053, 1975

Senn MJE: Speaking Out for America's Children. New Haven, CT, Yale University Press, 1977

Preventive Interventions With Infants and Young Children

Introduction

Joel Yager, M.D.

The chapters in this section address clinical problems in the earliest phases of life that have stimulated the interests and activities of prevention-oriented pediatricians, psychiatrists, psychologists, and other health professionals. Several common themes emerge that transcend the specific topics of the individual chapters.

First, all available information indicates that our society suffers from a high prevalence of serious problems in prenatal, neonatal, and early child development that render an astounding number of children vulnerable to the subsequent development of major psychiatric disturbances. The overwhelming numbers of mothers-to-be with alcohol and drug abuse, AIDS-related infections, poor coping skills, impaired social supports (with absent or conflicted relationships both with their own parents and with the fathers-to-be), little preparation for parenthood, and inadequate financial and social resources, numb the sensibilities of those who would attempt to intervene at an early stage.

Second, anyone aware of these problems can see the virtue of attempting to reduce these factors that so predictably promise a host of negative sequelae, frequently resulting in lives of anguish and pain for the children and their parents, and considerable expense to the community in the form of medical, psychiatric, welfare, criminal justice, and other social costs.

Third, the problems are heterogeneous and complex, and each one requires a careful assessment and an individualized treatment plan.

Fourth, all of the interventions attempted thus far are extremely labor-intensive. These interventions require the development of trust in sometimes hostile environments; the establishment of personal relationships with children, mothers, and families, with the involvement required often exceeding both the superficially professional and the usual working hours; and the willingness to give in ways that are instrumental, practical, educational, and emotionally supportive.

Fifth, to date, our information about the effectiveness of these interventions rests entirely on reports of relatively few individual case series and small demonstration research programs. While the available outcome data suggest that such interventions are often helpful, the problems are frequently so overwhelming that even time-intensive, ongoing relationships are insufficient to deter the development of subsequent catastrophes.

Sixth, research is urgently needed to establish exactly what can and cannot be accomplished by various forms of intervention, so that in the real world of limited resources intelligent triage decisions can be made as to what interventions should be assigned with what priority to which problems with what anticipated results.

Seventh, given our present society, it seems unlikely that sufficient resources will be made available in the foreseeable future to allow us simply to use what is already known to have a meaningful impact on the extensive problems we face. This realistic, not cynical, appraisal should not demoralize those who envision the value of additional research in this area.

With this preamble in mind, the chapters in this section fall into several groups.

The chapters by Beckwith, Heinicke et al., Howard and Kropenske, and Drotar include the discussion of children whose increased potential for serious difficulties can be identified before, at, or shortly after birth, by virtue of the presence of some fairly strong predictors of subsequent problems: prematurity, high-risk parents and early mother-child interactional difficulties, maternal alcohol and drug abuse, and nonorganic failure to thrive. In these chapters the available literature in each area is reviewed to detail the way in which each of the respective vulnerability factors leads to subsequent developmental difficulties. Each chapter also includes descriptions of the specific intervention programs developed and utilized by the authors, often illustrated with clinical vignettes, and discussion of the authors' understanding of the effective elements in these interventions.

Brill and Cohen, in the final chapter of this section, consider an intervention program aimed at children with chronic illness that also involves these children's families and the hospital staff so that potential negative sequelae are kept to a minimum.

For clinicians and behavioral scientists both, preventive interventions offer formidable challenges and exciting prospects, all of which are clearly conveyed by the authoritative chapters in this section.

CHAPTER 3

Preventive Interventions With Parents of Premature Infants

Leila Beckwith, Ph.D.

Because of the major technological and scientific advances that have been made in the last decade in neonatal intensive care, most prematurely born infants survive, and many do so without major handicaps (Hack et al. 1983; Saigal et al. 1984). There remains, however, an increased incidence of major sensory, motor, and mental handicaps for some children and decreased competence in intellectual tasks and school achievement for many (Drillien et al. 1980; Fitzhardinge 1985; Hunt 1981). The causes of these problems are to be found in the biological events of the prenatal and perinatal periods, the medical procedures required for survival, the physical and social environment of the hospital, and the social environment of the home (Kopp and Parmelee 1979). Complex interactions of these factors produce great heterogeneity in cognitive and socioemotional development for preterm infants. The range of outcomes is as varied within preterm infants as within normal-term infants.

IMPORTANCE OF THE HOME ENVIRONMENT

After hospital discharge, the home social environment is of primary importance for understanding the development of preterm infants for three reasons. First, research indicates that preterm infants are more difficult to care for and are less enjoyable social partners than are full-term infants, at least in the first year of life (Goldberg and DiVitto 1983). Second, preterm birth and the ensuing weeks in the hospital are often traumatic experiences for the parents. Third, naturally occurring differences in how

This research was supported by the Prevention Research Branch, National Institute of Mental Health, Grant MH-36902.

parents interact with their infants result in developmental difficulties being mitigated in some families but not in others. Some family environments are so supportive that they compensate completely for risk factors and prevent later developmental problems, whereas other family environments have insufficient emotional, educational, or economic resources to adapt to even slight perinatal problems. Children from the latter environments tend to maintain deficits into later stages of development (Sameroff and Chandler 1975; Werner and Smith 1977, 1982). Our research has focused on how different environments help or hinder infants with respect to overcoming early medical and developmental problems (Beckwith and Cohen 1984).

It has long been known that parent-infant relationships greatly influence later development of children born full-term and healthy (Gottfried 1984; Maccoby and Martin 1983). It was not clear, however, that infants suffering early biological trauma were equally malleable and equally subject to social environmental forces. Some researchers thought that anoxia, for example, caused irreparable brain damage, and that such brain damage could not be altered by experience. Now, however, considerable evidence demonstrates that the family environment and particularly the parent-infant relationship, operating after the trauma has occurred, can mitigate or exacerbate the adverse effects of the prior medical events and influence the later development of infants at risk as well as healthy full-term infants (Sameroff and Chandler 1975).

DIFFICULTIES IN CARING FOR PRETERM INFANTS

Although preterm infants vary greatly, they are less likely to be adequate social partners than are healthy, full-term infants. They are more likely than full-term infants to have disorganized sleep and feeding rhythms (Parmelee 1976) and to be more unpredictable, less responsive, and more fussy during social interaction (Field 1987). Preterm infants tend to be less alert, more difficult to soothe, and more likely to avert their gaze during face-to-face interaction. They smile less, show less positive affect, and vocalize less (Brachfeld et al. 1980; Brown and Bakeman 1979; Goldberg et al. 1980).

EFFECT OF PREMATURE BIRTH ON PARENTS

For most parents, premature birth and the ensuing perinatal problems are experienced as a prolonged crisis that increases anxiety, stress, grief, disappointment and guilt, and for some people, anger and blame; they reduce parents' self-confidence and confidence in the infant (Kaplan and Mason 1960; Seashore et al. 1973). Hospitalization of the infant in intensive care is a traumatic event. Fearing that their infant will die, parents are grieved for themselves and their child. They are fearful for the child's future health and development, and feel as though they have lost control over their own lives and their infant's life (Caplan 1960). Moreover, the infant's stay in the neonatal intensive care unit interferes with the parents' early contact with the infant, this early contact being an experience that may facilitate parental bonding (Klaus and Kennell 1976; Minde 1980).

Discharge from the hospital adds new anxieties, including the additional difficulties involved in caring for a less responsive, less predictable, more fragile infant, who may have continuing health problems and often delays in development (Goldberg and DiVitto 1983).

Furthermore, parents of preterm infants, just like parents of full-term infants, are subject to stresses within their own lives. These stresses may originate independently of the infant, but eventually may affect the relationship with the infant. Difficulties in parenting may result from depression, impaired judgment, or projection of distorted and negative images onto the infant. Parents who are distressed because of poverty, immigrant status, other small children to nurture, lack of support from others, unstable educational, work, and/or living arrangements, severe marital conflict, and/or disrupted and abusive relationships with their own parents are more likely to form deficient patterns of interactions with their infant (Maccoby and Martin 1983).

PARENT INTERACTION WITH PREMATURE INFANTS

Variations in the infant's ability to emit signals and to respond to the parents' behaviors, and variations in the parents' tendencies to respond promptly, appropriately, and tenderly, influence the course of the parent-infant relationship. Because characteristics of both parents and infants contribute to the relationship, difficulties occur when atypical parents or atypical infants disrupt the reciprocity of the relationship (Brazelton and Yogman 1986; Goldberg 1978). Parental interaction with prematurely born infants is both similar to and different from parental interaction with full-term infants (Brown and Bakeman 1979; Crawford 1982; Field 1977, 1979; DiVitto and Goldberg 1979). Parents tend to be more active, more persistent, and more likely to initiate and to continue behavioral exchanges with preterm infants than with full-term infants. Even when the infants grow older and contribute more to the interaction, parents of preterm infants continue to assume a disproportionate level of responsibility. Preterm infants may appear more distractible, or fussy and less organized during feeding and play, so their mothers stimulate and coax them more. Parents tend to show less pleasure during interaction. Moreover, differences in affect regulation occur in both the parents and the infants, so that fewer occasions of mutual smiling occur (Field 1987).

Although many studies have found that these differences in interaction style have disappeared by the second year of life (Brown and Bakeman 1980), some professionals are concerned that the early patterns of increased parental control may continue and may interfere with these infants' ability to take the initiative and assert independence, one of the developmental tasks of the second year of life. Research findings to date are conflicting. Some researchers have found that parents who make the most effort and succeed in engaging their infants in frequent mutually responsive social interactions promote competence in their children that continues throughout early childhood (Beckwith and Cohen 1984). Other researchers have found that parents may interact too actively, overwhelm the infant, and thereby interfere with the infant's competence (Field 1987).

PARENT-INFANT INTERACTION ACTS AS A PROTECTIVE FACTOR

Despite the difficulties involved in making and maintaining a positive relationship with a preterm infant, many parents do succeed, and such relationships act as a protective factor, buffering the child's later development against adverse effects associated with early traumas. This point is illustrated with data from a longitudinal, prospective study of 126 infants born prematurely during the years 1972–1974 (Parmelee et al. 1976). This group of infants was studied intensively in the first 2 years of life and was then assessed again with cognitive tests at ages 5 and 8. (The children are also being studied at age 12.) Among this group of children born in the years 1972–1974 with heavier birthweights and fewer medical complications than preterm infants surviving today, there were no relationships between neonatal medical problems and mental development at any age (Cohen and Parmelee 1983). Adverse perinatal events—for most of the children—were less powerful than had been expected in determining later competence. That is not to say that being born early and sick did not matter. Although major disabilities such as cerebral palsy, blindness, and severe mental retardation were few in number, they did occur, and at an increased incidence compared to infants born at term. These findings indicate that perinatal illness cannot be ignored, but does not necessarily determine outcome. Being born too soon, subject to complications of labor and delivery, perinatal illness, and potentially adverse medical intervention, does not necessarily eventuate in problems in mental functioning or socioemotional development, although for some children handicaps may result (Friedman and Sigman 1981; Sameroff 1981).

Moreover, the nature of the parent-infant relationship for those children without major handicaps was directly associated with the children's intellectual competence at ages 2, 5, and 8. This association between the parent-infant relationship and the children's cognitive functioning held true despite the presence for some infants of neonatal behavioral indicators of vulnerability. Within our study, sleep-state organization and EEG patterns, assessed at term date, identified a subgroup of children who were likely to show later difficulties in intellectual performance (Parmelee et al. 1976). In general, IQ scores were lower at ages 2, 5, and 8 for those children who had been less able to organize physiological and brain wave patterns of quiet sleep as newborns (Beckwith and Parmelee 1986). However, children who had experienced very attentive, responsive interactions with their mothers as infants were intellectually very capable later on. As a group, their IQs were no different from those of children who had been able as newborns to organize quiet sleep (Beckwith and Parmelee 1986). For the children experiencing responsive interactions, the good parent-infant relationship seemed to uncouple neonatal vulnerability from later performance.

EARLY INTERVENTION WITH PARENTS OF PRETERM INFANTS

A variety of early preventive intervention programs have been generated for parents of preterm infants in the last 10 years. These programs differ in the degree to which a structured curriculum is used, the extent to which education versus emotional support is stressed, and the extent to which the focus is on the infant versus the parents and family. The programs also differ in duration and frequency of contacts. Aims and approaches have included the following: bringing parents and infants together in the newborn nursery to facilitate mutual bonding; teaching parents how to care for their infants; encouraging cognitive mastery through learning about preterm infants in general and about the specific needs of their own infants in particular; and giving emotional support through home visits or self-help groups.

THE UCLA PROJECT

A very popular, widely used approach that we use in our own work employs professional home visitors who can individualize the program and provide emotional support to the parents, while highlighting the infant's needs, cues, and competencies.

We selected a group of infants who were at double jeopardy, both biologically and socially, i.e., sick preterm infants being reared by low-income parents. A professional home visitor began meeting with the parents before the infant was discharged from the hospital, and continued to meet regularly with them throughout the first year. This intervention focused primarily on the relationship between mothers and their infants, although the father was included if he wished, or if he became, as happened in two families, the primary caregiver.

Nature of the Intervention

The intervention was individualized and parent-directed. We did not use an infant curriculum (which ordinarily consists of a predetermined sequence of activities for skill development) because we were concerned that prescriptive teaching might interfere with the sensitivity of the mother to the infant, her responsiveness to the infant as a separate person, and her own spontaneity in interacting with the infant. Additionally, we considered and have found that multiproblem parents cannot focus on the infant until they themselves have been nurtured. Nor did we use a parent education model, because we did not consider it sufficient for the needs of our multiproblem parents with their sick preterm infants. Moreover, we believed that the effectiveness of intervention depended more on the relationship between the parent and the intervenor than on the curriculum.

We set out to develop a trusting, supportive relationship by mediating between the family and community resources such as child care, family planning, and medical care, and by providing concrete help to the family in the form of clothes, equipment, toys, photographs, and transportation. We also attempted to help parents develop observational skills in relation to their infant, and to help them place the infant's behavior in the context of normal development. The program was designed to increase parental self-confidence and competence by nurturing the parents and modifying their perceptions of the infant, making the infant more understandable in terms of normal development.

The intervenors were a pediatric nurse and an early childhood educator. Each possessed personal characteristics of sensitivity, flexibility, empathy, and commitment, which made them available to the families when needed, even evenings and weekends.

Attrition

Ninety-two subjects were recruited and randomly assigned, 37 to the intervention group and 55 to the control group. By the end of the study's first year there were 35 subjects in each group. Although monetary reimbursement and gifts were provided for every family at each laboratory visit, there was a differential attrition rate in the control group as compared to the intervention group. Many families dropped out of the control group; however, almost every family stayed in the project if they received home visitor services.

Differential attrition in the control and intervention groups resulted in the intervention group being at higher risk on the continuum of care-taking casualty than the control group. The possible effects of attrition in biasing the control group characteristics were tested in subjects who reached 13 months corrected age by comparing those individuals who had to those who had not participated in the 13-month testing. No significant differences were revealed between stayers and dropouts with respect to their infant's gestational age, birthweight, perinatal complications, length of hospitalization, and sex, or with respect to parity, maternal age, education, socioeconomic status, and marital status. The individuals who dropped out of the control group were characterized as follows: (a) women who had received no prenatal care in the first half of pregnancy, and (b) women whose own families of origin were unstable and/or abusive. Thus, a higher percentage of women in the intervention group than in the control group either had not received prenatal care or had come from more disrupted families of origin, or both.

Therefore, despite these two groups being matched initially for gestational age, birthweight, perinatal complications, birth order, maternal age, education, socioeconomic class, and marital status, differential attrition resulted in the intervention group being at higher risk on the continuum of caretaking casualty than the control group. By providing a trusting relationship, the intervention was able to keep in the program women with potentially more problematic relationships with their infants.

Evaluation of the Intervention

The next test of effectiveness was to see if parent-child interactions were altered by the intervention. As had been done in our previous work, mothers' involvement and level of reciprocal interactions were operationally defined from naturalistic home observations made when the infants were 1 and 9 months corrected age. The observer did not know the infants' medical histories, previous test data, or whether the family was receiving intervention. The observer used a precoded checklist, and every 15 seconds he or she recorded infant behavior, mother behavior, contingent or reciprocal interactions between mother and child, and behaviors of other persons toward the infant.

Using this method, the intervention group was found to be significantly more responsive to their infants than the control group by 1 month, and this difference was maintained at 9 months. Because the groups did not differ on most indices prior to intervention—and differences that

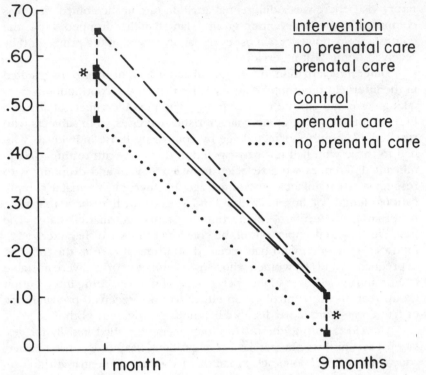

Figure 3-1. Comparison of mothers who did and did not receive intervention as to percent of observed time holding their infants. Asterisks indicate significance level $P < .05$.

did exist indicated potentially more problematic parent-child relationships in the intervention group—the findings suggest that intervention, given the crisis nature of the early months with a premature infant, had a significant effect within a very short period. Intervention appeared to unhook maternal behavior from predisposing adverse prenatal factors. That is, women who showed ambivalence, rejection, or poor adaptation to their pregnancies by not seeking prenatal care were able, with intervention, to show high involvement with their infants, but did not do so without intervention. Control group women who had not sought prenatal care for themselves in the first half of pregnancy held their infants less than women who had received prenatal care (Figure 3-1). However, women who had not sought prenatal care but who had received our intervention held their infants significantly more.

When amount of talking to the infants was used as the measure of involvement, the findings were similar. Control group women who had not received prenatal care in the first half of pregnancy talked to their infants less than women who had received prenatal care. However, women

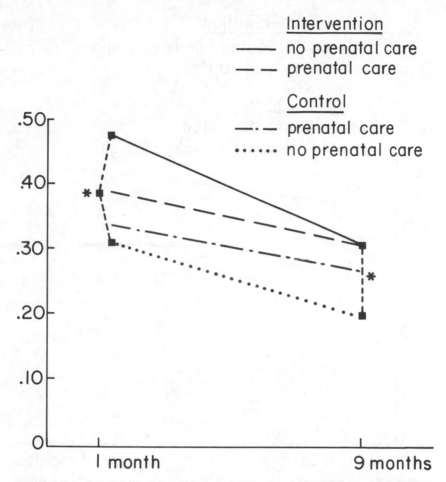

Figure 3-2. Comparison of mothers who did and did not receive intervention as to percent of observed time talking to their infants. Asterisks indicate significance level $P < .05$.

who had not received prenatal care but who *had* received the intervention spoke significantly more to their infants (Figure 3-2).

Similarly, women who had grown up in abusive, alcoholic, or disrupted families of origin were able, with intervention, to engage in increased reciprocal interactions with their infants, but did not do so without intervention. Responsive interactions were significantly fewer for control women from disrupted families of origin than for similar women who had received intervention (Figure 3-3).

Intervention had also acted to influence these women's attitudes about themselves as parents. An independent clinician, naive as to group membership, rated the typescripts of the initial interviews conducted at

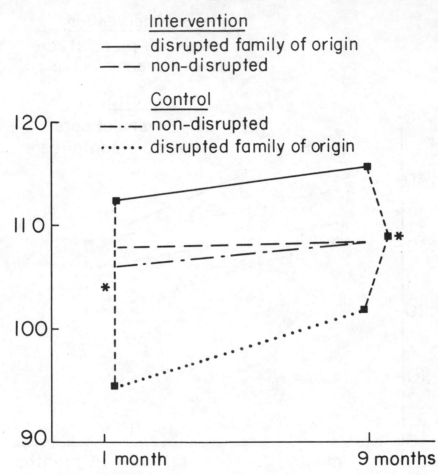

Figure 3-3. Comparison of mothers who did and did not receive intervention on summary score of responsive interactions with their infants. Asterisks indicate significance level $P < .05$.

entry into the project and of the interviews conducted 13 months later. The clinician made four-point ratings of the mother's emotional stability, the role of the infant in her life, the mother's developmental expectations of the child, and the mother's appraisal of the impact of the infant on her life. Women who received intervention were judged to have significantly increased emotional stability, and to have more realistic appraisals of the impact of the child on their lives and more appropriate developmental expectations of the children.

Examination of the ratings suggested that interventions with the mothers had promoted a more realistic appraisal of themselves and their children, so that both positive and negative feelings were expressed and

Table 3-1. Test performance at 13 months of children whose parents did and did not receive intervention

| | Intervention | | Control | |
| | Prenatal care | | Prenatal care | |
	Yes	No	Yes	No
Bayley Mental Development Index	110.1	103.2	107.1	107.8
Task mastery persistence	35.4	29.3	32.2	37.6
Symbolic play	.90*	1.08*	.57*	.00*
Secure attachment (% B)	47	33	64	60

*$P < .03$.

integrated. These findings contrasted with those of the control group—the individuals in the control group showed more denial, fragmentation, and contradiction in their attitudes.

An additional aim of the study was to demonstrate the extent to which the intervention would enhance the infants' quality of attachment to the mother, play behavior, mastery motivation, and developmental test performance at 13 months, and promote the children's acquisition of language, mastery motivation, and positive sense of self at age 2. However, intervention effects for these dependent variables were slight.

Intervention and control infants showed similar behavior at 13 months (Table 3-1). Of all the measures, only one showed a significant difference: intervention infants showed higher levels of symbolic play but no differences in task mastery persistence, Bayley Mental Development Index (MDI; Bayley 1969), or security of attachment. However, by 20 months, intervention subjects did show significantly higher developmental test scores on the Bayley MDI (Table 3-2). Moreover, intervention children continued spontaneously to engage in more symbolic play.

CONCLUSIONS

In sum, intervention did appear to promote a more attentive, responsive relationship between parent and infant. However, intervention effects in

Table 3-2. Bayley Mental Development Index (MDI) scores at 13 and 20 months for children whose parents did and did not receive intervention

| | Intervention | | Control | |
| | Prenatal care | | Prenatal care | |
	Yes	No	Yes	No
Bayley MDI				
13 months	110	103	107	108
20 months	102*	101*	91*	90*

*$P < .05$.

the infants' development were very modest. Intervention and control infants showed beginning divergences in cognitive functioning, with the intervention infants being more advanced in symbolic play and developmental level by 20 months. It will be important to assess the durability of these differences.

Thus, the effects of the intervention were positive in some ways and disappointing in others. For example, there was no link between intervention and children's security of attachment; both the control and the intervention groups showed the same proportion of infants who were and were not secure in their attachment to their mother. However, attachment is only one aspect of the relationship between parent and infant. That relationship includes physiological need satisfaction, protection and vigilance, teaching and learning, as well as play and fun (Emde 1988). It may be that our intervention influenced parents in their role as teachers, but did not affect other aspects of the parent-infant relationship. It also may be that various approaches to intervention differentially affect components of the parent-infant relationship. It would be useful in future studies to better conceptualize what aspects of the parent-infant relationship are expected to change for which families with what specific aspects of intervention, and how these changes may be linked to specific aspects of children's development. These preliminary research findings urge us to greater specificity in examining differences in families, the intervention relationship, dimensions of parenting, and separate behavioral systems within the developing child.

REFERENCES

Bayley N: Bayley Scales of Infant Development. New York, Psychological Corporation, 1969

Beckwith L, Cohen SE: Home environment and cognitive competence in preterm children during the first 5 years, in Home Environment and Early Cognitive Development. Edited by Gottfried A. New York, Academic, 1984, pp 235–271

Beckwith L, Parmelee AH Jr: EEG patterns of preterm infants, home environment, and later IQ. Child Dev 57:777–789, 1986

Brachfeld S, Goldberg S, Sloman J: Parent-infant interaction in free play at 8 and 12 months: effects of prematurity and immaturity. Infant Behav Dev 3:289–305, 1980

Brazelton TB, Yogman MW (eds): Affective Development in Infancy. Norwood, NJ, Ablex Publishing, 1986

Brown JV, Bakeman R: Relationships of human mothers with their infants during the first year of life, in Maternal Influences and Early Behavior. Edited by Bell RW, Smotherman WP. Jamaica, NY, Spectrum, 1979

Brown JV, Bakeman R: Early interaction: consequences for social and mental development at 3 years. Child Dev 51:437–447, 1980

Caplan G: Patterns of parental response to the crisis of premature birth. Psychiatry 23:365–374, 1960

Cohen SE, Parmelee AH: Prediction of five-year Stanford-Binet scores in preterm infants. Child Dev 54:1242–1253, 1983

Crawford JW: Mother-infant interaction in premature and full term infants. Child Dev 53:957–962, 1982

DiVitto B, Goldberg S: The development of early parent-infant interaction as a function of newborn medical status, in Infants Born at Risk. Edited by Field TM, Sostek AM, Goldberg S, et al. Jamaica, NY, Spectrum, 1979, pp 311–322

Drillien CM, Thoman AJM, Burgoyne K: Low-birthweight children at early school-age: a longitudinal study. Dev Med Child Neurol 22:26–47, 1980

Emde R: Risk, intervention and meaning. Psychiatry 51:254–260, 1988

Field T: Effects of early separation, interactive deficits, and experimental manipulation on mother-infant interaction. Child Dev 48:763–771, 1977

Field T: Interaction patterns of preterm and fullterm infants, in Infants Born at Risk. Edited by Field TM, Sostek AM, Goldberg S, et al. Jamaica, NY, Spectrum, 1979, pp 333–356

Field T: Affective and interactive disturbances in infants, in Handbook of Infant Development. Edited by Osofsky JD. New York, John Wiley, 1987, pp 972–1005

Fitzhardinge PM: Follow-up studies on infants, in Mother and Infant. Edited by Winick H. New York, John Wiley, 1985, pp 147–161

Friedman SL, Sigman M (eds): Preterm Birth and Psychological Development. New York, Academic, 1981

Goldberg S: Prematurity: effects on parent-infant interaction. J Pediatr Psychol 3:137–144, 1978

Goldberg S, DiVitto BA: Born Too Soon. New York, WH Freeman, 1983

Goldberg S, Brachfield S, DiVitto B: Feeding, fussing, and play: parent-infant interaction in the first year as a function of prematurity and perinatal medical problems, in High-Risk Infants and Children: Adult and Peer Interactions. Edited by Field T, Goldberg S, Stern D, et al. New York, Academic, 1980, pp 133–153

Gottfried A (ed): Home Environment and Early Cognitive Development. New York, Academic, 1984

Hack M, Caron B, Rivers A, et al: The very low birthweight infant: the broader spectrum of morbidity during infancy and early childhood. J Dev Behav Pediatr 4:243–249, 1983

Hunt JV: Predicting intellectual disorders in childhood for high-risk preterm infants with birthweights below 1501 gm, in Preterm Birth and Psychological

Development. Edited by Friedman S, Sigman M. New York, Academic, 1981, pp 329–351

Kaplan DN, Mason EH: Maternal reactions to premature birth viewed as an acute emotional disorder. Am J Orthopsychiatry 30:539–552, 1960

Klaus MH, Kennell JH: Maternal-Infant Bonding. St. Louis, MO, CV Mosby, 1976

Kopp CB, Parmelee AH: Prenatal and perinatal influences on infant behavior, in Handbook of Infant Development. Edited by Osofsky JD. New York, John Wiley, 1979, pp 29–75

Maccoby EE, Martin JA: Socialization in the context of the family: parent-child interaction, in Handbook of Child Psychology, 4th Edition (edited by Mussen PH), Vol 4, Socialization, Personality, and Social Development. Edited by Hetherington EM. New York, John Wiley, 1983, pp1–101

Minde K: Bonding of Parents to Premature Infants: Theory and Practice. Monographs in Neonatology Series. Edited by Taylor PM. New York, Grune & Stratton, 1980

Parmelee AH: Neurological and behavioral organization of premature infants in the first months of life. Biol Psychiatry 10:501–512, 1976

Parmelee AH, Kopp CP, Sigman M: Selection of developmental assessment techniques for infants at risk. Merrill-Palmer Q 22:177–199, 1976

Saigal S, Rosenbaum P, Stoskopf F, et al: Outcome in infants 501–1,000 gm birth weight delivered to residents of the McMaster Health Region. J Pediatr 105:969–976, 1984

Sameroff AJ: Longitudinal studies of preterm infants: a review of chapters 17–20, in Preterm Birth and Psychological Development. Edited by Friedman SL, Sigman M. New York, Academic, 1981, pp 387–393

Sameroff AJ, Chandler MJ: Reproductive risk and continuum of caretaking casualty, in Review of Child Development Research, Vol 4. Edited by Horowitz FD, Hetherington EM, Siegel M, et al. Chicago, IL, University of Chicago Press, 1975, pp 187–244

Seashore ML, Leifer AD, Barnett CT, et al: The effects of denial of early mother-infant interaction on maternal self-confidence. J Pers Soc Psychol 26:269–378, 1973

Werner EE, Smith RS: Kauai's Children Come of Age. Honolulu, HI, University of Hawaii Press, 1977

Werner EE, Smith RS: Vulnerable but Invincible. New York, McGraw-Hill, 1982

CHAPTER 4

Expanding Pediatric Care Through Family Intervention With At-Risk Parents

Christoph M. Heinicke, Ph.D.
Anne Thompson, Ph.D.
Elizabeth Carlin, Ph.D.

The most prevalent behavior problems confronted by parents and teachers are found in children who cannot sit still, cannot concentrate, or cannot modulate their angry feelings, and in children who exhibit all these behaviors. Preventing the development of these maladaptive behaviors can conceivably be structured in relation to the DSM-III (American Psychiatric Association 1980) diagnoses of hyperactivity, attention deficit disorder, and/or oppositional disorder. However, the research bases of making these differential diagnoses in a valid manner need further development. More importantly, very different clusters of antecedents or causes are likely to lead to the same outcome, which, for example, we may eventually label as an oppositional disorder in a 7-year-old. An alternative to the direct prediction and prevention of school-age symptomatology is to determine what intermediate preschool behaviors anticipate that symptomatology, and then determine what early parent and infant characteristics anticipate those preschool criteria. Having determined these associations, the preventive intervention can be focused on a significant aspect of the early parent-infant system. Below, we will first document the association of the preschool criteria and the school-age symptoms, and then in the next section cite the evidence linking pre- and postbirth antecedents to the preschool criteria.

PRESCHOOL PREDICTORS OF SCHOOL-AGE BEHAVIOR

In following the above prevention strategy it is necessary to hypothesize intermediate preschool criteria that are likely to anticipate behaviors associated with attention and oppositional disorders. Our research selected the child's task orientation, sustained attention, and capacity for positive relationships—three factors that can be shown to evidence considerable stability from preschool to the early school-age period. Heinicke's (1980) review of the research literature concluded that task orientation as assessed at 3 years of age is predictive of both later task orientation and intellectual achievement. Longitudinal studies conducted by Kagan and Moss (1962), Schaefer and Bayley (1963), and Block and Block (1977) support this conclusion.

For example, Kagan and Moss (1962) define task mastery as the child's persistence with challenging task games and problems and his or her involvement in activities in which a standard of excellence is applicable. These authors' general index of task mastery for the interval from ages 3 to 6 years correlated significantly with the same index for the interval from ages 6 to 10 years; and, unlike more specific intellectual-achievement variables, this index correlated with IQ scores obtained at ages 3, 6, 10, and adulthood in both sexes. Variations in task mastery are therefore very likely to be relevant to the development of hyperactivity and attention deficit disorder.

Similarly, Block and Block (1977) stressed the continuity from ages 3 to 7 of functions labeled "ego control" and "ego resiliency." Children scoring high on measures judged to be relevant to each of these constructs at age 3 also scored higher on them at age 7. The experimentally derived index of undercontrol at age 4 correlated negatively and significantly with the following teacher rating items at ages 3 and 4: "Is Attentive"; "Able to Concentrate"; "Is Planful"; "Thinks Ahead"; "Is Dependable"; "Is Reflective." These items are clearly all relevant to task orientation and sustained attention.

More specifically, in regard to ADD-H (attention deficit disorder with hyperactivity), several projects have reported the continuity of the core symptoms of this diagnosis from preschool to school age (Campbell et al. 1986; Palfrey et al. 1985). Research reported by Jacobvitz and Sroufe (1987) further documents the continuity of inattention from 42 months to 6 years and serves as a model of linking preschool intermediate criteria to school-age assessments of the psychopathology that is to be prevented. By following children from birth to age 6, Jacobvitz and Sroufe were able to examine psychogenic and certain endogenous factors. They demonstrated a significant correlation between measures of distractibility and inattention at 42 months and a hyperactivity scale derived from the Teacher Achenbach "Child Behavior Checklist" (Achenbach and Edelbrock 1986) for the same children at age 6. This scale includes inattention and impulsivity. A maternal overstimulating care scale at 42 months also anticipated the hyperactive kindergartners. Only one of 38 early (newborn to 30 months) child measures, namely motor maturity on the Brazelton Neonatal Behavioral Assessment Scale, was a predictor. Jacobvitz and Sroufe (1987) concluded that a number of different routes to attention deficit disorder exist and that further study of the varying etiologies and the search for homogeneous subgroups are needed.

Similarly, it has been shown that another intermediary criterion, namely, the young child's capacity to develop a trusting relationship with his or her caretaker, with the child's associated ability to modulate aggressive feelings, shows considerable continuity from the first year to early school age. Thus, in their critical review of research on mother-child attachment as measured by the Ainsworth Strange Situation procedure (Ainsworth et al. 1978), Lamb and his associates (1984) concluded that there does appear to be some reliable relationship between security of attachment as measured at 1 year of age and children's later preschool peer competence. In addition to alerting investigators to the importance of considering the context in which these developing relationships are studied, Lamb et al. emphasized that temporal continuity in children's characteristics is present only when these characteristics are maintained by the continuity in the characteristics of the rearing environment.

More recent reports further support the stability of individual differences in the child's active capacity to form positive trusting relationships. Main et al. (1985) correlated the behavior of 1-year-old children in the Ainsworth Strange Situation with various indices of relationship functioning at age 6. The children classified as secure at 1 year showed more active positive responses to various simulated separation situations at 6 years. This continuity in response was particularly striking in relation to the mother. This research underlines the importance of the association between the modulation of affect (and aggression modulation in particular) and the capacity to form positive relationships. Main et al. further found that the more secure 6-year-old children when shown pictured separation situations could confront and resolve the emotional facts more readily than the children who had been classified as insecure at 1 year of age. Finally, in our search for preschool criteria that show continuity with school-age behavior, aggression has repeatedly been shown to be stable across this time span (Beach and Laird 1968; Robins 1978).

PARENT-INFANT ANTECEDENTS OF PRESCHOOL BEHAVIOR

Wishing to intervene early in the developing family, we next asked: What key pre- and postbirth antecedents significantly anticipate the variation in preschool criteria just shown to anticipate early school-age behavior?

Various studies have shown that the predominant influences on pre-school sustained attention are maternal IQ and such stable infant char-acteristics as 1-month positive vocalization and previous measures of sustained attention (Heinicke et al. 1986; Heinicke and Lampl 1988). Given these particular antecedents and the implication of genetic sources of variation (for documentation, see Heinicke et al. 1986; Heinicke and Lampl 1988), the potential for early intervention is more limited.

The next intermediate criterion—preschool task orientation—is an-ticipated by the amount of 24-month parent stimulation and the child's verbal expressiveness. The more the parents stimulate the cognitive de-velopment of their 2-year-old child, and the more verbal the child is at that age, the more likely that child's task orientation is going to be well developed at 4 years of age (Heinicke and Lampl 1988). Task orientation in the 4-year-old child is also indirectly influenced by prebirth maternal adaptation and maternal verbal IQ, and directly anticipated by prebirth positive marital quality (Heinicke and Lampl 1988). The nature of this profile of antecedents shows some potential for influencing environ-mental conditions and thus enhancing the development of task orien-tation.

A preventive intervention strategy with the greatest potential would appear to involve modification of the child's capacity for positive rela-tionships, and the associated aggression modulation. These associated intermediate criteria are influenced by the pre- and postbirth positive marital quality and by the earliest parent responsiveness to need as they in turn interact with variations in infant visual attention and fretting (Heinicke et al. 1986; Heinicke and Lampl 1988). These findings suggest that promoting the positive parent-infant mutuality in the first weeks after birth would be an appropriate focus of preventive intervention.

The question next becomes one of finding a "window of opportu-nity" for facilitating that positive parent-infant mutuality. There are var-ious possibilities, but the first postnatal pediatric visits clearly provide one such opportunity. Issues of physical development frequently lead to discussions of how to soothe the infant and how to develop an adequate sleep-wake cycle with the young infant. It is important for the pediatrician to hear how the parent defines any experienced difficulty and to relate that to caretaking and infant responses. In many instances the positive enhancement given by the pediatrician is sufficient to enable the family to provide "good enough parenting." Sometimes the family expresses concerns and/or the pediatrician observes behavior that requires further clarification and intervention. If the pediatrician is unable to pursue the matter, referral to a home-visiting child mental health professional may be the most appropriate intervention.

UCLA FAMILY DEVELOPMENT SERVICE

The UCLA Family Development Service, a home-visiting intervention, is available to families receiving care in the UCLA Obstetrical-Gynecological and Pediatric Continuity Care Clinics. Referral to the service is facilitated by a pediatric clinical social worker, thus ensuring continuing liaison between the pediatric house staff and the home-visiting intervenor. Families are recruited if they are asking for help in the nonmedical care of their physically normal infant, and they are at the same time at risk for maladaptive parenting because they are average or below average in areas of perceived social support, husband or partner adaptation, and such personality characteristics as ego strength, anxiety, mood states, capacity for relationships, and confidence in themselves as parents.

Following the referral, a preventive intervention plan consisting of the following elements is formulated: (1) initial relationship-building with the family and problem identification; (2) objective assessments of the family's functioning; and (3) the actual intervention. These steps are spelled out in three operational manuals (UCLA Family Development Service 1989).

The first manual describes the home visitor's initial response to the family's interest in the service. In various ways we convey that promoting early infant development involves enhancement of the parents' parenting, their more general family functioning, and their environmental supports. A first task of the home visitor is to listen to and help the parents clarify what they feel good about and what they experience as difficult. Listening and shared observation help to clarify areas of distress and their antecedents. Priority is given to building an ongoing relationship by the home visitor offering to be available on a regular (usually weekly) and convenient basis, and encouraging telephone contacts. Expertise is kept in the background except when advice or reassurance is appropriate to enhance the family's experience of receiving support. Before leaving the house, great care is taken by the home visitor to schedule the next contact.

The initial contacts permit subjective definition of the experienced difficulty and offer a committed, enhancing relationship. These contacts also permit observation of the salient features of the infant's caretaking environment. Although the primary observational stance is to note whatever emerges, the following five domains that are important in family development are observed: (a) the social and economic support available to the family; (b) the quality of the marital or partner relationship; (c) the individual personality of each parent, including his or her adaptation competence; (d) the quality of the transaction between parent and infant, including their positive mutuality; and (e) the early emerging and relatively stable characteristics of the infant, such as his or her soothability. Further guidelines for observation are defined within these five foci. The initial approach to gathering valid knowledge is to have the family members define through words and actions what is important rather than having them respond to a set of prestructured questions.

Somewhat by contrast but clearly as a complement to the above initial picture, a further step is to continue our evaluation using objective assessment techniques. A second manual defines ratings covering the five data domains discussed above and also guides the administration of four inventories filled out by the parents. Thus, the initial and ongoing naturalistic observations are complemented by systematic and reliable measurement techniques. The parents' functioning, the parent-infant interaction, and the infant's functioning are rated. Ratings have been developed for the parents' general capacity for empathic responsiveness, the specific transaction of parental responsiveness to the needs of the infant, and the infant's soothability. One inventory filled out by the parents is the Spielberger Anxiety State Scale (Spielberger 1977), which measures the manifest anxiety verbalized by the parent.

On the basis of the above subjective and objective assessments, a plan for intervention is formulated and initiated as guided by the third manual. Intervention begins by reflecting back on the parents' area of greatest concern. Below we describe specific interventions with two families. Both interventions begin with forming the initial relationship, identifying the developmental problems, and making initial assessments.

DEVELOPMENT OF RUTH, PAUL, AND SHEILA

Having moved to their present neighborhood from outside California, and lacking family or social support, Ruth and Paul reached out eagerly to the Family Development Service when told about it as part of Ruth's obstetric-gynecological prenatal care. Following a difficult delivery, they were elated with Sheila, their healthy, first-born infant. The parents readily formed a trusting relationship with the intervenor, and the objective assessments revealed a generally well-functioning couple that had little confidence in their parenting. The parents' efforts to respond to their infant left them very helpless. Ruth felt that the best way to comfort her desperately and frequently crying 3-week-old infant was to breast feed as often as every 2 hours. But she found herself exhausted. Our intervention explored what other solutions she had tried and what advice she had been given. One authority told her to simply let the infant cry; the mother tried but rejected this approach. Discussion with the home visitor revealed how important it was for the mother to be the sole source of comfort for her infant and how much she enjoyed the intimacy of breast feeding. Thus, a personality determinant had to be considered in dealing with the crying. The mother's need to be the all-giving person very likely stemmed from some unresolved needs in the mother herself. Other possible antecedents to the difficulty in managing the crying were studied. Potentially supportive relatives were available but had been perceived by the parents as critical: "You are spoiling the child," the relatives said. The parents felt further pressure to resolve matters themselves. A variety of nutritional and health antecedents were reviewed. Further focusing on the infant also led to the recognition that Sheila might well have been more difficult to comfort than some other 3-week-old babies, and that the parents blaming themselves for their inadequacies was not helpful.

This initial review then suggested that modifications in the area of the marital and parent-infant interaction might be most fruitful to counter the mother's tendency to want to be the sole source of comfort. What alteration in the caretaking system could be made to find alternate modes of satisfying the infant? A differentiated response to the different cries and alternate modes of comforting were modeled by the home visitor, who was heavily influenced by observing the marital interaction. The husband felt left out of the caretaking and resented his wife's excessive involvement with their daughter. This aspect of their relationship had been clearly repeated with the home visitor. Although both parents felt positively toward the home visitor, time and again an effort had to be made to avoid the mother's exclusion of her husband.

We have found that a central guide to the salient changes that need to take place in the parents' interaction with each other and the infant is the manner in which the parents relate to the home visitor. In addition to the mutually satisfying aspects of the parent–home visitor relationship, transference phenomena—namely, tendencies to repeat in new and ongoing relationships patterns of relating developed in present and past relationships—are also recognized. In this context, our experience is similar to the pioneering work reported by Fraiberg (1980). Although not interpreted, actions and discussions are designed to counter the maladaptive aspects of these repetitions and to substitute more adaptive views and actions. Thus, it was deemed important to suggest ways of soothing the infant that would draw on the strength of the father and bring him emotionally closer to his wife and daughter. Because the father could more easily tolerate his daughter's crying, he was in a better position to try various ways of comforting her. This case study illustrates the importance in all our intervention efforts of enhancing understanding of the differential meaning of cries. Also central to our intervention is the modeling of alternate modes of soothing and need satisfaction. It was suggested that instead of the mother always breast feeding, the father rock the baby or take her for a ride in the carriage. Both during the initial intervention and the weeks to follow, it was possible to model and observe the effectiveness of this approach.

The intervention plan also included discussion of the couple's sense of togetherness, and especially their need to find time to be by themselves.

> Although the regular home visiting contacts stopped at 7 months, when at 9 months the mother had difficulty putting the child to bed, a long follow-up telephone conversation and a follow-up home visit at 12 months provided support and confidence. Authoritative advice given by another source suggested that the parents abruptly leave the child to cry it out. We recognize that this approach often works well, but it did not in this case. Extensive exploration during the telephone conversation revealed the mother's ongoing reluctance to give up breast feeding, a recently unsettling trip to another state, and the husband's discomfort with his wife's overinvolvement with their daughter. Gradual weaning both from her breast and from her presence, alternate modes of satisfaction (including the father staying for a limited time with the child), and discussion of their recognized need to spend more time with each other again emerged as the core components of the intervention plan. Follow-up at 12 months revealed that the parents' difficulty in putting the daughter to bed and the distance in their marital relationship had both greatly diminished.

DEVELOPMENT OF LISA AND HER SON DAVID

An intervention with another at-risk parent, carried out by one of the coauthors of this chapter (A.T.), further illustrates our procedure:

> Lisa is a 19-year-old single woman on welfare who lives at home with her own mother. She sought help from her UCLA house staff pediatrician because she was not sure how to make her infant son David feel good about himself. She generally doubted her ability to raise him. During the first home visits she mentioned that she tended to leave him alone and let him cry loudly for a long time before she picked him up.
>
> Consistent with our general approach, our first goal with this young mother was to initiate a listening, accepting, and caring relationship. At times her distress and incoherent speech were so profound that it was difficult to both listen and know where help might be effective. Further clarification of the mother's experienced difficulty was urgently needed. Her need to develop some distance from her own possessive, controlling, alcoholic mother had to be confronted immediately. Lisa's mother would not permit home visits, so the intervenor's office was used as a place to which Lisa could bring her baby. Not meeting in her mother's home represented Lisa's wish to move away from her, but also aroused a fear that the mother might reject her.
>
> The first sessions helped further define the difficulties as experienced by Lisa and as observed by the home visitor. Although Lisa could talk of the baby's excessive crying, she was unable to articulate a way of soothing him. When David began to suck his fist during a session, Lisa did not recognize that he might be hungry, but said that she fed him before the visit. Nor did she consider that he might be sleepy rather than hungry. In brief, though David was an alert and soothable baby, Lisa was unable to determine his

needs and act accordingly. Rather, her actions seemed to be governed exclusively by her own feeling state, which fortunately she could talk about. She wanted to be a good mother and wondered how she could get her own good feelings into David. She saw him as "empty and vulnerable," and felt his crying would at least make him "feel surrounded by something."

On the whole, we were concerned about Lisa's level of emotional disturbance. We soon realized that the sense of isolation that she projected onto the infant could be related to a combination of stressors. We planned the intervention to initially focus on these sources of stress and on the disorganization manifest in her anxious, and at times incoherent, speech. Although we recognized her potential disturbance, a timely opportunity for enhancing her strength became the challenge. Further subjective clarification of her sources of stress and the objective assessment of these sources through ratings and inventories led to a treatment plan that evolved as follows:

Lisa lived with her possessive, emotionally and physically ill mother who required Lisa's welfare monies and daily caring, thus impeding her daughter's autonomous growth. A healthy sister who had left the home to pursue her education served as a model of how Lisa might escape the mother's constant criticism of her out-of-wedlock birth and what her mother perceived as Lisa's poor mothering. Meeting the intervenor away from her mother's home helped to encourage the psychological move to autonomy and also helped to confront and resolve her sense of obligation to and need of her mother. As she could trust the support of the intervenor and become psychologically less dependent on her mother, Lisa could more objectively evaluate what to expect of her mother. As Lisa freed herself from having to mother her own mother, she became receptive to another issue—the need to feed herself properly so that through her milk she could strengthen her infant. As she experienced the caring "good" beginning with the home visitor, Lisa recalled her own "good" childhood beginnings and became concerned that the "good" would vanish. How could she sustain the "good" for David? While acknowledging these concerns, the home visitor initially focused on the importance of attending to David's immediate and practical needs. How could Lisa provide him with enough calories now in order to ensure a future of good feelings? Lisa became increasingly responsive to the home visitor's encouragement to expose David to various "interesting cognitive experiences." However, while Lisa's social responses to her infant increased and she became more effective in feeding and stimulating him, effective empathy was often still wanting.

Before Lisa's relationship with the home visitor and David could become more positive, and the work of enhancing her empathic responsiveness could continue, a major negative transference expectation had to be recognized. In various ways Lisa communicated her expectation that just as in her early relationship with her parents, the new "good" experiences with the intervenor would cease or be spoiled. Consequently, the major thrust of the intervention shifted to show Lisa through discussion and action (not interpretation) that her negative predictions need not come true. For example, she feared that having "sinned" sexually, with an out-of-wedlock birth, her good David would be taken away from her. Accordingly, she and the home visitor extensively discussed her fear that David would be kidnapped, especially by his biological father. Parallel to these discussions, the home visitor continued her encouragement and modeling of a relaxed, positive mother-infant mutuality; Lisa became increasingly able to respond effectively to the baby.

Discussions of Lisa's conscious feelings that she was undeserving of her emerging satisfying relationship with her son were consistent with her less conscious communications that she did not deserve the home visitor. Lisa would be late to appointments, but always came; if she canceled appointments, she notified the home visitor. Her behavior suggested that it was safer to trust her controlling mother than this reliably giving person. Through determined patience and some accommodation, the home visitor gradually passed these tests. Lisa increasingly came regularly, expressed her gratitude for the home visitor's help, and during subsequent contacts sorted out what she could reliably expect from David's father and her own mother. How could she best take care of herself and enhance David's development? The intervention process allowed her to experience not being trapped and helpless in the face of a feared rejection from her former partner.

Before we further summarize this work, which mostly occurred in the second half of David's first year, we will describe observations of Lisa and David done at 6 months. The Bayley Development (Bayley 1969) revealed David's excellent motor skills and his reaction to being separated from his mother. An extension of the Bayley Scales was developed to assess the quality of the mutuality between mother and infant. The infant's positive affect, as opposed to anxiety and defensiveness, was estimated from the reaction to the examiner and to a planned brief separation from the mother that occurred at the end of the testing. These observations were combined with ratings of the mother's responsiveness to the child's needs in the home. David and Lisa's positive mutuality at 6 months was classified as "Parent Shows a Medium Level of Responsiveness and the Infant Shows Positive Affect" (see Oates and Heinicke 1986, for mode of classification). We feel David definitely reacted to his mother's departure but then turned to the examiner and to the manipulation of various objects. These various observations showed that David's development at 6 months was average or, especially for the motor items, above average. He scored 116 on the motor scale and 102 on the mental scale. Lisa seemed proud of her mothering, but at times she was still suspicious and distant.

We shall now return to the further work done by Lisa in relation to her son's father and her own mother:

Lisa longed for the affection that David's father had once given her, but she gradually realized that he could not be counted on. Several sessions were devoted to recounting various experiences with him. Lisa concluded that she wanted to provide some contact between David and his father, but that his father would have to initiate it.

In regard to her mother, Lisa began increasingly to realize that she would have to find her own residence away from her mother and a sufficiently well-paying job to move off welfare. Part of Lisa's ability to leave her mother and not be negatively bound to her resulted from her developing a more positive and realistic view of her mother. Lisa realized that her mother had endured a hard life with a physically abusive husband who had sexually abused Lisa's older sister. Also very important in facilitating the plan to move out was the increasing positive relationship that had developed between Lisa and the home visitor. As opposed to her initial sense of needing to contain Lisa's intense anxiety, the home visitor experienced the pleasures of a positive exchange. This positive base enabled the home visitor to conceive and plan Lisa's increasing contacts with other young mothers through a mother-infant group and charity work in a religious organization.

Although a termination point for the fairly frequent contacts with the home visitor was discussed, Lisa needed to be able to structure continuous contacts until David was 12 months old. She quietly but firmly resisted the idea of terminating contacts before that point and also requested the continuity of an occasional contact afterward. As she risked the autonomy of a job and her own apartment, she needed to maintain a positive base with the home visitor.
As termination approached, Lisa described how the home visitor's encouragement enabled her to experience motherhood as a valuable, worthwhile "job." Lisa now had many warm positive feelings about her son and his interactions and progress. She held a joyous celebration of his first birthday. When David was 14 months old, Lisa moved out of her mother's home and started to look for employment as a live-in housekeeper, a job in which she could also accommodate David. It remains difficult for her to imagine no ongoing contact with the home visitor, but the mother-infant group provides Lisa with continuing support.

Responding to Lisa's needs, the home visitor has maintained some contact with her and with David. Repeat evaluation using the modified Bayley scale examination revealed Bayley scores for David that were similar to those obtained in the first evaluation: 107 on motor performance and 99 in mental development. Comparison of the mother-infant relationship shortly after birth with the relationship at 6 and 12 months revealed an increase in the positive mutuality between mother and child. When David was separated from his mother at 12 months, he again made it clear that he missed her by running to the door, but he did not fret. Instead David preoccupied himself with the Bayley examiner and greeted his mother with a smile as she reached for him during the reunion.

Systematic reliable ratings done at 1, 6, and 12 months revealed that Lisa was more responsive to a variety of her child's needs and more positive and less tense with him. Although the ratings revealed no clinically dramatic changes in her experienced support or general coping, both of these areas also improved to a statistically significant extent.

David's positive development from birth to 1 year of age was quite striking. By 12 months he was more alert, more responsive, actively exploring the world, and in general showing a greater sense of making an impact on the world. He was less irritable and enjoyed a greater positive mutuality with his mother. Although some of these developments may have occurred without intervention, we believe further research will show that the intervention made a significant impact. Plans for such research are discussed below.

In summary, the intervention plan focused on restoring and maintaining a sense that a good experience is not disrupted, and particularly that a good relationship can continue and can be the basis of greater autonomy. In parallel, the home visitor's modeling of specific responses to David helped the mother build her repertoire of skills related to feeding, social stimulation, and overall responsiveness to the needs of her infant. Lisa said that she really liked the home visitor because the visitor did not give her advice, just helpful hints.

FAMILY DEVELOPMENT AS A FUNCTION OF THE DURATION OF THE CONTACT WITH THE INTERVENOR: A PILOT RESEARCH PROJECT

The development of a trusting working relationship between the parents and the home visitor is central to the formulation of the preventive intervention discussed above. We have outlined how we use this relationship to effect change. In addition, we have asked, more generally, what other factors allow this relationship to be used most effectively.

The quality of this relationship is affected by the quality of the family's initial functioning and the parents' capacities for developing a working relationship. The personal qualities of the individual home visitor and the specific style of intervention are also important contributors. Moreover, the ecological and supportive context of the family clearly affects the developing relationship. Much evidence indicates that the frequency and duration of contacts by the home visitor are also important. Therefore, we decided to study the effect on family development of varying the duration in number of months of home visitor contacts. We hypothesized that the duration of the home-visiting contacts influences the extent to which trusting relationships are formed. This trust in turn provides for real relationship and transference developments, as well as sufficient opportunity to resolve the maladaptive aspects of the relationships and move the families to greater independence. A review of 20 controlled studies has revealed that a greater number of components of the family system are changed when there are at least 11 contacts with the intervenor during the infant's first year of life (Heinicke et al. 1988). As a result of our review of the experience of ongoing projects (Barnard et al. 1988), combined with the above review of previous research, our new project will include families seen for 1, 12, or 24 months. Contacts will average one per week during the first year and approximately two per month during the second year.

Combining our expectations about the impact of duration of contact with consideration of the initial characteristics of the family, we formulated the following hypotheses in relation to three intermediate criteria, namely, sustained attention, task orientation, and the capacity to form relationships as reflected in aggression modulation:

1. The child's sustained attention in the interval from ages 2 to 4 years will be minimally affected by even the 24-month home visitation intervention.
2. Task orientation will be affected by the 24-month home intervention, but especially so if the variables predicting task orientation are subject to change in response to the intervention. These variables include husband-wife adaptation, parental-adaptation, competence, and warmth, parental stimulation and responsiveness to need, and child verbal expressiveness and aggression modulation.
3. Aggression modulation and the transactionally associated parental responsiveness to need will be affected by the 24-month intervention contact and also by the 12-month contact if the variables influencing the transaction are subject to change. These variables include husband-wife adaptation, parental adaptation-competence and warmth, and parental responsiveness to the needs of the child.

Four types of systematic assessment are being used to test the impact of duration of contacts:

1. *Parent, parent-infant, and infant ratings* based on the in-home observation at 1, 6, 12, and 24 months. This rating methodology has been previously tested for reliability (Heinicke et al. 1986) and will be checked by parallel observation.
2. *A structured interview with the mother* focused on deriving personality dimensions and a DSM-III Axis II personality diagnosis (Loranger 1988). These assessments will parallel the parent personality factor scores derived from the parent ratings.
3. *Four inventories completed by the parents* at 1, 6, 12, and 24 months: the Spielberger Anxiety State Scale (Spielberger 1977); the Cutrona Support Inventory (Cutrona 1984); the Locke-Wallace Marital Inven-

tory (Locke and Wallace 1959); and the Beck Depression Inventory (Beck et al. 1961).

4. *The Bayley Scales of Infant Development* (Bayley 1969) and an associated procedure of assessing the parent-infant positive mutuality described above (Oates and Heinicke 1986).

CONCLUSIONS

This chapter presents the rationale for a specific preventive family intervention beginning shortly after birth. A salient focus has been on the parent's responsiveness to the needs of the infant, which in turn is seen as crucial to the development of the child's capacity for positive relationships. The development of a trusting working relationship between the parents and the home visitor is central to the effectiveness of the home-visiting intervention in enhancing this responsiveness. A design for studying the influence of the initial status of the family and the duration of the intervenor contact on the development of that working relationship has been outlined and is being pursued.

REFERENCES

Achenbach T, Edelbrock C: Manual for Teacher's Report Form. Unpublished manuscript. Burlington, VT, University of Vermont, Department of Psychiatry, 1986

Ainsworth MDS, Blehar MC, Waters E, et al: Patterns of Attachment. Hillsdale, NJ, Erlbaum, 1978

American Psychiatric Association: Diagnostic and Statistical Manual of Mental Disorders, 3rd Edition. Washington, DC, American Psychiatric Association, 1980

Barnard K, Booth CL, Spieker S, et al: Comparison of two infant prevention models: interactions between maternal characteristics and program type. Abstract of paper presented at the biannual meeting of the International Conference on Infant Studies, Washington, DC, April 1988

Bayley N: Bayley Scales of Infant Development. New York, The Psychological Corporation, 1969

Beach CF, Laird JD: Follow-up study of children identified early as emotionally disturbed. J Consult Clin Psychol 32:369–374, 1968

Beck AT, Ward CH, Mendelson M, et al: An inventory for measuring depression. Arch Gen Psychiatry 4:561–569, 1961

Block J, Block JH: The developmental continuity of ego control and ego resiliency. Abstract of paper presented at the biannual meeting of the Society for Research in Child Development, New Orleans, April 1977

Campbell SB, Breaux AM, Ewing LJ, et al: Correlates and predictors of hyperactivity and aggression: a longitudinal study of parent-referred problem preschoolers. J Abnorm Child Psychol 14:217–234, 1986

Cutrona CE: Social support and stress in the transition to parenthood. J Abnorm Psychol 93:378–390, 1984

Fraiberg S (ed): Clinical Studies in Infant Mental Health: The First Year of Life. New York, Basic Books, 1980

Heinicke CM: Continuity and discontinuity of task orientation. J Am Acad Child Psychiatry 19:637–653, 1980

Heinicke C, Lampl E: Pre and post-birth antecedents of three and four-year-old attention, I.Q., verbal expressiveness, task orientation and capacity for relationships. Infant Behav Dev 11:381–410, 1988

Heinicke CM, Diskin SD, Ramsey-Klee CM, et al: Pre and postbirth antecedents of 2-year-old attention, capacity for relationships, and verbal expressiveness. Dev Psychol 22:777–787, 1986

Heinicke CM, Beckwith L, Thompson A: Early intervention in the family system: a framework and review. Infant Ment Health J 9:111–141, 1988

Jacobvitz D, Sroufe LA: The early caregiver-child relationship and attention-deficit disorder with hyperactivity in kindergarten: a prospective study. Child Dev 58:1488–1495, 1987

Kagan J, Moss H: Birth to Maturity. New York, John Wiley, 1962

Lamb MH, Thompson RA, Gardner WP, et al: Security of infantile attachment as assessed in the "strange situation": its study and biological interpretation. Behav Brain Sci 7:127–171, 1984

Locke H, Wallace K: Short marital adjustment and prediction tests: their reliability and validity. Marriage Fam Living 21:251–255, 1959

Loranger AW: Personality disorder examination (PDE) manual. Yonkers, NY, DV Communications, 1988

Main M, Kaplan N, Cassidy J: Security in infancy, childhood, and adulthood: a move to the level of representation, in Growing Points of Attachment Theory and Research. Edited by Bretherton I, Waters E. Monographs of the Society for Research in Child Development, Vol 50. Chicago, IL, University of Chicago Press, 1985, pp 66–104

Oates DS, Heinicke CM: Pre-birth prediction of the quality of the mother-infant interaction in the first year of life. J Fam Issues 6:523–542, 1986

Palfrey JS, Levine MD, Walker DK, et al: The emergence of attention deficits in early childhood: a prospective study. Dev Behav Pediatr 6:339–348, 1985

Robins LN: Sturdy childhood predictors of adult antisocial behavior: replications from longitudinal studies. Psychol Med 8:611–622, 1978

Schaefer E, Bayley N: Maternal Behavior, Child Behavior, and Their Intercorrelations From Infancy Through Adolescence. Monographs of the Society for Research in Child Development, Vol 28. Chicago, IL, University of Chicago Press, 1963

Spielberger CD: Self Evaluation Questionnaire. Palo Alto, CA, Consulting Psychologists Press, 1977

UCLA Family Development Service: Operational Manuals for Preventive Intervention Plan. Los Angeles, CA, University of California, Department of Psychiatry and Biobehavioral Sciences, 1989. [The three operation manuals are available from the author (CMH), Department of Psychiatry and Biobehavioral Sciences, University of California, Los Angeles, 760 Westwood Plaza, Los Angeles, California 90024-1759.]

CHAPTER 5

A Preventive Intervention Model for Chemically Dependent Parents

Judy Howard, M.D.
Vickie Kropenske, P.H.N.

The problems of illicit drug and alcohol abuse in our society, particularly involving parents, have continued to escalate in spite of national and international attempts to halt this growing concern. It has been estimated that within the United States, more than 15 million individuals abuse drugs or alcohol on a regular basis (Abelson and Miller 1985; Adams et al. 1986; National Commission on Marijuana and Drug Abuse 1973). Drug and alcohol dependency continues to be a pervasive and increasingly destructive problem, affecting all aspects of an individual's personal and family life. However, at no time is the impairment of functioning more critical than when the chemically dependent adult becomes a parent. As commentators in a 1988 *Newsweek* magazine article noted, "It is important to begin to think of addiction not only as an illness that affects bodily organs but as an illness that affects families" (Leershen and Namuth 1988).

Increasingly large numbers of women, most of whom are of child-bearing age, admit to problems of chemical dependency. In the majority of cases, these women are unable to shake their addiction, even with the assistance of drug and alcohol treatment programs. As this pattern of prenatal drug use has escalated, hospitals throughout the country have documented a disturbing increase in reports of infants exposed prenatally to drugs (U.S. House of Representatives 1989). The chemically dependent neonate has now become a common occurrence in the newborn nurseries and neonatal intensive care units of community hospitals and major medical centers across the United States.

71

During the past decade, mass education through the news media and professional journals has alerted the general population to fetal alcohol syndrome, a consequence of maternal ethanol abuse. There is extensive evidence showing that infants who have had in utero exposure to alcohol frequently are born prematurely, are of low birth weight, and are at risk for medical problems postnatally (Leershen and Namuth 1988). Mental retardation, neurological impairments, growth retardation, and behavioral disorders have also been well documented in longitudinal studies of children of alcoholic mothers (Clarren and Smith 1978; Jones et al. 1974; Streissguth 1978). O'Connor et al. (1986) examined middle-class professional women and showed that the intellectual abilities of these women's offspring varied directly according to the women's average daily alcohol consumption.

Within the past ten years, as women in particular have begun to abuse drugs as well as alcohol, research efforts have focused on identifying and documenting the effects of prenatal exposure to illicit drugs of abuse such as opiates, phencyclidine (PCP), and cocaine.

Extensive documentation exists describing the withdrawal syndrome commonly seen in infants prenatally exposed to heroin and the synthetic opiate methadone. These newborns are typically tremulous, irritable, and hypertonic, and often suffer from vomiting, diarrhea, and dehydration (Finnegan 1986; Wilson et al. 1973). Furthermore, there is also growing evidence that prenatal exposure to opiates is related to fine motor incoordination, short attention spans, sleep disturbances, and low frustration tolerance in children followed up to 5 years of age (Finnegan 1986; Kaltenbach et al. 1979; Rosen and Johnson 1982; Wilson et al. 1973, 1979).

Studies of infants prenatally exposed to PCP have demonstrated that this drug also produces increased irritability, tremors, darting eye movements, and increased sensitivity to environmental stimuli (Strauss et al. 1981). The long-term sequelae observed in children exposed to PCP include global developmental delays, impaired spatial orientation, clumsy gross and fine motor movements, unclear speech, and poor interpersonal relationships in spite of nurturing and stable environments (Howard et al. 1986).

Finally, the much publicized abuse of cocaine and "crack" cocaine has prompted studies of the prenatal effects of this widely used stimulant. Cocaine, once thought to be a harmless, recreational drug, has been shown to have serious and severe effects on adults (Gawin and Ellinwood 1988). Infants who have been exposed in utero have a higher incidence of spontaneous abortion and abruptio placentae related to their mothers' prenatal cocaine use (Chasnoff et al. 1985; Ryan et al. 1987; Smith and Deitch 1987). Other researchers have reported decreased birth weights and an increase in premature deliveries and stillbirths, as well as higher malformation rates (Bingol et al. 1987; Chasnoff et al. 1987; Madden et al. 1986; Ryan et al. 1987; Yonekura et al. 1987). In addition, studies have reported ocular abnormalities in the neonatal period (Isenberg et al. 1987), as well as an increase in sudden infant death syndrome (SIDS) during the first 6 months of life (Chasnoff et al. 1987). These complications also place the infant at far greater risk for later medical problems.

In addition to the biological risk that results from prenatal drug exposure, chemically dependent infants may also be environmentally at risk. Frequently, these medically compromised infants have caretakers with limited knowledge about their special care needs, and few skills for providing appropriate oversight. The majority of drug-exposed infants have significant feeding and sleeping problems throughout the first 6 months of life. Many infants who have been exposed to heroin and/or methadone suffer vomiting and diarrhea, as well as excessive movements that burn up calories and contribute to poor growth and weight gain during the first year of life. Protracted high-pitched cries, frantic sucking of fists, tremors, excessive movements, and inability to organize normal sleep-wake periods are commonly observed (Finnegan 1986; Oro and Dixon 1987; Rosen and Johnson 1982; Wilson et al. 1973).

These prolonged withdrawal behaviors are disruptive for the family and exhausting for caretakers, who can become more and more frustrated by their inability to soothe and comfort the irritable infant. When a caretaker is "turned off" by a demanding and emotionally labile infant and is unfamiliar with how to practically care for the withdrawing neonate, he or she may leave the infant alone to cry in a distant room of the house, or may return the child as a "failed" placement.

Infants may also be at environmental risk when placed in the home of the biological parent(s). New federal and state legislation places increased emphasis on family maintenance and reunification. However, some states, such as California, recommend that these newborns be reported for child abuse if they demonstrate withdrawal behaviors following birth, although family reunification still remains the short-term goal. The courts have responded by placing affected infants in their parental homes following delivery or within a few weeks after birth as long as the parents are willing to consider attendance at—let alone actually attend—a drug treatment program.

Consequently, such infants may be environmentally at risk because of their parents' multiple social and health problems and addicted lifestyles. Frequently, the biological parents serve only as intermittent caretakers and are unable to fully attend to their children's emotional and physical needs. The parents' physical need for "drugs," compounded by their "high" psychological state, makes them inaccessible both emotionally and physically to their infants' or children's needs.

Although a pregnant addict may have the best intentions to remain drug-free, the strong grip of addiction, the chaotic life-style associated with drug use, the lack of appropriate support systems, and ineffective coping skills make this task nearly impossible. Extensive studies of these families have described the continuing poverty, personal demoralization, physical and mental illness, and social instability of chemically dependent parents (Fanshel 1975; Lawson and Wilson 1980; Nichtern 1973).

Many women who abuse drugs and/or alcohol were themselves victims of physical, sexual, and/or emotional abuse as children, and the majority were raised in households where one or both parents were also addicted to drugs and/or alcohol (Mayer and Black 1977; Steele 1987). As parents, these women often utilize the same poor coping mechanisms modeled by their own parents in dealing with life's problems and frustrations, including their struggles with childrearing. They lack a strong, positive parenting model for use in raising their own children (Regan et al. 1987).

It is often a struggle to engage this population in treatment, and their life-style makes long-term follow-up a particular challenge. Families may actively request referrals and resources, with the intention of seeking assistance and treatment. However, lack of follow-through is prevalent, and motivation for seeking treatment is usually temporary. Parents may not utilize traditional systems, or may use systems inappropriately. Correspondingly, long-term planning, intervention, and follow-up with these families is essential, especially given the chronic nature of chemical dependency.

A PREVENTIVE INTERVENTION MODEL

As a result of our growing awareness of the problem of substance abuse among pregnant women, the deleterious effects of prenatal drug and alcohol exposure on the unborn, and the lack of appropriate services and resources for caretakers of these infants, in 1985 the UCLA Department of Pediatrics received a 3-year grant from the U.S. Department of Education to develop and implement a model demonstration program to serve this at-risk population of infants and their caretakers.

The model was designed and developed within an ecological framework that addresses and integrates the unique problems of the parents, the special issues and vulnerabilities of the child, family dynamics, and the roles and services of community agencies and systems. This ecological approach to intervention has provided a strong and comprehensive scaffold, well-suited to the complex support needs of chemically dependent families and the multiple agencies that serve them.

The model project, which provided for development and refinement of an earlier comprehensive intervention program, served 20 infants until

Table 5-1. Maternal drug use during pregnancy ($N = 20$)

Drug	n (%)
Cocaine	16 (80)
Heroin	9 (45)
Marijuana	5 (25)
Methadone	4 (20)
Phencyclidine (PCP)	4 (20)
Other	7 (35)
(codeine, Valium, Darvon, Quaalude, phenothiazine, imipramine)	

Note. Fifty-five percent of mothers gave a history of intravenous drug use; 50% of mother/infant pairs had positive toxicology screens for more than one drug.

18 months of age, 25 biological parents, 28 siblings, 16 extended family members, and 20 foster parents who served as caretakers for these children. The two goals of the model program were (a) to promote a stable and appropriately responsive environment for these infants, and (b) to ensure continuity in their health care.

IDENTIFICATION OF FAMILIES

In selecting families for this project, priority was given to serving women during the prenatal period. However, because so few women sought prenatal care, the majority of our mother-infant pairs were identified postdelivery. Three women were identified prenatally in the UCLA Obstetrics Clinic and 17 infants postnatally in the UCLA Newborn Nursery.

The characteristics of this randomly selected population of mothers and infants were strikingly similar to those reported in the literature. Fifty percent of the mothers had experienced serious obstetrical complications during delivery. These included preterm delivery (45%), prolonged rupture of membranes (20%), placenta previa (10%), and chorioamnionitis (10%). All mothers were poly-drug abusers, and 55% gave history of intravenous drug use (Table 5-1).

Socially, 75% of mothers had grown up in households where there had been a history of parental drug or alcohol abuse, and 40% had experienced physical and/or sexual abuse. Eighty percent of the women chose a spouse or partner who also abused drugs and alcohol, and at the time of delivery three mothers (15%) reported a supportive relationship with the infants' fathers. Of the 15 mothers who previously had had children, 45% currently had another child in foster care or in the care of a relative.

The characteristics of the nine preterm and 11 full-term infants born to these medically and socially high-risk mothers are described in Table

Table 5-2.   Characteristics of infants

	Preterm (N = 9)	Full-term (N = 11)	Combined (N = 20)
Sex			
Male	6	2	8
Female	3	9	12
Gestational age	32	39	36
(in weeks)	(26–36)	(37–41)	(26–41)
Birth weight	1,804	2,665	2,278
(in grams)	(730–2,690)	(2,100–3,300)	(730–3,300)
Apgar scores			
≤6 at 1 minute	6(67)	3(27)	9(45)
≤6 at 5 minutes	2(22)		2(10)
Mean length of	35.1	5	18.6
hospital stay			
(in days)			

Note.   Parenthetical figures represent the range.

5-2. These infants exhibited a variety of medical and neurobehavioral complications. Neurobehavioral effects included tremors (60%), lethargy (40%), hypertonia (35%), irritability (20%), abnormal eye movements (20%), clonus (15%), and high-pitched cry (15%). Significant medical complications were seen in 50% of the infants: retinopathy of prematurity (20%), chronic lung disease (15%), small size for gestational age (15%), and dysmorphology (15%). Intraventricular hemorrhage, porencephalic cyst, cerebral infarct, retinal detachment, seizure disorder, and cardiac arrhythmia were additional complications seen within this cohort of infants. Significantly, nine of these infants were hospitalized for a total of 316 days in the UCLA Medical Center intensive care unit.

At the time of discharge from the hospital, 40% of the infants were placed in foster care, 35% were placed in the care of a relative, and 25% were discharged to a parent.

ASSESSMENT

Within the model program, each staff member had a specific role to play in assessing the families' health care, social, and environmental status:

1. The social worker met with each mother and, through interviews, obtained information about her family and childhood, her introduction to drugs, her drug and alcohol use, her school history, her previous pregnancies and their outcomes, her medical and obstetric history, and her hopes for her family.

2. The pediatricians reviewed each infant's and mother's medical records, examined the newborns to determine neurobehavioral status, looked for evidence of dysmorphology, and served as consultants to the primary care pediatricians and neonatologists.
3. The public health nurse was responsible for acquiring information about the health of all family members, home environments, the mothers' caretaking experiences, and the newborns' evolving feeding and sleeping schedules.

DEVELOPMENT OF INDIVIDUAL AND FAMILY INTERVENTION PLANS

Following the initial assessments as described above, the staff identified strengths, needs, and problem areas for each family. Incorporated into this information were important data gained from collaboration and consultation with involved public and community agencies. At 6-month intervals these intervention plans were adjusted following team case presentations to meet the changing needs of the infants, family members, and caretakers.

To implement the intervention plan, we focused on the identified infant, making him or her the "center" of our ecological model. This perspective of the environment aided us in planning for the infant's total needs, while still addressing the ongoing problems and needs of the biological and/or foster family.

The three primary objectives of intervention were as follows: (a) providing developmental assessment for the identified infant and his or her siblings, as well as coordinating their health care and services; (b) providing education to the parents, foster parents, and extended family about fetal and infant development, child health and immunization needs, safety, and nutrition; and (c) providing social work intervention for the parents, foster parents, and extended family in terms of crisis intervention counseling, referrals, and interagency coordination and collaboration.

IMPACT OF MODEL

The most salient outcomes of this model and their impact on service delivery to this biologically and environmentally at-risk population are as follows:

1. The program ensured continuity of medical services for all infants, including those infants who experienced changes in foster placement. Prior to this project, there was no systematic follow-up or tracking system within Los Angeles County to coordinate and monitor the

Table 5-3. Developmental outcome at 12 months ($N = 20$)

Disability (n)	n (%)

Physically handicapped
  Cerebral palsy (3)
  Visual impairment (1)
	3 (15)

Global developmental delay	2 (10)

Delay within a specific area
  Gross motor (1)
  Fine motor (4)
  Adaptive (1)
  Language (1)
  Personal/Social (1)
	5 (25)

Note. Some children had more than one disability.

medical care of infants born to substance-abusing mothers. Consequently, these infants were frequently lost to follow-up or received only sporadic and inconsistent medical care. In contrast, all infants followed by this model project received routine well-baby care, were enrolled in the Supplemental Food Program for Women, Infants, and Children (WIC), and received current immunizations. When there was a change in a court-ordered placement, our staff facilitated the transfer of medical services and information. Private pediatricians providing well-baby care for many project infants were sent complete medical histories and were periodically informed of our developmental findings.

2. Early identification of neurological and developmental problems was made possible. Formal developmental assessments for all infants were completed by the project pediatrician, who has a subspecialty in child development. At 12 months of age, 50% of the children within the project showed developmental disabilities (Table 5-3): 15% had cerebral palsy, 10% were globally delayed, and 25% exhibited significant delays in at least one area of development. Because of this careful developmental follow-up, we were able to initiate early in-home intervention services for these affected children as well as facilitate their entry into systems that could provide for their ongoing developmental needs.

3. All infant caretakers (parents, foster parents, relatives) received extensive education regarding the clinical manifestations of prenatal drug exposure and the special care needs of this population. Withdrawing infants are difficult to care for, and in Los Angeles County such children experience an average of five home placements per year because of foster parent and relative "burnout." Caretakers generally receive no training in the care of the chemically dependent

Table 5-4. Home environment of infants ($N = 20$)

	Discharge n (%)	6 Months n (%)	12 Months n (%)
Foster care	8 (40)	6 (30)	7 (35)
Care of relative	7 (35)	6 (30)	6 (30)
Parental home	5 (25)	8 (40)	7 (35)

Note. Infants averaged 2.1 placements during the first year.

infant and are often unaware of the child's unique needs. In contrast, infants served by our project averaged only two home placements during the first 12 months. Our home intervention provided the biological parents, the foster parents, and the extended family members with sufficient support to decrease burnout in the care of these irritable infants with their erratic sleep schedules. (The home environments of the infants during the first year are described in Table 5-4.)

4. Siblings with previously undiagnosed medical, developmental, and learning problems were identified. The medical, developmental, and social assessments completed by project staff resulted in the identification of 13 siblings with significant untreated medical, developmental, and/or emotional problems. For example, within one household a 5-year-old sibling had not received any immunizations, was not currently enrolled in state-mandated kindergarten, and was found to have indistinct speech, language delays, and poor socialization skills. For each of these at-risk siblings our staff also developed an individual intervention plan that resulted in these children obtaining appropriate treatment and services.

5. Project staff remained with the program through the entire 3-year grant period. The design of the project enabled staff to provide each other with support, professional assistance, and alternative perspectives throughout the intervention process. This "team" support created staff stability and consistency and helped to counter the feelings of frustration and ineffectiveness that are common in this work.

DISCUSSION

Our success in attaining the basic goals set forth in the 3-year model demonstration program serving chemically dependent infants may seem insignificant in light of what is known about the theoretical approaches to early intervention and the implementation of such programs (Bricker and Dow 1980; Haskins et al. 1978; Hayden and Haring 1977; Tjossem 1976). Our goals were purposefully basic: ongoing health care and maintenance for all infants; developmental assessment and referral to appropriate community programs for infants and their siblings; support and assistance to caretakers; and in-service training and support for program staff. These accomplishments may be taken for granted by professionals working with developmentally high-risk populations of young children. However, infants exposed prenatally to drugs present a unique set of circumstances for professionals who plan preventive intervention programs for these compromised infants and their families.

The basic principles of intervention include home- and community-based services, a comprehensive approach to the individual child and the needs of the family, and a multidisciplinary approach with interagency collaboration and coordination. Yet, the staff involved in the UCLA model program found that these infants and their caretakers differed significantly from those nondrug-exposed infants and families who have been traditionally served by early intervention programs.

One of the most striking differences is the caretaker's lack of commitment to the child. Any professional who works with high-risk children must be acutely aware of the importance of enlisting the parents as partners when planning intervention goals and strategies aimed at optimizing the child's development. However, parents who are substance abusers have a priority (i.e., drugs) that precedes that of their child. Their days' activities are often planned around their biological need for the next fix. Furthermore, while under the influence of drugs, it is difficult for these individuals to organize their own basic needs, let alone the needs of their children. Compounding this problem is the staggering percentage of substance-abusing parents who themselves were reared by parents who abused drugs and alcohol. Thus, the intergenerational cycle of parenting style is perpetuated.

A second reason for lack of caretaker commitment is based on the fact that these children are frequently placed with different foster parents for varying lengths of time. The foster parents' role is to care for the children on a temporary basis until the biological parents have received treatment for their addiction and are able to "parent" on a daily basis. Under such circumstances, how is it possible for the foster parent, no matter how nurturing, to develop a total commitment to the child's emotional, physical, and developmental needs? What psychological approach would a foster parent take in order to commit emotionally to a child he or she stands to lose in 6 or 12 months?

Several unique issues must be considered when working with substance-abusing families:

1. *The parents' mental status.* Individuals who are under the influence of drugs and/or alcohol experience broad alterations in mental alertness. How does the professional evaluate the parents' alert state? For example, the acute effects of cocaine cause the user to feel a sense

of control and be hypervigilant. If a discussion with the professional takes place during such a state, will the parent still recall salient points the next day, after the period of dysphoria has set in? Adults who chronically use PCP are known to be mentally impaired, and even schizophrenic. Is a mother who has used PCP for 5 years and brings her child to the clinic capable of day-to-day parenting? Drugs and alcohol eventually damage the adult user's memory, learning, and emotional responses as well. In the group of 20 children whom we served, 50% of the mothers had either abandoned their children or had only infrequent contact with them. Where do we draw the fine line between mental capability and mental impairment?

2. *Environmental inconsistency.* The parents are often physically and emotionally unavailable. As substance abusers, they tend to neglect their own health care, failing to obtain treatment for venereal disease, malnutrition, and anemia. Multiple caretakers are involved with the children even within the biological parents' residence. While the parents' fluctuating mental status makes them emotionally unavailable, foster family placements only add to this pattern of environmental inconsistency.

3. *Extensive involvement of community-based systems.* A comprehensive intervention program for such families must include a variety of agencies. The children are often dependents of the courts and are invariably involved with children's protective services. In addition, professionals from other programs are frequently involved, e.g., visiting nurse associations for home visits, foster parents, drug treatment counselors, and WIC program officials. During a 12-month period the staff involved in the model demonstration program worked with an average of five agencies per family, contacting them an average of 52 times, and holding an average of two case conferences per year. Multiple agencies have multiple policies that require completion of separate forms and development of separate family treatment plans. Furthermore, many agencies have limited knowledge about the medical and developmental issues affecting the care of these at-risk children.

4. *Safety of the children and of involved professional staff.* Drugs and alcohol decrease inhibitions and may be associated with acts of aggression and violence. The sale of illicit drugs is also associated with violence. Professionals who make home visits to substance-abusing families are in jeopardy of being in the right place at the wrong time. Additionally, the incidence of child abuse increases when family members use drugs and alcohol (Fanshel 1975). How do staff members working with such families balance their professional knowledge with the anger they must feel at some level regarding their concern for the children's safety, their own safety, and implementation of a family

intervention plan aimed at improving this generation's chances for a better life?

These issues are present in each substance-abusing family. There are more questions than answers. Yet, tens of thousands of such children and parents exist in this nation who require preventive intervention services. Perhaps acknowledgment of these issues will allow us to proceed with caution and a realistic approach. Our expectations for success and change with these families cannot be too far reaching.

REFERENCES

Abelson HI, Miller JD: A decade of trends in cocaine use in the household population, in Cocaine Use in America: Epidemiologic and Clinical Perspectives. Edited by Kozel NJ, Adams E. Washington, DC, National Institute on Drug Abuse Research Monograph Series, Vol 61, 1985, pp 35–49

Adams EH, Gfroerer JC, Rouse BA, et al: Trends in prevalence and consequences of cocaine use. Adv Alcohol Subst Abuse 6:49–71, 1986

Bingol N, Fuchs M, Diaz V, et al: Teratogenicity of cocaine in humans. J Pediatr 110:93–96, 1987

Bricker D, Dow M: Early intervention with the young severely handicapped child. J Assoc Severe Handicaps 5:130–135, 1980

Chasnoff IJ, Burns WJ, Schnoll SH, et al: Cocaine in pregnancy. N Engl J Med 313:666–669, 1985

Chasnoff IJ, Burns KA, Burns WJ: Cocaine use in pregnancy: perinatal morbidity and mortality. Neurotoxicol Teratol 9:219–293, 1987

Clarren S, Smith D: The fetal alcohol syndrome. N Engl J Med 298:1063–1067, 1978

Fanshel D: Parental failure and consequences for children: the drug-abusing mother whose children are in foster care. Am J Public Health 65:604–612, 1975

Finnegan LP: Neonatal abstinence syndrome: assessment and pharmacotherapy, in Neonatal Therapy Update. Edited by Rubaltelli FF, Granati B. New York, Excerpta Medica, 1986, pp 122–146

Gawin FH, Ellinwood EH Jr: Cocaine and other stimulants: actions, abuse, and treatment. N Engl J Med 318:1173–1182, 1988

Haskins R, Finkelstein NW, Stedman DJ: Infant stimulation programs and their effects. Pediatr Ann 7:99–105, 1978

Hayden A, Haring N: The acceleration and maintenance of developmental gains in Down's syndrome and school-age children, in Research to Practice in Mental Retardation: Care and Intervention, Vol 1. Edited by Mittler P. Baltimore, MD, University Park Press, 1977, pp 129–141

Howard J, Kropenske V, Tyler R: The long-term effects on neurodevelopment in infants exposed prenatally to PCP, in Phencyclidine: An Update. Edited by Clovet DH. Washington, DC, National Institute on Drug Abuse Research Monograph Series, Vol 64, 1986, pp 237–251

Isenberg SJ, Spierer A, Inkelis SH: Ocular signs of cocaine intoxication in neonates. Am J Ophthalmol 103:211–214, 1987

Jones K, Smith D, Streissguth A: Outcome in offspring of chronic alcoholic women. Lancet, June 1, 1974, pp 1076–1078

Kaltenbach K, Graziani LJ, Finnegan LP: Methadone exposure in utero; developmental status at one and two years of age. Pharmacol Biochem Behav 2 (suppl):15–17, 1979

Lawson M, Wilson G: Parenting among women addicted to narcotics. Child Welfare 59:67–70, 1980

Leershen C, Namuth T: Alcohol and family. Newsweek, Jan 18, 1988, pp 62–68

Madden JD, Payne TF, Miller S: Maternal cocaine abuse and effects on the newborn. Pediatrics 77:209–211, 1986

Mayer J, Black R: Child abuse and neglect in families with an alcohol or opiate addicted parent. Child Abuse Negl 1:85–91, 1977

National Commission on Marijuana and Drug Abuse: Drug Use in America: Problem in Perspective. Washington, DC, National Institute on Drug Abuse, 1973

Nichtern A: The children of drug users. J Am Acad Child Psychiatry 12:24–31, 1973

O'Connor MJ, Brill NJ, Sigman M: Alcohol use in primiparous women older than thirty years of age: relation to infant development. Pediatrics 78:444–450, 1986

Oro AS, Dixon SD: Perinatal cocaine and methamphetamine exposure: maternal and neonatal correlates. J Pediatr 3:571–578, 1987

Regan DO, Ehrlich SM, Finnegan L: Infants of drug addicts: at risk for child abuse, neglect, and placement in foster care. Neurotoxicol Teratol 9:315–319, 1987

Rosen T, Johnson H: Children of methadone-maintained mothers: follow-up to 18 months of age. J Pediatr 101:192–196, 1982

Ryan S, Ehrlich S, Finnegan L: Cocaine abuse in pregnancy: effects on the fetus and newborn. Neurotoxicol Teratol 9:295–299, 1987

Smith JE, Deitch KV: Cocaine: a maternal, fetal, and neonatal risk. J Pediatr Health Care 1:120–124, 1987

Steele B: Psychodynamic factors in child abuse, in The Battered Child, 4th Edition. Edited by Helfer RE, Kempe RS. Chicago, IL, University of Chicago Press, 1987, pp 81–114

Strauss AA, Modanlou HD, Bosu SK: Neonatal manifestations of maternal phencyclidine (PCP) abuse. Pediatrics 68:550–552, 1981

Streissguth A: Fetal alcohol syndrome: an epidemiological perspective. Am J Epidemiol 107:467–468, 1978

Tjossem TD: Intervention Strategies for High Risk Infants and Young Children. Baltimore, MD, University Park Press, 1976

U.S. House of Representatives: Born hooked: confronting the impact of perinatal substance abuse. Hearing before the Select Committee on Children, Youth, and Families, April 27, 1989. Washington, DC, U.S. Government Printing Office, 1989

Wilson GS, Desmond MM, Verniaud WM: Early development of infants of heroin-addicted mothers. Am J Dis Child 126:457–462, 1973

Wilson JS, McCreary R, Kean J, et al: The development of pre-school children of heroin-addicted mothers: a controlled study. Pediatrics 63:135–141, 1979

Yonekura LY, Inkelis SH, Smith-Wallace T: Cocaine intoxication during parturition: maternal and neonatal complications. Abstract of paper presented at the annual meeting of the Society of Perinatal Obstetricians, Las Vegas, NV, February 1987

CHAPTER 6

Prevention of Emotional Disorders in Children With Nonorganic Failure to Thrive

Dennis Drotar, Ph.D.

NONORGANIC FAILURE TO THRIVE AS A POPULATION AT RISK

The target population of the prevention activities described in this chapter is comprised of children with nonorganic failure to thrive (NOFT), which is defined as a significant deceleration in rate of weight gain to below the 5th percentile, that is not primarily accounted for by organic influences (Bithoney and Rathbun 1983). NOFT is only one of a spectrum of conditions that result from environmental and organic influences on physical growth (Bithoney and Dubowitz 1985). However, NOFT is a well-recognized clinical entity that can be reliably identified by detailed assessment of physical growth and health status (Altemeier et al. 1985a).

The advantages of NOFT as a condition in which to study the effects of early preventive intervention include the frequency of occurrence, the association with both acute and chronic behavioral and developmental disorders, and the potential for early recognition and intervention. Surveys indicate that NOFT frequently presents in outpatient medical settings and emergency rooms (Massachusetts Department of Public Health 1983; Mitchell et al. 1980) and accounts for a relatively large number (1–5%) of pediatric hospital admissions of infants and young children (Hannaway 1970).

The preparation of this chapter and the research reported herein were supported by grants from the National Institute of Mental Health (MH-30274) and the Bureau of Maternal and Child Health Resources Development (MCJ-390557), U.S. Public Health Service.

85

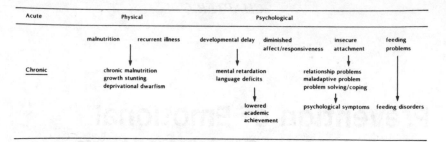

Figure 6-1. Psychological and physical sequelae of nonorganic failure to thrive.

As shown in Figure 6-1, the wide range of physical health problems and psychological deficits that can accompany NOFT either as acute problems or as chronic sequelae underscores the need for preventive intervention. By definition, all NOFT children are malnourished, at least to some extent (Bithoney and Dubowitz 1985). The nutritional deficits of NOFT children range from the severe, life-threatening deficiencies usually associated only with developing countries (Lozoff and Fanaroff 1975) to milder undernutrition that can affect the child's behavior and physical health (Frank 1985). Partly because of their malnutrition, some NOFT children are subject to recurrent infections (Bithoney and Dubowitz 1985) or other health problems (Kotelchuck 1980; Sherrod et al. 1984).

Children who fail to thrive are also at risk for deficits in cognitive and socioemotional development. Many children with NOFT initially present with deficient motor and language development (Drotar et al. 1979), lowered social responsiveness, and diminished affect (Powell and Low 1983; Powell et al. 1987). Although additional information from controlled studies of long-term psychological outcomes of NOFT children is certainly needed, available information from retrospective and prospective studies indicates relatively high rates of severe cognitive deficits, including mental retardation, as well as behavioral disturbances in preschool and school-age children who were initially diagnosed with NOFT as infants and young children (Drotar 1988; Drotar et al. 1979, 1980). Psychological problems that have been noted among NOFT children include attachment and feeding disturbances (Woolston 1983) and depression (Berkowitz 1985). Higher frequencies of behavior problems relative to controls have been noted in both preschool and school-age children with early histories of NOFT (Pollitt and Eichler 1976; Hufton and Oates 1977; Oates 1987; Oates et al. 1985).

Treatment of the physical and psychological problems of NOFT children entails significant economic costs to society. For example, NOFT children are frequently admitted to pediatric acute care and rehabilitation hospitals (Sills 1978; Singer 1985). Some NOFT children are admitted to psychiatric or psychosomatic units for the treatment of severe feeding and behavioral disorders (Chatoor et al. 1985). In some instances, the chronic and psychological problems associated with NOFT necessitate foster care placement (Hopwood and Becker 1979; Money et al. 1972). Finally, costs are also incurred by outpatient treatment of developmental and behavioral disorders, pediatric care, and special education for academic problems.

From the standpoint of prevention, one of the most important features of NOFT is the potential for early recognition. By comparing the child's physical growth to norms (Hammill et al. 1979) and conducting a comprehensive physical and psychosocial assessment, NOFT can be identified during the first year of life. In contrast to psychological disorders, which cannot be detected during critical phases of early development, NOFT can be identified prior to the development of chronic health and/or psychological problems. However, the potential for early recognition of NOFT does not ensure that serious psychological sequelae will be prevented. The large numbers of children who present to pediatric hospitals and clinics with a diagnosis of NOFT (Frank et al. 1985) and the relatively high rates of psychological and health problems encountered in NOFT children attest to the difficulties of prevention within current patterns of care.

ETIOLOGY AND PATHOGENESIS OF NOFT: HETEROGENEOUS CONDITIONS

In order to design effective preventive interventions for NOFT, one needs to understand the factors that contribute to the development of this problem and its sequelae. Unfortunately, the specific processes and vulnerabilities in the person-environment system that trigger NOFT and associated sequelae are very difficult to observe directly. Moreover, the factors that trigger NOFT may differ from those that maintain this condition or affect the development of chronic physical and emotional disorders. NOFT is a complex heterogeneous set of conditions that have varying psychological outcomes. The fact that the processes that give rise to NOFT and subsequent psychological deficits can occur simultaneously at different levels, including the family context, parent-child relationship, or biologic (especially nutritional) level, limits our understanding of etiology. Finally, the scientific data base for preventive interventions for NOFT children and their families is limited by the difficulties of involving and maintaining the families of children with NOFT in research.

The data that provide a preliminary framework for prevention in NOFT come from several sources, including the following: (a) studies of

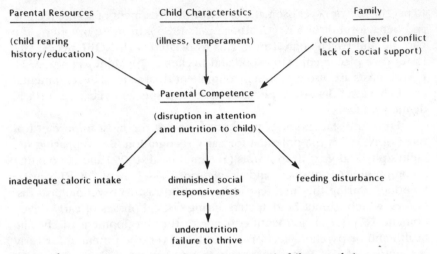

Figure 6-2. Factors that contribute to nonorganic failure to thrive.

factors that influence parental competence (Belsky 1984; Belsky et al. 1984); (b) research concerning the psychological effects of child abuse and neglect (Ammerman et al. 1986; Schneider-Rosen et al. 1985); (c) the results of preventive intervention studies with disadvantaged (Ramey et al. 1984) and malnourished children (Grantham-McGregor et al. 1983; Hicks et al. 1982); (d) prospective studies of maltreated (including NOFT) children (Altemeier et al. 1985a); and (e) case descriptions and intervention studies with NOFT children (Ayoub and Milner 1985; Lieberman and Birch 1985; Drotar 1988; Drotar et al. 1985a; Drotar and Sturm 1988).

INFLUENCES ON THE DEVELOPMENT OF NOFT

PARENTAL COMPETENCE

Based on empirical studies, Belsky's process-oriented model of parental competence (Belsky 1984; Belsky et al. 1984) suggests a useful conceptualization of the factors that give rise to NOFT. In this model, parental competence (defined as sensitivity and involvement) is based on three sets of factors: (a) the parents' personal resources, such as education, developmental history, and intellectual ability; (b) the current family context, especially the degree of family stress relative to support; and (c) child characteristics such as temperament and illness.

As shown in Figure 6-2, parental competence is multiply determined but is assumed to be most vulnerable when all three domains (parent, child, and family) are compromised. Prior research has suggested that the competence of parents of NOFT infants is limited by multiple factors.

For example, Altemeier and his colleagues (1985a) have demonstrated that the presence of problems in the mother's childhood (e.g., conflict with parents, unhappy childhood, feelings of rejection by parents) is associated with the occurrence of NOFT in a high-risk sample and may contribute to maternal relationship and childrearing difficulties. Deficits in parental intellectual abilities, education, or personality also contribute to NOFT (Breunlin et al. 1983). Child characteristics may also play a role in the development of NOFT. For example, NOFT infants' physical problems may intensify maternal childrearing burdens and heighten perceptions of the child as sickly (Sherrod et al. 1984; Kotelchuck 1980).

Finally, problems in the family context may deplete maternal resources and limit access to emotional support. Families of NOFT infants have lower economic levels (Kanawati and McClaren 1973), higher family stress (Altemeier et al. 1985a), less available extended family for help with childrearing, and greater social isolation (Bithoney and Newberger 1987) than comparison groups. In some families, highly conflictual relationships are a source of additional strain and depletion (Drotar et al. 1985c). Such competing family claims may interfere with the mother's ability to effectively deploy her nutritional resources and attention to the child. Family influences may disrupt the child's weight gain by limiting the amount of food that is available or offered to the child, the quality of the mother's interactions, or the consistency of feeding patterns. Controlled studies of maternal-child interaction suggest that NOFT is mediated by deficiencies in maternal behavior, including responsivity (Pollitt et al. 1975; Bradley et al. 1984) and contingent responsiveness (Ramey et al. 1972; Linscheid and Rasnake 1985). However, we do not have good prospective evidence for the specific processes that contribute to NOFT.

The best evidence for a multifactorial causal pathway for NOFT comes from the Nashville prospective studies in which high-risk mothers were followed from pregnancy (Altemeier et al. 1979, 1985b). In these studies, families in which children were subsequently diagnosed with NOFT were compared with high-risk families in which no such problem was identified. Mothers whose children developed NOFT were more likely to identify problems in their own childhood, especially feelings that they were not loved and were neglected. In addition, mothers of NOFT infants identified more frequent current life stresses during the preceding year than comparison group families, especially problems in the immediate family context such as arguments with the child's father, separations from the father, the father leaving a job, and the father being arrested. Single risk factors were not necessary or sufficient for NOFT to occur. However, once the number of risk factors reached a threshold level, maltreatment was likely to occur (Sherrod et al. 1985). Although studies have identified family risk factors that heighten a child's vulnerability for NOFT, the factors that account for the development of NOFT

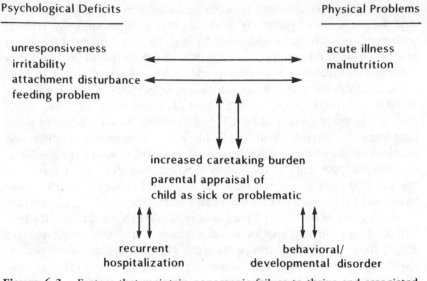

Psychological Deficits   Physical Problems

unresponsiveness   acute illness
irritability   malnutrition
attachment disturbance
feeding problem

increased caretaking burden
parental appraisal of
child as sick or problematic

recurrent   behavioral/
hospitalization   developmental disorder

Figure 6-3. Factors that maintain nonorganic failure to thrive and associated risk.

versus other infant mental health or maternal-child relationship problems are not well documented.

FACTORS THAT MAINTAIN NOFT

As shown in Figure 6-3, the factors that trigger NOFT overlap with, but should be differentiated from, those that maintain this condition and/or contribute to the development of chronic psychological problems. For example, once the child's nutrition is compromised, the mother's caretaking burden can be increased by the child's deficits in social responsiveness, feeding problems, or irritability (Pollitt 1973; Powell and Low 1983; Powell et al. 1987). Clinical observations suggest that the child's response to feeding, play, or caretaking may be disrupted by what he or she learns in the course of interaction with the mother or other family caretakers (Fraiberg 1980; Linscheid and Rasnake 1985). By the time the child is diagnosed with NOFT, mother and child may have become progressively disengaged from each other. In other cases, mother and NOFT child may demonstrate high levels of conflictual interaction, especially in the feeding situation (Chatoor et al. 1985).

Although there is little empirical information concerning the factors that contribute to the development of psychological deficits in NOFT children, studies of maltreated children suggest possible mechanisms (Aber and Allen 1987). Maladaptive maternal-child interactions may perpetuate a vicious cycle of maladaptive attachments and social relationships that threaten the child's cognitive and sociocmotional development. Thus, it is not surprising that NOFT children have been found to have a higher than average frequency of insecure attachments at 12 months of age (Crittenden 1987; Gordon and Jameson 1979). The early development of insecure attachments may contribute to affective disturbances, feeding problems, and problematic coping patterns that are reinforced in the family environment and become increasingly unresponsive to intervention over time.

Pediatric evaluations, diagnostic tests, and hospitalization for NOFT also have an impact on the family, especially on parental attitudes concerning the child and appraisal of the child's problem. For example, it is not uncommon for parents of NOFT children to come to perceive the child as physically ill, as "quiet," or as not needing as much food as other children in the family (Ayoub and Milner 1985; Kotelchuck 1980).

Finally, the child's chronic nutritional deficits may contribute to psychological risk (Frank 1985). Given the multiple risk factors that are often associated with NOFT, a cumulative cycle of continuing psychological risk may be very difficult to interrupt. Improvement in physical growth patterns that can follow nutritional treatment does not reduce the NOFT child's risk for psychological problems, which may necessitate preventive psychosocial intervention (Bithoney and Rathbun 1983).

PREVENTION PROGRAMS: PREVIOUS REPORTS

This preliminary framework for the etiology of NOFT and associated psychological risk suggests possible points for preventive intervention prior to the development of NOFT or very early in the course of the condition. For example, primary prevention programs can be designed to reduce the impact of risk factors that have been described for high-risk mothers during pregnancy or during the newborn period. Although primary prevention of NOFT has not been empirically demonstrated, the results of intervention studies that have employed outcome measures related to physical growth, health, or psychological status suggest that primary prevention of NOFT is possible.

For example, O'Connor et al. (1980) found that early postpartum maternal-child contact and rooming-in were associated with fewer (10 versus 2) cases of parenting inadequacy as measured by physical or sexual abuse, NOFT, relinquishment of parental responsibilities, or neglect. Field et al.'s (1980) home-based parent training intervention resulted in more optimal face-to-face interaction, cognitive development, and maternal attitudes, as well as better physical growth in young infants of adolescent mothers, than were evidenced in a comparison group.

Olds and his colleagues (1986a) found that high-risk unmarried adolescent mothers from low-income families who were visited by nurses during their pregnancy made more extensive use of nutritional supplements than mothers who did not receive home visitation. In a subsequent study, Olds et al. (1986b) noted that home visitation that began during pregnancy and the child's first 2 years of life resulted in a lower frequency of abuse and neglect, fewer emergency room visits for infectious illness during the child's first year, and fewer accidents than alternative interventions such as transportation for parents or home visitation that began subsequent to pregnancy.

KEY FEATURES OF PRIMARY PREVENTION PROGRAMS

Unfortunately, available evidence from primary prevention programs does not permit strong inferences about the components of intervention that were most effective. However, key features of many successful primary prevention programs for infants at risk include the following:

1. Intervention at a critical point in the family life cycle prior to the development of NOFT
2. Parent education concerning infant development and nutrition
3. Involvement of multiple family members in addition to the mother
4. Advocacy and support
5. Provision of concrete resources, especially nutritional supplementation
6. Emphasis on enhancing parental competencies
7. Linkage between hospital services and community health agencies
8. Outreach to promote access to parents and their engagement with the program

Prevention-minded practitioners can function effectively as advocates for families by encouraging utilization of primary prevention services that are available in their communities, including maternal and infant health programs for pregnant women that provide comprehensive nutritional, educational, health, family planning services, and home visitation support. During the neonatal period, liberal rooming-in opportunities, support services, home visitation, and nutritional supplementation are useful preventive interventions. During early childhood, parents and children at risk for neglect and NOFT may benefit from additional anticipatory guidance, nutritional supplements, compensatory education, and stimulation. However, the opportunities for primary prevention of NOFT vary considerably as a function of available community services.

GENERAL PRINCIPLES OF PREVENTION MANAGEMENT

Relatively few primary prevention programs for NOFT have been implemented on a wide-scale basis. In addition, the risk factors that contribute to NOFT have not diminished (Frank et al. 1985). For this reason practicing clinicians from many professional disciplines are faced with the considerable challenge of managing infants and young children who are already showing symptoms of NOFT.

The question that will now be addressed is: How can one best intervene early in the course of the condition to prevent the chronic physical and psychological disturbances associated with NOFT? Our research (Drotar et al. 1989; Drotar et al. 1985a; Drotar and Sturm 1988) and descriptions of clinical intervention (Ayoub and Jacewitz 1982; Chatoor et al. 1985; Lieberman and Birch 1985; Linscheid and Rasnake 1985) suggest the following general principles of preventive management:

1. Early diagnosis
2. Assessment of the child's physical and psychological status, the parent-child relationship, and family context
3. Stabilization or reversal of the child's acute physical symptoms by physical and nutritional intervention
4. Addressing specific problems in the parent-child or family system that are maintaining NOFT and contributing to risk for emotional disorders

Early recognition depends upon the physicians' or nurse practitioners' abilities to identify deceleration in the child's rate of weight gain. Evidence for the importance of early identification of NOFT comes from several sources. Experienced pediatricians and nurse practitioners can intervene effectively at the first signs of poor weight gain by providing education, support, and close monitoring of the child's physical status (Schmitt 1980). Reversal of serious growth deficits and prevention of chronic failure to thrive may be easier to accomplish with young infants, most of whom have not developed feeding and behavioral disorders severe enough to affect weight gain (Sturm and Drotar 1989). Our research has indicated that infants who develop NOFT early in life and who are not diagnosed for a number of months show a higher frequency of insecure attachments than children who have a somewhat later onset and who are recognized relatively early in the course of the condition (Drotar 1985). Finally, early recognition of NOFT and intervention can lessen the time the child is exposed to the effects of undernutrition.

On the other hand, obstacles to early recognition of NOFT include the fact that family problems may divert parental attention from the child who is failing to thrive. Moreover, parents may not comply with recommendations for diagnostic tests or well-child visits. Because some parents do not recognize the severity or potential developmental significance of NOFT, practitioners must assume the difficult burden of identification. However, the pediatric practitioner's diagnostic dilemma is heightened by the difficulty of distinguishing organic versus environmental influences on growth and accurately assessing environmental influences. Our experience and that of others (Berkowitz 1985) suggest the utility of a comprehensive evaluative approach that considers the following: (1) characteristics of NOFT such as onset, duration, and severity of the child's nutritional status; (2) the child's functional problems, including accompanying developmental, feeding, and behavioral deficits; and (3) the child's interactional context and family resources (Bithoney and Rathbun 1983; Drotar 1985; Woolston 1983).

Another goal of prevention concerns identification and correction of the physical and nutritional deficits that affect the child's behavior (Bithoney and Dubowitz 1985; Pollitt 1973) and parental attitudes about the child. The beneficial effects of early nutritional intervention on psychological development have been demonstrated in several studies (Hicks et al. 1982; Klein et al. 1976; Joos et al. 1983). With the exception of NOFT children who have serious feeding disorders (Chatoor et al. 1985), it is often possible to achieve improved weight gain on an outpatient basis with nutritional supplementation (Peterson et al. 1984) or by pediatric hospitalization. However, the results of follow-up studies suggest that with the exception of mild cases, medical or nutritional intervention alone does not necessarily prevent chronic NOFT or psychological problems (Drotar et al. 1979; Kristiansson and Fallstrom 1987; Singer 1985; Sturm and Drotar 1989). One obvious reason is that medical care does not address the underlying factors that perpetuate NOFT and associated psychological risk.

Our experience and that of others (Ayoub and Jacewitz 1982; Lieberman and Birch 1985) suggest that effective secondary prevention requires a concerted effort to engage the parents, intervention that addresses parenting problems that are maintaining the child's NOFT, and close and continuous follow-up. Engaging the parents is a critical but very difficult component of secondary prevention. Many parents are threatened by the diagnosis of NOFT and are not easily accessible. To enhance parental participation in intervention, we have found it useful to actively initiate contact with parents, emphasize parents' unique role in helping their child, address parents' specific concerns about their child and about the child's medical treatment, understand parents' concepts of their child's condition, emphasize parental strengths, and create a sense of optimism concerning the child's recovery from NOFT and his or her future potential.

Another important principle is to enhance parents' sense of control through a process of negotiating the child's diagnosis and treatment (Katon and Kleinman 1981). The following steps are useful in this process:

1. Eliciting parents' ideas of the causes and consequences of NOFT
2. Considering parents' ideas about diagnosis and treatment
3. Presenting information and treatment recommendations to family members such as fathers and grandparents whose significant influence on family life may not be readily apparent
4. Openly acknowledging differences in opinions about what is wrong with the child and what needs to be done
5. Working out a compromise with parents when conflict arises
6. Monitoring communication and providing ongoing feedback to parents concerning the goals of intervention and the child's progress

Our experience suggests that the overwhelming majority of parents of NOFT infants will accept home visitation intervention if follow-up is actively maintained (Drotar et al. 1985a).

LEVELS OF INTERVENTION: CLINICAL EXAMPLES

While an effective working relationship with parents of NOFT infants is a cornerstone of preventive clinical management, it should be accompanied by remediation plans that are targeted to specific problems. Recent research has suggested that NOFT is a heterogeneous condition that subsumes several subtypes differing in such parameters as etiology, age of onset, and nature of risk to the child (Chatoor et al. 1985; Drotar 1985; Drotar 1988; Linscheid and Rasnake 1985; Woolston 1983). The condition of NOFT may be conceptualized as a continuum of problems that includes relatively discrete and time-limited influences as well as more pervasive, chronic, or interlocking influences on physical growth and psychological development. As shown in Table 6-1, specific strategies of preventive intervention can be based upon hypothesized etiology of breakdown in the maternal-child relationship, the duration of this breakdown, and anticipated effects on the child.

Nutritional Support

One type of NOFT is a product of underfeeding that reflects a lack of knowledge concerning the child's nutritional needs or that may relate directly to depletion of family economic resources (Frank et al. 1985). In some cases, families who run out of food at the end of the month may be forced to limit the child's caloric intake. Parents who underfeed their

Table 6-1. Preventive intervention with nonorganic failure to thrive

Etiology	Major presenting problem	Goal(s) of intervention
Underfeeding owing to lack of knowledge of child nutrition as well as to financial problems	Undernutrition	Nutritional education advocacy
Dysfunctional parent-child relationship	Understimulation; feeding disorder	Reinforce maternal involvement in modifying feeding patterns
Severe family dysfunction	Understimulation; disorganized feeding	Enhance family support; reduce level of family conflict; promote family cooperation concerning the child's feeding

children may benefit from education concerning children's nutritional needs and/or advocacy to help them to obtain food for their children.

For example, Johnny presented with NOFT at 3 months of age. Although the factors that influenced his growth deficit were initially not apparent, a careful review of his history indicated that he had an earlier infectious illness. At that time his mother was advised to feed him clear liquids. However, she kept him on clear liquids for longer than necessary because she felt this would help him. She was reluctant to feed him too much following this incident because she viewed him as physically vulnerable. When his growth deficit was identified, she attributed it to a physical illness. When the cause of his problem was pointed out to her, she became concerned, she fed him more frequently, and his weight gain improved.

In another case, the child's NOFT reflected acute nutritional depletion secondary to a family financial crisis. For example, Alice's father was laid off unexpectedly, which exhausted the family's financial reserves. To save money, the parents reduced their own food intake and did not see the harm in diluting Alice's formula. Alice's NOFT improved when the family was referred to the emergency food center and Alice began to receive benefits from the Supplemental Food Program for Women, Infants, and Children (WIC) that paid for her formula.

Maladaptive Mother-Child Relationships

In some situations NOFT reflects a maladaptive maternal-child relationship that limits the child's caloric intake. In other cases the deficit is characterized by a lack of maternal responsiveness, especially contingent responses to the child (Linscheid and Rasnake 1985; Ramey et al. 1975). In still other cases the problem involves a conflictual relationship and high levels of aversive stimulation (Chatoor et al. 1985). Depending on the developmental origins of these problems, i.e., focalization of attachment (3–7 months) or separation and individuation (8–24 months), different intervention approaches may be required (Chatoor et al. 1985; Lieberman and Birch 1985). To deal with these issues, Fraiberg (1980) and her colleagues have advocated developmentally oriented guidance that combines education, support, and therapy to help mothers to address the impact of conflicts experienced during their own childhood and improve their capacities to respond to specific signals or demands from their children. Others have utilized parent training to help mothers modify specific maladaptive behaviors (Linscheid and Rasnake 1985). For example, mothers who have low rates of contingent interaction with their infants might be encouraged to increase their rate of contingent responses. On the other hand, mothers who engage in aversive feeding interactions with their children may be encouraged to increase their attention to adaptive feeding behaviors (Chatoor et al. 1985).

Family Interventions

Some cases of NOFT respond favorably to intervention at the level of the mother-child dyad. However, dysfunctional parent-child relationships may reflect broader problems in the family, such as conflicts with the child's mother and her parenting partner (spouse, boyfriend, or mother) (Drotar and Malone 1982; Drotar et al. 1985c). Family problems may affect the child directly by increasing the conflict and disorganization during mealtimes or indirectly by depleting the mother's energy for childrearing or attention to her child (Wahler 1980; Wahler and Dumas 1984). In such cases, focusing intervention solely on maternal-child relationship difficulties without attending to serious family dysfunction may not result in permanent treatment gains. Family problems can also interfere with the mother's capacity to follow through with interventions focused on improving her relationship with her child (Drotar et al. 1985c). In such cases family-centered intervention involving multiple family members can enhance the quality of the child's nurturing by (a) improving the overall organization and planning concerning the allocation of family resources; (b) reducing family conflicts, thus improving the quality of exchanges within the family; and (c) helping family members to protect the child from dysfunctional family influences.

In some cases the child's NOFT reflects a family crisis that needs to be managed. For example, it came to light that Bobby's NOFT related to his parents' marital problems. Bobby's mother was involved in a conflictual marital relationship with her husband who abused her. Although she had wanted to separate from her husband, she needed support to accomplish this action. The major focus of intervention was to help her obtain legal and emotional support to initiate and follow through with this separation.

Family-centered intervention can also help the mother to make positive changes in her relationships with family members, thereby freeing up her energies for her child, as in the following case: Rashita, the mother of a young NOFT infant, was engaged in a highly conflicted relationship with two men that affected her ability to nurture her infant, as well as her access to financial resources. When her relationships with men were going well, she was able to provide relatively well for her child's needs. However, when things became more difficult between her and her boyfriends, she would miss her pediatric appointments, and her relationship with the child suffered. Intervention helped Rashita to mobilize a more adaptive social network. Eventually, she moved in with her sister, who helped care for the infant. As she began to distance herself from her boyfriends and develop positive sources of social support within her family, her ability to care for her child improved.

Families in which the child's caretaking is disorganized and dispersed among many caretakers and family members may need help to focus their caretaking more effectively, as in the case of Randy, who presented with NOFT at 2 months of age. Randy's complex assortment of caregivers included his mother, who lived alone with her four children, and four other adults—his great-grandmother, two uncles, and an aunt. Randy's mother was stressed by the burden of his care and often asked the other adults to help feed him. However, this pattern of group childrearing reduced her overall level of involvement with Randy and resulted in highly inconsistent care, culminating in decreased caloric intake and two hospitalizations. Following Randy's hospitalization, the family was encouraged to change their patterns of care by increasing Randy's mother's involvement in his care, decreasing the overall number of caretakers, and enhancing the overall organization of his care. One effective approach to restructuring Randy's care was to encourage his great-grandmother to support his mother's primary involvement by helping to feed Randy's very active siblings (Drotar and Malone 1982).

INTERVENTION RESEARCH IN NOFT

Thus far, empirical evidence for various models of intervention is largely restricted to case reports (Chatoor et al. 1985; Lieberman and Birch 1985). Additional research concerning the effects of preventive interventions on the long-term psychological development of children with early histories of NOFT is needed.

We have assessed the efficacy of three alternative forms of time-limited outreach intervention with the parents of infants ($n = 68$) who were hospitalized for NOFT at a young age (5 months). Parents were randomly assigned to one of three time-limited intervention plans. One of these—family-centered interventions—involved members of the family group (mother, father, or grandparents) in weekly home visits directed toward enhancing family coping skills, supporting the child's mother, and lessening the impact of dysfunctional family influences such as marital conflict. A second group received parent-centered intervention that included supportive education focused on improving the quality of the mother's interactions, nutritional management, and relationship with the child. In the third intervention plan, the child's mother was seen for an average of six home visits focused on providing emotional support to help her stabilize the child's weight gain following hospitalization and obtain necessary economic and community resources. In each group, intervention was terminated after one year's duration, when the NOFT child was 18 months old on the average. Type of intervention did not affect physical growth, cognitive development, attachment, or ratings of behavior at 12–48 months (Brinich et al. 1989; Drotar et al. 1985b; Drotar and Sturm 1988; Sturm and Drotar 1989). However, the parent-centered intervention was associated with a lower frequency of behavioral disorders in 4-year-old children. Consistent with the results of other follow-up studies (Fryer 1988), improvements in physical growth and nutritional status were generally maintained (Sturm and Drotar 1989), while cognitive development declined over time (Drotar and Sturm 1988).

Several issues need to be considered in interpreting our findings. For example, the nonspecific effects of intervention, including support for the mother, continuity of intervention from hospital to home, and outreach, may have made it difficult to demonstrate specific intervention effects. Moreover, the level of within-sample variation in onset and duration of NOFT and family demographics may have also limited the detectability of intervention effects (Drotar and Sturm 1988; Sturm and Drotar 1989).

Our research has consistently documented the importance of individual difference factors on prognosis. For example, risk factors concerning psychological deficits within the NOFT population include low income and characteristics of the NOFT condition, especially onset and duration. Children with earlier-onset NOFT have shown a greater level of risk for cognitive deficits and attachment disturbances (Drotar et al. 1985a, 1985b; Drotar and Sturm 1988). Families who experienced chronic relationship problems such as severe marital conflict, those in which the mother was being abused by the child's father, or those in which a parent had a substance abuse problem, did not respond well to our outreach intervention. Children in these families required continued surveillance and intervention by protective service agencies, and in some cases foster care.

DIRECTIONS FOR FUTURE RESEARCH

The present analysis of preventive intervention in NOFT is admittedly incomplete. It is ironic and unfortunate that a condition such as NOFT that occurs frequently and is so compelling in its costs to children has resisted empirical scrutiny. There is a considerable agenda for future research. Prospective studies of the factors within high-risk populations that contribute to the development of NOFT versus other infant mental health disorders are needed. Prospective data are also needed concerning the factors that increase or lessen the longer-term psychological risk of children with early histories of NOFT (Rutter 1984, 1987). One priority area is the study of influences on key developmental parameters such as feeding behavior or security of attachment that appear to be vulnerable to disruption and are potential mediators of long-term psychological outcomes.

Finally, preventive intervention needs to be evaluated by well-documented case studies and randomized controlled studies of the efficacy of preventive interventions directed toward specific subtypes of NOFT (Ayoub and Milner 1985). The efficacy of preventive intervention should be enhanced by a more precise match between the type of NOFT and the specific model of intervention (Drotar et al. 1989). Parent training programs, which have been developed for abused and neglected children (Brunk et al. 1987) and parent-infant psychotherapy (Fraiberg 1980; Lieberman and Birch 1985), may be promising intervention approaches for NOFT that should be evaluated in controlled studies.

REFERENCES

Aber JL, Allen JP: Effects of maltreatment on young children's socioemotional development: an attachment theory perspective. Dev Psychol 23:406–414, 1987

Altemeier WA, Vietze P, Sherrod KB, et al: Prediction of child maltreatment during pregnancy. J Am Acad Child Psychiatry 18:205–219, 1979

Altemeier WA, O'Connor S, Sherrod KB, et al: A strategy for managing nonorganic failure to thrive based on a prospective study of antecedents, in New Directions in Failure to Thrive: Implications for Research and Practice. Edited by Drotar D. New York, Plenum, 1985a, pp 211–222

Altemeier W, O'Connor S, Sherrod KB, et al: Prospective study of antecedents for non-organic failure to thrive. J Pediatr 106:360–365, 1985b

Ammerman RJ, Cassisi JE, Hersen M, et al: Consequences of physical abuse and neglect in children. Clin Psychol Rev 6:291–310, 1986

Ayoub C, Jacewitz MD: Families at risk of poor parenting: a model for service delivery, assessment, and intervention. Child Abuse Negl 6:351–358, 1982

Ayoub CC, Milner SS: Failure to thrive parental indicators, types and outcome. Child Abuse Negl 9:491–499, 1985

Belsky J: The determinants of parenting: a process model. Child Dev 55:83–96, 1984

Belsky J, Robins E, Gamble W: The determinants of parental competence: toward a contextual theory, in Beyond the Dyad. Edited by Lewis M. New York, Plenum, 1984, pp 251–279

Berkowitz C: Comprehensive pediatric management of failure to thrive: an interdisciplinary approach, in New Directions in Failure to Thrive: Implications for Research and Practice. Edited by Drotar D. New York, Plenum, 1985, pp 193–211

Bithoney WB, Dubowitz H: Organic concomitants of nonorganic failure to thrive, in New Directions in Failure to Thrive: Implications for Research and Practice. Edited by Drotar D. New York, Plenum, 1985, pp 47–68

Bithoney WB, Newberger EH: Child and family attributes of failure to thrive. J Dev Behav Pediatr 8:32–36, 1987

Bithoney WB, Rathbun JM: Failure to thrive, in Developmental Behavioral Pediatrics. Edited by Levine MD, Carey WC, Crocker AD, et al. Philadelphia, PA, WB Saunders, 1983, pp 557–572

Bradley RH, Casey PM, Wortham B: Home environments of low SES non-organic failure to thrive infants. Merrill Palmer Q 30:393–402, 1984

Breunlin DC, Desai VJ, Stone ME, et al: Failure to thrive with no organic etiology: a critical review. Int J Eating Disorders 2:25–49, 1983

Brinich E, Drotar D, Brinich P: Relationship of security of attachment to the physical and psychological outcome of preschool children with early histories of nonorganic failure to thrive. J Clin Child Psychol 18:142–152, 1989

Brunk M, Henggeler SW, Whelan JP: Comparison of multisystemic therapy and parent training in the brief treatment of child abuse and neglect. J Consult Clin Psychol 55:171–178, 1987

Chatoor I, Dickson L, Schaefer S, et al: A developmental classification of feeding disorders associated with failure to thrive: diagnosis and treatment, in New Directions in Failure to Thrive: Implications for Research and Practice. Edited by Drotar D. New York, Plenum, 1985, pp 235–259

Crittenden PM: Nonorganic failure to thrive: deprivation or distortion? Infant Ment Health J 8:51–64, 1987

Drotar D: Environmentally based failure to thrive: diagnostic subtypes and early prognosis, in Slow Grows the Child: Psychosocial Aspects of Growth Delay.

Edited by Stabler B, Underwood L. Hillsdale, NJ, Erlbaum, 1985, pp 151–167

Drotar D: Failure to thrive, in Handbook of Pediatric Psychology. Edited by Routh DK. New York, Guilford, 1988, pp 71–107

Drotar D, Malone CA: Family-oriented intervention in failure to thrive, in Birth Interaction and Attachment, Johnson and Johnson Pediatric Round Table, Vol 6. Edited by Klaus M, Robertson MO. Skillman, NJ, Johnson and Johnson, 1982, pp 104–112

Drotar D, Sturm L: Prediction of intellectual development in children with early histories of non-organic failure to thrive. J Pediatr Psychol 13:281–295, 1988

Drotar D, Malone CA, Negray J: Psychosocial intervention with the families of failure to thrive infants. Child Abuse Negl 3:927–935, 1979

Drotar D, Malone CA, Negray J: Environmentally based failure to thrive and children's intellectual development. J Clin Child Psychol 9:236–240, 1980

Drotar D, Malone CA, Devost L, et al: Early preventive intervention in failure to thrive: methods and early outcome, in New Directions in Failure to Thrive: Implications for Research and Practice. Edited by Drotar D. New York, Plenum, 1985a, pp 119–138

Drotar D, Nowak M, Malone CA, et al: Early psychological outcome in failure to thrive: predictions from an interactional model. J Clin Child Psychol 14:105–111, 1985b

Drotar D, Woychik J, Mantz-Clumpner C, et al: The family context of failure to thrive, in New Directions in Failure to Thrive: Implications for Research and Practice. Edited by Drotar D. New York, Plenum, 1985c, pp 295–310

Drotar D, Wilson F, Sturm L: Parent intervention in the management of failure to thrive, in Handbook of Parent Training. Edited by Schaefer LE, Briesmeister JM. New York, John Wiley, 1989, pp 364–391

Field TM, Widmayer SM, Stringer S, et al: Teenage lower class black mothers and their preterm infants: an intervention and developmental follow-up. Child Dev 51:426–436, 1980

Fraiberg S (ed): Clinical Studies in Infant Mental Health. New York, Basic Books, 1980

Frank DA: Biologic risks in "nonorganic" failure to thrive: diagnostic and therapeutic implications, in New Directions in Failure to Thrive: Implications for Research and Practice. Edited by Drotar D. New York, Plenum, 1985, pp 17–20

Frank DA, Allen D, Brown JL: Primary prevention of failure to thrive: social policy implications, in New Directions in Failure to Thrive: Implications for Research and Practice. Edited by Drotar D. New York, Plenum, 1985, pp 337–358

Fryer GE: The efficacy of hospitalization of nonorganic failure to thrive children: a meta-analysis. Child Abuse Negl 12:375–381, 1988

Gordon AH, Jameson JC: Infant-mother attachment in parents with non-organic failure to thrive syndrome. J Am Acad Child Psychiatry 18:96–99, 1979

Grantham-McGregor S, Schofield W, Harris L: Effect of psychosocial stimulation on mental development of severely malnourished children: an interim report. Pediatrics 72:239–243, 1983

Hammill PVV, Drizd TA, Johnson CL, et al: Physical growth: National Center for Health Statistics percentages. Am J Clin Nutr 32:607–629, 1979

Hannaway PJ: Failure to thrive—a study of 100 infants and children. Clin Pediatr 9:96–99, 1970

Hicks LE, Langham RA, Takenaka J: Cognitive and health measures following early nutritional supplementation: a sibling study. Am J Public Health 12:1110–1118, 1982

Hopwood N, Becker DJ: Psychosocial dwarfism: detection, evaluation and management. Child Abuse Negl 3:439–447, 1979

Hufton IV, Oates RK: Nonorganic failure to thrive: a long-term follow-up. Pediatrics 59:73–79, 1977

Joos SK, Pollitt E, Mueller WH, et al: The bacon chow study: maternal nutritional supplementation and infant behavioral development. Child Dev 54:669–676, 1983

Kanawati AA, McClaren DS: Failure to thrive in Lebanon. II. An investigation of the causes. Acta Paediatr Scand 62:571–576, 1973

Katon W, Kleinman A: Doctor-patient negotiation and other social science strategies in patient care, in The Relevance of Social Science for Medicine. Edited by Eisenberg L, Kleinman A. Dordrecht, The Netherlands, Reidel, 1981, pp 153–282

Klein RE, Arrenabes P, Delgado H, et al: Effects of maternal nutrition on fetal growth and infant development. Bull Pan Am Health Organ 10:301–316, 1976

Kotelchuck M: Nonorganic failure to thrive: the status of interactional and environmental theories, in Advances in Behavioral Pediatrics, Vol 1. Edited by Camp BW. Greenwich, CT, Jai Press, 1980, pp 29–51

Kristiansson B, Fallstrom SP: Growth at the age of 4 years subsequent to early failure to thrive. Child Abuse Negl 11:35–40, 1987

Lieberman AF, Birch M: The etiology of failure to thrive: an interactional-developmental approach, in New Directions in Failure to Thrive: Implications for Research and Practice. Edited by Drotar D. New York, Plenum, 1985, pp 259–287

Linscheid TR, Rasnake LK: Behavioral approaches to the treatment of failure to thrive, in New Directions in Failure to Thrive: Implications for Research and Practice. Edited by Drotar D. New York, Plenum, 1985, pp 279–294

Lozoff E, Fanaroff A: Kwashiorkor in Cleveland. Am J Dis Child 129:710–711, 1975

Massachusetts Department of Public Health: Massachusetts Nutrition Survey. Boston, MA, Massachusetts Department of Public Health, 1983

Mitchell WG, Gorell RW, Greenberg RA: Failure to thrive: a study in a primary care setting: epidemiology and follow-up. Pediatrics 65:971–977, 1980

Money J, Wolff G, Annecillo C: Pain agnosia and self injury in the syndrome of reversible somatotropin deficiency (psychological dwarfism). J Autism Childhood Schizophr 2:19–27, 1972

Oates R: Child Abuse and Neglect: What Happens Eventually. New York, Brunner/Mazel, 1987

Oates RK, Peacock A, Forest D: Long-term effects of non-organic failure to thrive. Pediatrics 75:36–40, 1985

O'Connor S, Vietze PM, Sherrod KB, et al: Reduced incidence of parenting inadequacy following rooming in. Pediatrics 66:176–182, 1980

Olds DL, Henderson CR, Tatelbaum R, et al: Improving the delivery of prenatal care and outcomes of pregnancy: a randomized trial of nurse home visitation. Pediatrics 77:16–28, 1986a

Olds DL, Henderson CR, Tatelbaum R, et al: Preventing child abuse and neglect: a randomized trial of nurse intervention. Pediatrics 78:65–78, 1986b

Peterson KE, Washington JS, Rathbun JM: Team management of failure to thrive. J Am Diet Assoc 84:810–814, 1984

Pollitt E: The role of the behavior of the infant in marasmus. Am J Clin Nutr 26:264–270, 1973

Pollitt E, Eichler A: Behavioral disturbances among failure to thrive children. Am J Dis Child 130:24–29, 1976

Pollitt E, Eichler A, Chan CK: Psychosocial development and behavior of mothers of failure to thrive children. Am J Orthopsychiatry 45:525–537, 1975

Powell GF, Low JL: Behavior in non-organic failure to thrive. J Dev Behav Pediatr 4:26–33, 1983

Powell GF, Low J, Speers MA: Behavior as a diagnostic aid in failure to thrive. J Dev Behav Pediatr 8:18–24, 1987

Ramey CT, Hieger L, Klisz D: Synchronous reinforcement of vocal responses in failure to thrive infants. Child Dev 43:1449–1455, 1972

Ramey CT, Starr RH, Pallas J, et al: Nutrition, response contingent stimulation and the maternal deprivation syndrome: results of an early intervention program. Merrill Palmer Q 21:45–55, 1975

Ramey CT, Yeates KO, Short EJ: The plasticity of intellectual development: insights from preventive intervention. Child Dev 55:1913–1925, 1984

Rutter M: Protective factors in children's responses to stress and disadvantage, in Readings in the Primary Prevention of Psychopathology. Edited by Joffe JM, Albee GW, Kelly LD. Hanover, NH, University Press of New England, 1984, pp 157–177

Rutter M: Psychosocial resilience and protective mechanisms. Am J Orthopsychiatry 57:316–331, 1987

Schmitt BD: The prevention of child abuse and neglect: a review of the literature with recommendations for application. Child Abuse Negl 4:171–177, 1980

Schneider-Rosen K, Braunwald VG, Carlson V, et al: Current perspectives in attachment theory: illustration from the study of maltreated infants, in Growing Points of Attachment Therapy and Research. Edited by Bretherton I, Waters E. Monograph Society for Research in Child Development, Vol 50. Chicago, IL, University of Chicago Press, 1985, pp 194–210

Sherrod KB, O'Connor S, Vietze PM, et al: Child health and maltreatment. Child Dev 55:1174–1182, 1984

Sherrod KB, O'Connor S, Altemeier WA, et al: Toward a semispecific multidimensional threshold model of maltreatment, in New Directions in Failure to Thrive: Implications for Research and Practice. Edited by Drotar D. New York, Plenum, 1985, pp 89–106

Sills RH: Failure to thrive: the role of clinical and laboratory evaluation. Am J Dis Child 132:967–969, 1978

Singer L: Extended hospitalization of failure to thrive infants: patterns of care and developmental outcome, in New Directions in Failure to Thrive: Implications for Research and Practice. Edited by Drotar D. New York, Plenum, 1985, pp 139–154

Sturm L, Drotar D: Prediction of weight for height following intervention in three-year-old children with early histories of nonorganic failure to thrive. Child Abuse Negl 13:19–28, 1989

Wahler RG: The insular mother: her problems in parent-child treatment. J Appl Behav Anal 13:207–219, 1980

Wahler RG, Dumas JE: Changing the observational coding styles of insular and noninsular mothers: a step toward maintenance of parent training effects, in Parent Training. Edited by Dangel RF, Polster RA. New York, Guilford, 1984, pp 379–416

Woolston JL: Eating disorders in infancy and early childhood. J Am Acad Child Psychiatry 22:114–121, 1983

CHAPTER 7

Meeting the Developmental Needs of Chronically Ill, Hospitalized Children

Nancy Brill, M.D.
Sarale Cohen, Ph.D.
Mary Fauvre, Ph.D.

Over the past 40 years pediatrics has changed dramatically. Many life-threatening diseases, particularly infectious diseases, have been brought under control with the use of antibiotics, the development of vaccines, and the widespread availability of health care. More recently, significant progress has been made in such areas as bone marrow transplantation, total parenteral nutrition, renal dialysis, organ transplantation, and cardiac surgery. Expertise and technology in these fields sometimes result in a cure, but more often they prolong a life that is less than perfect from medical, social, and emotional standpoints. The children who benefit from the new technology are subjected to frequent hospitalizations and multiple medical procedures.

Since the early 1970s it has been known that any hospitalization of duration greater than 1 week, or repetitive hospitalizations, may result in a psychosocial disturbance that does not terminate with the end of the hospital stay, but may tend to persist throughout life. Studies comparing the nonhospitalized child with children hospitalized 1 week or more show a higher incidence of behavioral problems, learning disabilities, and difficulties in forming healthy relationships in the hospitalized group (Douglas 1975; Quinton and Rutter 1976). Although types of illnesses have changed and hospital practices have been altered since

This research was supported by the U.S. Department of Education, Handicapped Children's Early Education Programs, Grant No. DE-G00-00789.

these reports, the same problems continue to exist. Understanding the needs of the developing child gives some insight into why hospitalization is traumatic for any child, and more strikingly so if it occurs repeatedly as with the chronically ill child.

NORMAL DEVELOPMENTAL TASKS

While infants and young children are subjected to the same difficulties that illness inflicts upon persons of all ages (e.g., unexpected separations, unexplained physical pain, unfamiliar people and surroundings, frightening events, family disruptions, and depression), they are particularly vulnerable because of their developmental stage (Vernon et al. 1965). Children with chronic illness have the same emotional needs as healthy children, but attainment of the major affective tasks of attachment, individuation, and mastery (Erikson 1950) is more complex. The task of the infant during the first year of life is to make a secure and selective attachment to a consistent caretaker, usually the mother. This process, which requires a state of well-being in both infant and mother, takes place during ordinary caretaking activities (e.g., feeding, changing, and holding) while smiles, vocalizations, and touches are contingently exchanged. As the infant grows, toys are introduced as objects of mutual interest between mother and child, and the child begins to play.

With the acquisition of mobility, the toddler goes on to practice exploration of his or her world as a separate being—hesitantly and for short periods, with frequent reference to the attachment figure. Play becomes an important need for emotional and cognitive development. The child's play continues to be facilitated by, and often shared with, the attachment figure.

As a preschooler, the child expands his or her world to social relationships and the development of associative play skills with other children. The attachment figure remains a reassuring support to be returned to in difficult, new, or threatening situations. In the ideal situation, the preschooler is becoming a trusting, autonomous being who can usually predict his or her environment, modify it, and feel secure and safe.

DEVELOPMENTAL BURDENS RELATED TO HOSPITALIZATION AND ILLNESS

How does the chronically hospitalized child fare in the pursuit of these essential tasks of childhood? In 1962, Provence and Lipton studied infants raised in an institutional environment during the first year of life. The care given to the infants was routine and not individualized. Babies' needs, such as feeding, diapering, and sleeping, were primarily determined by the institutional schedule. Few contingency experiences existed for the infants. Care was provided at the convenience of the staff, irrespective of the infants' demands. Toys were available but were placed about the babies and not used as objects of shared interest. Babies were expected to play alone. At the end of the year, the infants were delayed or showed atypical behavior in motor, socioemotional, and language development, and in the development of object play.

Hospitals as institutions often run on rigid schedules. As recently as the early 1980s a population of chronically ill infants living for much of the first year at UCLA were observed to have similar motor delays and atypical behaviors (Ralston et al. 1984). These infants were depressed, disinterested in toys, and indiscriminate in smiling and vocalizations. Current studies summarized by Thompson (1985) support older studies in demonstrating the persistent problems that emerge when the child's lack of contingency experiences interferes with emotional needs.

In addition to its impact on the infant, hospitalization also influences the mother's feelings of competence in her role as caregiver. In the same way that infants derive feelings of efficacy from mother-infant contingency experiences, the mother derives feelings of competence from contingency experiences provided by her infant. An infant who is weak, sick, or depressed by being separated from the parents may be unable to respond in a positive manner to his or her mother when she visits. The infant may respond in a similar way to all caretakers without showing preference for the mother. Some young infants purposefully avoid eye contact with the mother under the stressful circumstances of hospitalization. Such situations make it difficult for the mother to continue to reach out to her infant to maintain an effective mothering role. While mothers are frequently encouraged to stay with their infants, many cannot do so because of ongoing family demands, long distance, or financial necessity. The infant is then abandoned for long periods. The mother's feelings in this situation often make it even more difficult for her to respond to her infant when they are together. Schaffer and Callender (1959), observing infants after discharge from the hospital, showed that hospitalization changes the infants' feeding, sleeping, and elimination pattern on return home for up to several weeks. A mother may feel she is a stranger to her own infant, and a negative feedback system can have deleterious long-term consequences.

Beyond the first year of life, toddlers and preschoolers have difficulty coping with the hospital setting. Although the normal toddler begins to move away from the attachment figure, during this life stage he or she needs a consistent figure to return to for reassurance. The separation and strange environment of the hospital is formidable. Just as the infant might appear depressed, the toddler is insecure, clinging, disinclined to explore, and unable to play creatively. The hospitalized preschooler may regress in toilet training and self-help skills, and have difficulty with peer socialization, associative play, and trust (Willis et al. 1982). He or she may be unable to move confidently into new situations. Cognitive as well as social and emotional growth suffers if this condition continues for any length of time after the chronically ill child is discharged.

Families are frequently unwilling to allow their toddler or preschool child to participate in available community resources. Fear of infections, injury, overexertion, and damage to necessary indwelling catheters are frequent reasons chronically ill children are kept house-bound. Play opportunities in the neighborhood, Regional Center services, Head Start programs, and local public schools often are not utilized. As a result the child falls even further behind in development of socialization and individuation. Continuation of a disturbance that begins in the hospital is more likely if the child comes from a stressed family or if the child's relationship with the family is poor. The way a parent responds to a child upon return from the hospital may determine whether the disturbance persists or is dissipated (Stacey et al. 1970).

CHILDREN AT RISK FOR DEVELOPMENTAL PROBLEMS

Observations of the growing number of chronically ill children at UCLA Medical Center have been made by the Child Development staff. Many of the children identified as being at risk for the developmental problems of chronic illness come from four pediatric subspecialty services: Hematology/Oncology, Gastroenterology, Cardiology, and Nephrology. Although all chronically ill children share many of the same problems, specific experiences are associated with specific groups of diseases.

HEMATOLOGY/ONCOLOGY

Children in this group have a primary diagnosis of leukemia or solid tumors. Treatment includes chemotherapeutic drugs and radiation therapy. These children are subjected to repetitive traumatic procedures, e.g., lumbar puncture, bone marrow aspiration, and intravenous medications.

In the event of relapse of the disease, bone marrow transplantation may be done, with repetition of chemotherapy and radiation therapy, plus additional procedures. Indwelling catheters are often placed into veins for access for frequent blood tests and medication. After the transplantation the child is kept in an isolation room accessible only to a few family members and medical personnel caring for him or her. Isolation, which is sometimes required for months, interferes with participation in normal activities and play with other children. Even after a successful transplant, activities and contacts at home remain restricted.

The children in this group are often diagnosed during the second to fifth year of life, and sometimes beyond. At this age the disease process and its treatment have an impact primarily on the child's attainment of separation, individuation, and peer socialization. Particularly difficult for this group of children is the change in physical appearance (e.g., hair loss) that occurs with chemotherapy. Nausea, vomiting, and weakness interfere with daily functioning. Nerve damage and central nervous system damage, which sometimes unavoidably result from therapy, can have a long-term sensory, motor and cognitive impact.

A bone marrow transplant can have such a traumatic effect on a child that his or her development can come to a standstill. For example, a 12-month-old child, developing normally at the time of the transplant, continued to develop in all areas except language, which remained at the same level for the next 2 years. With or without a bone marrow transplant, the long-term care of these children is punctuated by periodic assessment with painful procedures, always with the possibility of relapse. Living with the threat of relapse is debilitating to both parent and child; they tend to approach life with a sense of vulnerability.

GASTROENTEROLOGY

This group includes infants and children who do not have a functional gastrointestinal system and have to be fed intravenously over an 8- to 12-hour period each day. With new techniques, these babies may be able to survive indefinitely without eating.

However, without oral intake, the attachment behaviors and the socialization that accompanies feeding are lost. These infants must stay in a sitting or lying position for long periods of time while the intravenous fluids are given. They have a permanent indwelling catheter attached to their abdomen or chest that discourages them from lying on their stomachs or creeping. These infants are often weak or malnourished for periods of time while an optimal level of nutrition is being worked out. Gross motor skills are almost inevitably delayed. Opportunity for play is restricted. Hospitalization is frequent and prolonged, sometimes occurring over much of the first year of life.

When the babies are home, parents have an overwhelming responsibility in maintaining the indwelling catheter and delivering the intravenous fluids. Frequent infections, often life-threatening, and equipment malfunctions occur. These children, as they grow, have a significant sense of life dependency on a machine. In their drawings of themselves, they often include magnified versions of their catheters connected to the machine, with the machine drawn as an extension of their bodies (M. O'Connor, January 7, 1983, personal communication). The development of a sense of independence and self-sufficiency is a complex issue for these children.

CARDIOLOGY

This group consists of an increasing number of infants and older children who undergo vascular or cardiac surgery early in life. Frequently, a palliative, or temporary, procedure is done early, while the definitive repair is done when the child has grown. These children are often subjected to frequent long hospitalizations for a series of surgeries as well as intervening assessments involving cardiac catheterization.

The parents of these children live with uncertainty about the eventual outcome. Often the level of oxygenation in these infants and children is marginal; they are chronically short of breath. They have feeding difficulties because of the exertion needed to suck; often they are gavage (tube)-fed to enable them to save their energy. Deprivation of the feeding experience has an effect on attachment behavior similar to that experienced by the gastroenterology group. Even a short interaction with a cardiac baby might overtax him or her and result in cyanosis, so these babies are frequently left in relative isolation. Use of an oxygen tent separates them even further from the environment. These infants have little opportunity to play or practice gross motor skills. Consequently, they have frequent delays in these areas.

As the children grow, parents are tremendously overprotective and fearful that their children will overtax themselves. Often parents will discourage the child from learning to walk, and certainly prevent running and climbing. Toddlers with the skills to walk are sometimes wheeled for hours around the ward in baskets or wagons by a worried parent. Separation, individuation, and peer socialization for these children remains a difficult process. Unnecessary infantilization of these children contributes to their frequent delay in language, motor, and self-help skills.

NEPHROLOGY

The children in this group have end-stage renal disease and are maintained even in the early infancy period on peritoneal dialysis. This procedure requires an indwelling abdominal catheter and dependency either on a peritoneal or a hemodialysis machine.

Many of the same issues that characterize the gastroenterology and cardiology infants are present in this group. The infants are weak, have poor appetites, and fail to grow. The long periods of time spent on a machine and the attachment of the machine to a catheter in the abdominal wall make placement of the infant in the prone position difficult. These infants have renal rickets, with fragile bones that may break even with normal handling. This combination of problems results in gross motor delay and little play experience. Parents have to cope with lengthy hospitalizations and a poor long-term prognosis in their infant. In addition, the infant's weak response to caregivers, as well as his or her poor feeding skills, puts him or her at risk for attachment problems.

Older children may be candidates for renal transplantation, go home on peritoneal dialysis, or return to the hospital every other day for hemodialysis. These children continue to have bone disease and to be at risk for fractures. They complain chronically of "feeling sick," with specific reference to nausea and poor appetites. They have severe dietary restrictions in terms of water and salt, and will go to great lengths to obtain forbidden foods and water. This behavior often results in another hospital admission. Children in this group who are maintained on peritoneal dialysis have more freedom from a machine during the day and more time at home, but their parents must maintain complex equipment. Infection and malfunction are constant worries. Rickets, food restrictions, malaise, and indwelling catheters are factors that impinge upon the child's life, giving him or her little opportunity for independence and control.

This group of children presents unique needs that have not yet been addressed. Twenty-five percent of these children will not survive the first 5 years of life. The rest will receive intensive medical intervention, with varying amounts of time in the hospital from a few weeks to 12 months a year. Even when at home, these children and their families live with the tremendous burden of a new brand of chronic illness that in intensity more closely resembles a continuous series of acute episodes rather than the background low-level chronicity produced by some diseases. By the time they are 5 years old, an age when normal children begin kindergarten, many of these children are no longer in the mainstream emotionally or cognitively.

MODEL DEMONSTRATION PROGRAM

FRAMEWORK AND FOCUS OF THE INTERVENTION

How can we help this group of children? There are several approaches that might mitigate the emotional and cognitive impact of their diseases, although none offers an absolute solution. Over the past 4 years we have developed a model demonstration program on the pediatric ward at UCLA Medical Center (Brill et al. 1987).

Our intervention, targeted at children from birth to age 5 years, includes a multidisciplinary team consisting of a pediatrician, psychologists, child development (child life) specialists, and volunteers. In addition, we draw from a broad community of university resources, including psychiatry, social work, and nursing services, all working together to provide service for these children and their families.

Guiding principles of the program include the following:

- A primary focus on emotional development
- Working with the entire family
- Continuous intervention
- Establishment of a long-term relationship

Our primary focus is on the emotional development of the child because we feel that the child's emotional needs must be met first before he or she can go on to other tasks. We work with the entire family, knowing that the impact of chronic illness is felt by every family member. Our intervention is continuous, whether the child is in the hospital or at home, because issues being addressed are long-term and do not dissipate when the child is discharged. Many of our program goals are met through the establishment of a positive long-term relationship with the child and his or her family. All members of the multidisciplinary team commit significant time to an individual family over the long course of the child's illness. The staff must be willing to function in a supportive role when parents can be present and in a parent-surrogate role when they are unable to be present.

PROGRAM COMPONENTS

Referral

The program provides continuous intervention with referral into the cycle at any point, and movement around the cycle in synchrony with the child's hospitalizations (Figure 7-1). A preferred starting point is with the child at home before his or her first hospitalization; but often the initial meeting of program staff and the patient and family is during an acute phase. Intervention before, during, and after hospitalizations is focused on support and guidance for the child and family, with the aim of optimizing the child's ability to continue with his or her developmental tasks.

Home Visit

Initial contact with a family prior to a hospitalization provides an opportunity to begin to establish a trusting relationship. A home visit is a comfortable setting where the staff can meet the child and the family and offer support, guidance, and education. At this time the family's chronic and short-term

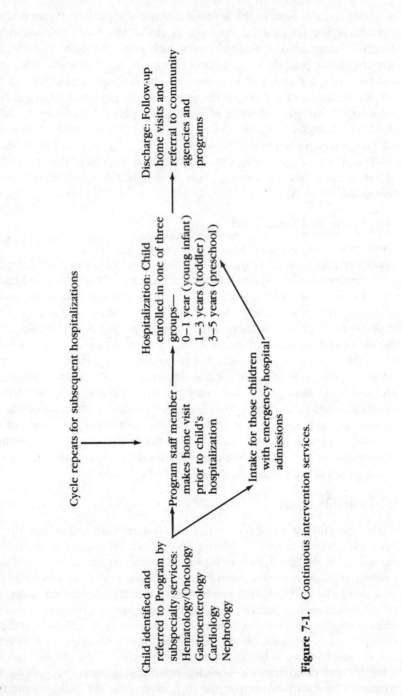

Figure 7-1. Continuous intervention services.

needs for the duration of the hospitalization are identified. Planned modifications of the hospital environment begin at this time. Discussion frequently centers around parental issues such as the likelihood of survival, preparation for painful events, sibling education, developmental questions, and preparing for and how to cope with the hospital setting. The child's developmental level and play skills, as well as the parent-child interaction, are assessed. An understanding of the parents' perceptions of their child's condition, prognosis, and developmental level is important to an effective intervention process. During this visit a videotape is made of the child and family and is available during the hospitalization to remind the child of his or her home, family relationships, experiences, and the skills he or she had previously mastered.

Visit to the Pediatric Ward

The family is also invited to visit the pediatric ward. This visit gives them an opportunity to explore the medical environment before they are faced with the threatening aspects of medical treatment. The child and family tour the unit and meet the staff. The emphasis is on orientation to the environment rather than an introduction to medical equipment. Preschoolers have questions about where things are and how they work, i.e., the lights, toilets, sink, automatic beds, where the food comes from, and where family members will sleep. A play session is arranged in the playroom that contains both conventional toys and medical play equipment. The child and siblings are encouraged to play and ask questions. Simple interpretations of a child's questions and modeling of appropriate responses are provided by the child development specialist. Many of the parents' questions are addressed at this time, as well as in subsequent conversations. Parents receive relevant literature, and children are given a play medical kit and hospital booklet to take home.

Inhospital Program

When the child is admitted to the hospital, a relationship has already been established with the family. The inhospital program has several components designed to meet the individual needs of the family by helping parents maintain confidence in parenting their sick child, by facilitating the child's maintenance of acquired developmental skills, and by creating an environment in which developmental progress can continue. Program services include individual work with children and parents, playroom sessions, parent group meetings, and support for siblings.

A major intervention element is the provision of a consistent caretaker for the child and a continuing relationship with the staff for the parents. The ability of the parents to remain with the child during hospitalization varies. If the parents cannot be present much of the time,

Table 7-1. Intervention strategies of the hospital infant program

---

Attachment is the central issue.

Encourage parents to stay in the hospital with infant.

Provide volunteer to act as surrogate parent and to support and relieve parent.

Modify hospital room with infant's toys, rocking chair, mobiles, nursery music, lowered hospital noise level.

Choose activities appropriate for infant's stress level, energy, state of well-being.

Position infant to optimize play opportunity and visual opportunity in spite of equipment or restraints.

Use comforting techniques, e.g., rocking, singing, eye contact, and touch.

Use infant's cues to facilitate reciprocal social games, vocalization, smiling.

Point out positive changes in infant's response.

Support parents in decision to be present or retreat from treatment procedure.

Encourage parents to dress infant in clothing from home and bring their own stroller and equipment.

Help parents become comfortable with machines and lines.

Provide consistent daily visiting schedule with rituals that will become familiar to infant.

Minimize number of casual visitors.

Work with medical staff on initiating oral feeding in the older infant.

Interpret infant's and parents' emotional needs to hospital staff.

---

volunteers who have been trained and supervised by program staff act as surrogate parents.

Summaries of the intervention strategies used during the inhospital program are given in Table 7-1 (infants), Table 7-2 (toddlers), and Table 7-3 (preschoolers).

Parent and Sibling Support

In addition to respite care and frequent contacts with project staff, parents have the opportunity to meet with other parents twice a week in a parent support group. Parents discuss specific concerns regarding their hospitalized child, and the effects on their children at home and on the total family. The meetings provide a forum for sharing reactions to hospitalization, as well as disappointments and successes in assisting their child. Parents build a support system and a network for friendship, thereby lessening the stress of isolation.

Siblings are included in intervention services, in prehospital visits, and in visits to the hospitalized child. In addition, individual play therapy sessions are arranged for siblings. Family members are encouraged to phone the patient and to provide video- and audiotapes.

Posthospital Program

The posthospital transition to home is difficult for parents who sometimes assume tremendous responsibilities for their sick child. Project staff main-

Table 7-2. Intervention strategies of the hospital toddler program

---

Separation and individuation are central issues.

Assure daily presence of parent and/or surrogate.

Facilitate maintenance and development of independent skills.

Structure opportunities for choices and control.

Structure predictable daily events; depict these events on wall calendar.

Ritualize greetings and departures.

Provide corner table with age-appropriate toys and music.

Encourage family to bring photographs and personal items of family and child.

Play videotapes/audiotapes from home.

Help child learn the workings of the hospital environment (e.g., bed, sink, toilet, food trays).

Incorporate playroom activities into daily schedule, providing hospital play and other play activities (music, tricycle, sand and water, playdoh, playhouse, guinea pig, celebrations).

Encourage play-motivated approach to physical and occupational therapy.

Accept regressive, angry, difficult behavior and interpret this behavior for parents.

Help parents with fair limit-setting.

Work with child and staff on difficult issues such as medicine taking and medical procedures.

Support and counsel parents in their decisions to participate or retreat.

---

tain close contact during this time by telephone, home visits, and attending medical appointments with the parents. Play sessions are offered on the pediatric ward or during a home visit, enabling children to work through troublesome experiences with the help of a familiar person. Project staff and parents continue to have developmental follow-up discussions on emotional and cognitive developmental issues. When appropriate, referrals are made to nursery schools, "mommy-and-me" groups, and Regional Center programs. When the next hospitalization is scheduled, the child and family visit the ward and project staff to become familiar once again with the hospital environment.

Individual Intervention Plan

An individual intervention plan is written by the project staff in conjunction with the family during the child's hospital stay. Writing the plan focuses the attention of the staff on the major areas of intervention with regard to the strengths and problems of a specific family. The individual intervention plan includes the following areas: child health, child environment, emotional development, attachment, individuation, socialization, adaptive behavior, language development, fine motor development, gross motor development, parent issues, and sibling issues. On the basis of the major strengths and problems, the staff formulates a program plan for the implementation of objectives in each area.

Table 7-3. Intervention strategies of the hospital preschool program

Socialization and mastery of independent skills are the central issues.

Encourage parents to stay in hospital with child.

Provide volunteer to act as surrogate parent and to support and relieve parent.

Structure predictable daily events; depict these events on wall calendar.

Provide opportunities in daily care to allow choices, participation, and development of competency.

Set up corner table with child, letting him or her choose favorite activities and music.

Encourage child to dress in his or her own clothes.

Set up opportunities for play activities with other children in playroom.

Ritualize greetings and departures.

Use videotapes/audiotapes from home; encourage photos and availability of personal items.

Have absent parent(s) or siblings call at same time each day.

Modify play environment to accommodate indwelling catheters, shunts, and intravenous equipment poles.

Organize small group activities involving games and taking turns.

Encourage cooking and eating together, and outings.

Provide materials for art projects, allowing child to decorate his or her room with products.

Encourage caretaking activities with guinea pig.

Help parents allow activities (e.g., jumping, running, tricycle riding) to expand child's physical endurance, as appropriate.

Bring activities to child's room if he or she is in isolation.

Structure play therapy sessions around medicine taking and medical procedures.

Prepare child for procedures with simple explanations, and conduct a play session shortly before each procedure takes place.

Interpret for parents the child's level of cognitive understanding.

This plan emerges from clinical observations, interviews, and standardized instruments as described below:

- The Gesell Developmental Schedules (Knobloch and Pasamanick 1974) are used to determine the level of cognitive function.
- The Functional Status Measure (Stein et al. 1981) is used to assess the child's ability to engage in age-appropriate social roles.
- A rating scale of the maternal-child interaction (adapted from Clarke-Stewart 1973) is administered during the home visit.
- The Parenting Stress Index (Abidin 1983) assesses parental attitudes, concerns, and adjustment.
- The child's behavior during developmental testing is also assessed using the Bayley Infant Behavior Record (Bayley 1969).
- Daily written clinical observations contribute to understanding child and family function.

CASE STUDIES

Two case studies are presented to demonstrate some of the issues and interventions present with the toddler and preschool child. The second case includes two excerpts from the child's individual intervention plan (Tables 7-4 and 7-5).

Sean

Sean was 15 months old when we first met him. Biliary atresia had been diagnosed in early infancy. His chronic illness resulted in repeated hospitalizations for recurrent infections and surgical procedures until liver transplantation could be undertaken at 19 months of age. His upper-middle-class parents were immersed in meeting the medical needs of their only child. A housekeeper was hired to stay in the hospital with Sean throughout his course of treatment. Every evening his parents drove 3–4 hours to visit him after work; they stayed with him on weekends.

Sean was referred by the medical staff who noted that he was developmentally delayed. At age 15 months he had no language skills. He could sit if placed in a sitting position, but could not crawl or pull to stand. No one had ever observed him picking up a toy, demonstrating curiosity, or initiating an activity. He was entirely bottle-fed, spending long periods of time at home and in the hospital sucking his thumb to soothe himself. He was extremely fearful and withdrawn; his eyes were wide and watchful when he was awake, and any approach was met with a look of terror and tears.

The staff noted that his parents and housekeeper continued to interact with Sean as if he were still an infant, being hypersensitive to his weakness and ill-health and fearful of stressing him by any playful interactions. New feeding experiences had been quickly abandoned when Sean showed the slightest resistance. He was fearful, passive, and offered no cues to those persons in his environment. The medical staff, in their busy routine, found this undemanding infant easy to care for.

Based on these early observations the staff felt that Sean's developmental delay and his behavior were secondary to his medical problems and consequent emotional issues. Frequent short play sessions were planned two to three times daily. These sessions took place at the same time every day with the same child development specialist to provide familiarity and predictability, and to establish a safe, trusting relationship. Interventions included encouraging the family to bring to the hospital Sean's own clothes, his stroller, and familiar objects from home; play with Sean in the fashion modeled in the hospital, rather than allowing him to spend hours in what they described as his favorite activity—"lying in bed, watching television"; and introduce soft foods and finger foods—items they believed their 16-month-old was too sick to enjoy.

Sean changed slowly. Throughout initial interactions he remained withdrawn and self-protective. There were no vocalizations or smiling, only a watchful gaze. He soon began to anticipate his play sessions and watch the door, waiting for the child development specialist. He would look toward her unsmiling and put his arms out, as though comforted by her presence. He watched her play, initially gesturing with his eyes and his hands. After several weeks he reached out to touch a toy. Following his successful transplant Sean was visibly stronger, healthier, and interacted with more energy. He vocalized and became more involved in reciprocal play.

Following hospital discharge the issues of autonomy and control remained important for Sean and his family. His parents understandably remained overprotective. For example, when Sean was 22 months old they talked about how they would bump heads racing to pick up a toy that Sean had dropped rather than allow him to retrieve it for himself. They described him as the "little king" who was pulled about in his wagon pointing to desired objects. Consequently, they wondered how they could ever let Sean take his first steps. At meals Sean gestured toward morsels and drink, receiving them without ever putting out a hand. His father asked the hospital staff whether Sean might pick up his own glass if his mother were not so quick to anticipate his thirst. Paradoxically, he expressed concern that Sean was late at toilet training, and wondered about starting training.

With time, guidance from the staff, and Sean's own increasing need for independence, Sean began to walk, run, and feed himself. His language skills emerged rapidly. He recently made a successful transition into nursery school. His parents look optimistically but cautiously toward the future and talk about how difficult the past has been.

Matthew

Matthew, aged 3½ years, and his family illustrate issues the preschooler may face when dealing with chronic illness and hospitalization. He was admitted to UCLA Medical Center for bone marrow transplantation treatment for neuroblastoma, a form of childhood cancer. His mother, an intensive-care-unit nurse in their home community, made plans to stay throughout the hospitalization. Relatives took care of the 6-year-old brother in their home. Matthew's father planned his vacation to be with him in the hospital, but otherwise was able to visit infrequently.

Matthew was referred to our program by hospital staff because they believed he needed medical intervention for hyperactivity. They were concerned about the problems associated with keeping him in an iso-

Table 7-4. Individual intervention plan: emotional domain

Name: Matthew	Age: 3½ years		
Strengths	Problems	Objectives	Plan
Responsive and playful	Anxious about own well-being	To decrease feelings of anxiety To create a more predictable environment	Implement regular play therapy sessions to provide emotional release and mastery around issues dealing with his illness, hospitalization, and lack of security. Help staff to view Matthew's behavior as anxiety rather than as noncompliance or aggression. Establish predictable daily routines by pictorial calendar. Help staff to give mother clear cues to anticipate forthcoming events.
Resilient	Anxious about procedures	To increase his tolerance of procedures	Prepare Matthew through play sessions by giving him opportunities to enact difficult procedures. Help Matthew to develop strategies to cope with treatment procedures, e.g., thinking about something pleasant, seeking emotional support, protesting by saying "ouch." Inform Matthew of progress during procedures. Interact with Matthew after procedures.

Well-developed sense of independence	Behavior problems around medication taking	To increase compliance	Encourage staff to be low-key in approach. Develop consistent approach for mother and staff to use regarding medicine taking:
			1. Matthew given choice of method when choice available, e.g., medicine in cherry syrup or applesauce, etc. (one choice given)
			2. Nurse to *give* medicine with mother present to praise and support Matthew; mother or nurse *not* to threaten mother's departure if Matthew does not comply
			3. Matter-of-fact approach to avoid prolonging of medicine taking, secondary gains, and manipulation of situation by Matthew; attention given after medicines are taken

Table 7-5. Individual intervention plan: parental domain

Name: Matthew   Age: 3½ years

Strengths	Problems	Objectives	Plan
Mother is able to stay at hospital and sleep in room.	Mother has difficulty dealing effectively with Matthew around separation.	Mother and Matthew to feel more comfortable with separation	Work out plan with mother for separation: 1. Matthew is to be told when mother is leaving. 2. Matthew is to be told when mother will return, using Matthew's pictorial schedule. 3. Mother is to leave without prolonging separation; this is to be modeled for mother. 4. Arrange for consistent staff/volunteer to be with Matthew when mother leaves.
Mother has confidence in child's verbal and cognitive skills.	Mother's explanations are above child's cognitive level.	To increase mother's awareness of Matthew's level of comprehension	Help mother to be aware of child's level of understanding. Help mother to ask Matthew questions. Help mother to answer Matthew's questions on his developmental level by modeling and by discussions with mother. Help mother to observe Matthew's response to events and conversations.
Mother is knowledgeable about hospital environment and medicine.	Mother's anxiety	To reduce and alleviate stress	Provide ongoing discussions with mother. Listen carefully to mother's concerns. Facilitate communication with medical staff. Build upon mother's suggestions regarding daily care routines. Encourage mother to perform routine care; but mother is not to be given medical care of child.

lation room, connected to an intravenous apparatus and monitors. The staff noted a positive, caring mother-child relationship. The mother valued Matthew's independence and autonomy, but she had difficulty setting limits. Developmental testing indicated that he was a competent child with a well-developed sense of independence.

Staff intervention revealed that Matthew did not feel safe. He was struggling to maintain the independent skills he had already mastered. He felt he had to be strong, active, and in control because he felt so threatened. This sense of vulnerability was affected by two issues. First, his mother was so upset by Matthew's situation that it was impossible for her to provide reassurance, consistency, firm limit setting, and age-appropriate explanations. Her nursing knowledge and awareness of the medical risks Matthew faced presented her with a terrible dilemma. She wondered if the right decision had been made in choosing the bone marrow transplant. Matthew quickly picked up her fears and ambivalence. The second issue was that Matthew's advanced verbal skills deceived others into expecting higher cognitive understanding than a 3½-year-old possesses. The astute questions he asked were often given answers too rational or complicated for him to understand. When he asked where the dinosaurs live, rather than wanting to be told they were extinct and did not live anymore, he actually wanted to know that he was safe from harm. So Matthew armed himself with guns, knives, and rubber alligators. He refused medicines despite his mother's desperate attempts to make them palatable and her logical explanations of their importance. He hit the physical therapist when she asked him, "Can you show me how strong you are?" Matthew was enraged and terrified when his mother tried to separate from him, and so she rarely did, intensifying his fears that he was not safe because she did not feel safe to leave him. To add to his difficulties the required isolation during treatment severely limited Matthew's normal social interactions for an extended period.

Interventions were aimed at helping Matthew and his mother feel more secure. The child development specialist met frequently with the mother. Matthew was seen daily for play therapy. In addition, a volunteer was assigned to visit on a regular schedule. Matthew's mother allowed herself daily breaks when the child development specialist or volunteer was with Matthew. These relationships provided social interaction and opportunities to allay fears and to model appropriate limit setting. Matthew responded positively to play sessions, exploring his feelings and concerns, and becoming more comfortable with medical treatments. He took his medicine with less difficulty. He remained active and maintained his independent skills. When discharged from the hospital after successful treatment, Matthew and his mother left feeling that they had mastered a difficult time. They were looking forward to renewing their life at home and in their community.

Tables 7-4 and 7-5 present the 'emotional' and 'parental' domains, respectively, of Matthew's individual intervention plan, demonstrating the application of this instrument.

EVALUATION OF THE INTERVENTION FAMILIES

We studied the characteristics of our intervention population and evaluated the accomplishment of our intervention goals over a 3-year period. The intervention study population consisted of a group of 46 children who were very sick at the time of referral. Most of them had a questionable or poor prognosis, scored low on a life activity scale, and were delayed in their growth parameters. Approximately 10% of the children showed significant progress in health status, whereas 25% of the children died during the course of the project. Many of the children spent more than 3 months in the hospital during the project and were hospitalized repeatedly. The maximum time that an individual child was hospitalized was 18 consecutive months.

The Functional Status Measure (Stein et al. 1981) indicated a range of functioning for the children in their ability to conduct daily routines, as well as a demonstration of common problems faced by these children. Forty percent of the children were dependent on medical equipment, 33% had eating problems, 23% had sleeping problems, and 48% were described as being in a difficult or bad mood.

The children were tested repeatedly during the project with the Gesell Developmental Schedules and the Peabody Picture Vocabulary Test, if appropriate. The children as a group functioned in the low normal range (developmental quotient = 83). Gross motor and language skills were the areas showing the greatest delay. Thirty-nine percent scored below 80 at final testing, and 29% scored above 100. The developmental quotient of individual children did not shift significantly from the beginning to the end of the project for the majority of the children followed. In spite of their severe illness, most of the children were able to progress in their development, but a few children improved dramatically in their cognitive development during the project. Seven percent decreased drastically as their disease progressed rapidly.

The Parenting Stress Index (Abidin 1983) was administered in order to assess parent-child systems at risk for dysfunctional parenting. The stress felt by parents was high and put a number of dyads at risk for dysfunctional parent-child systems. Those dyads that were at risk had children who were less cognitively competent and who showed less reciprocal interactions during child care and play. The older the child, the more stress the parents experienced, probably reflecting the duration of time the parents have had to cope with the child's health problems.

The study indicated that the families were usually multiproblem families with financial problems (56%), marital difficulty (50%), and emotional instability (44%) as common sources of stress. Only 24% of our families did not report serious problems in addition to chronic illness. Assessment of family functioning indicated that those families that appeared to be coping well, regardless of number of problems, were able to be more responsive to their children and were less stressed.

Each family that participated in the model demonstration program was evaluated as to the number of intervention goals accomplished for the child and the family system. A high percentage of intervention goals were accomplished overall. Families for whom intervention was more successful were also rated, independently, as showing a more reponsive home environment, and had children who were performing better at final developmental testing at the end of the project. The actual health status of the child was related to the number of goals that were achieved for the child, but the success in achieving family goals was independent of the severity of the child's illness.

CONCLUSIONS

The above data indicate the cognitive and emotional fragility of this group of children and their parents and the need for a comprehensive approach to psychosocial issues. The opportunity to help these children maintain cognitive skills and to support highly stressed families with multiple problems is evident. Our observation is that the intervention strategies of the model demonstration program are effective in supporting and guiding these families, reducing potential stress, increasing parental awareness of their child's cues, and increasing responsivity to these cues, thus facilitating a more effective parent-child relationship and optimal emotional and cognitive functioning in the child. Our observations were confirmed by parental report and comments by referring physicians, nurses, and other hospital staff. Parents have expressed gratitude to the program staff for providing emotional support and valuable information for them and their child. Nurses who consulted program staff for suggestions, such as ways to improve compliance with medication, reported success in applying the techniques based on an understanding of the child's needs. Physicians have reported improved interactions in working with the child and family.

The multifaceted program interventions have addressed a range of needs and issues for chronically ill, hospitalized children and their families. The program was designed so that replication in other sites is possible. Program services can be adapted and implemented to meet the needs of children in a variety of hospital settings.

REFERENCES

Abidin RR: Parenting Stress Index. Charlottesville, VA, Pediatric Psychology Press, 1983

Bayley N: Bayley Scales of Infant Development. New York, The Psychological Corporation, 1969

Brill N, Cohen S, Fauvre M, et al: Caring for chronically ill children: an innovative approach for care. Children's Health Care 16:105–113, 1987

Clarke-Stewart KA: Interaction Between Mothers and Their Young Children: Characteristics and Consequences. Monographs of the Society for Research in Child Development, Vol 38 (serial no 153), 1973

Douglas JWB: Early hospital admissions and later disturbances of behaviour and learning. Dev Med Child Neurol 17:456–480, 1975

Erikson E: Childhood and Society. New York, WW Norton, 1950

Knobloch H, Pasamanick B: Gesell and Amatruda's Developmental Diagnosis, 3rd Edition. New York, Harper & Row, 1974

Provence S, Lipton RC: Infants in Institutions. New York, International Universities Press, 1962

Quinton D, Rutter M: Early hospital admissions and later disturbances of behavior: an attempted replication of Douglas' findings. Dev Med Child Neurol 18:447–459, 1976

Ralston C, O'Connor M, Ament M, et al: Somatic growth and developmental functioning of children on prolonged home total parenteral nutrition. J Pediatr 105:842–846, 1984

Schaffer HR, Callender WM: Psychological effects of hospitalization in infancy. Pediatrics 24:528–539, 1959

Stacey M, Dearden R, Pill R, et al: Hospitals, Children and Their Families: The Report of a Pilot Study. London, Routledge & Kegan Paul, 1970

Stein REK, Reissman CK, Jessop DJ: Functional status measure. Unpublished manuscript, 1981

Thompson RH: Psychological Research on Pediatric Hospitalization and Health Care. Springfield, IL, Charles C Thomas, 1985

Vernon DTA, Foley JM, Sipowicz RR, et al: The Psychological Responses of Children to Hospitalization and Illness. Springfield, IL, Charles C Thomas, 1965

Willis DJ, Elliot CH, Jay JM: Psychological Effects of Physical Illness and Its Concomitants, in Handbook for the Practice of Pediatric Psychology. Edited by Tuma JM. New York, John Wiley, 1982, pp 20–66

Preventive Interventions With Older Children

Introduction

Robert S. Pynoos, M.D., M.P.H.

The following chapters reflect the increasing diversity of psychiatric issues relevant to school-age and adolescent children that confront the prevention-oriented psychiatrist. Although these chapters discuss a more diverse set of issues than those in Section II, a number of common themes emerge from them as well.

First, programs previously established for adults may not be suitable for children. Programs for early identification of suicidal persons, and model suicide intervention programs for adults, may not be the most appropriate for children and adolescents with similar problems. Likewise, postdivorce interventions, which might often entail long-term individual psychotherapy for adults, might not be as good as alternatives such as "pulsed interventions" for children. Therefore, research findings from the adult prevention literature cannot simply be generalized to children. Additional specific research is necessary to identify areas of difference as well as areas of similarity.

Second, considerable research is required to improve our abilities to identify potential problems, including depression and suicidality, particular vulnerability to the stressors of divorce or natural disasters, and speech and language problems likely to predict subsequent psychiatric disorders. Because resources for intervention will never approach the demands, we need to have the best possible understanding of where and when intervention is likely to be most useful.

Third, in spite of our many good intentions and kind wishes to prevent all sorts of bad consequences from following unfortunate circumstances, we must take a hardheaded (but not hardhearted) look at the results of our intervention programs. If our best shot using strategy A fails to prevent negative sequelae for condition B, perhaps we are wasting energy and resources by continuing to throw more resources down the same type of holes—the results of other intervention programs using strategies similar to A for problems similar to B are not likely to be more robust. In some instances we should acknowledge the limits that current concepts and tools impose on us, and radically alter our research strategies and intervention efforts—seeking strategies C and D, for example.

Fourth, carefully designed evaluation programs with control groups who receive no interventions are needed in all subsequent studies if we are ever to convincingly demonstrate the ultimate worth of such programs to policymakers. Although naturalistic experiments may be possible, they are rarely as convincing as preplanned designs.

With these general observations in mind, let us turn to the individual chapters in Section III.

Shaffer and his associates, in Chapter 8, address the difficulties in simply applying traditional adult prevention programs to adolescents. Shaffer's work over the past decade has provided much needed empirical evidence documenting who, among adolescents, are at most risk for suicide. As this chapter points out, some of these factors—impulsivity, drug abuse, and severe psychopathology—make it unlikely that the suicidal adolescent will utilize suicide hotlines as traditionally offered. While acknowledging the potential usefulness of hotlines, Shaffer and his associates suggest that alternative approaches must be considered because timely access is a cornerstone of prevention.

This research raises a fundamental question about adolescent suicide prevention. Do we rely on a voluntary or self-referral program or do we pursue known epidemiological leads and actively seek out those individuals at risk? Even though adolescent suicide now accounts for a significant percentage of deaths in this age group, it is still a rare phenomenon. Therefore, we may be going in the wrong direction in our efforts to reach the whole student body through generic school-based suicide prevention programs. Those teenagers with the lowest risk already have a positive attitude toward help-seeking behavior, while, unfortunately, those at highest risk may be the least inclined to seek help, and their attitudes may not significantly improve after participation in such a program.

Because critical at-risk features (e.g., prior suicide behavior in the family) are difficult to address in a classroom setting, should we not look for ways to identify, gain access to, and provide assistance to these at-risk youngsters, rather than expand limited public funding for more widespread suicide prevention programs? While the public has demanded that action be taken, prevention may rest on strategic interventions rather than a broad policy that responds to every parent's fear that it could happen to his or her child.

In Chapter 9, Wallerstein describes a comprehensive clinical intervention program for children of divorce, based on an extensive longitudinal study. Divorce, in contrast to adolescent suicide, is so frequent an occurrence that often in child psychiatric clinics, a history of parental divorce is lost as background noise. Wallerstein reminds us of the profound and enduring distress caused by marital discord and rupture, and that the goal of prevention may not be so much to ease the acute pain, but to ameliorate or substantially reduce the long-lasting detrimental effects. In previous work she has outlined how the developing child faces an ongoing series of complex psychological tasks after parental divorce. In this chapter Wallerstein expands these notions by substituting for the usual dichotomy of crisis versus long-term therapy, an example of a pulsed intervention strategy. This model rests both on the knowledge of what is psychologically most accessible and on the capacity for an adaptive response at different intervals over the years. In doing so, she underscores a major principle of preventive work with children, namely, to help maintain normal developmental progress.

Cantwell and Baker take a different starting point. They begin not with a psychiatric outcome like suicide behavior or an intrafamilial stress like parental divorce, but with a pediatric developmental disorder that involves language and communication. They closely follow the psychiatric sequelae, showing how careful discrimination of the type of communication disorder reveals significantly different risks of psychiatric morbidity. In some ways this research is the most disturbing of the studies reported in this section, while at the same time being the most sophisticated. It is disheartening that children can be identified early as having a specific communication disorder, can be provided with substantial speech therapy, and yet still can go on to develop psychiatric problems. However, this method of extracting out from a larger pediatric population a specific group of children at risk for developmental psychopathology is an important instrument in targeting preventive mental health efforts.

Pynoos and Nader provide still another approach to preventing psychiatric morbidity in children and adolescents. In this instance a relatively normal population of children is confronted with a major external adverse event—a natural or technological disaster. Careful interventions with the children, their families, and sometimes their larger communities are needed to ensure that the potential negative sequelae of this trauma are kept to a minimum. The authors demonstrate that data-based preventive strategies (e.g., understanding the critical importance of exposure) seem quite promising, especially following time-limited traumas that befall previously normal children with family supports. Some of the authors' recommendations involve the recognition and avoidance of emotionally detrimental decisions, such as protecting adolescents from unnecessary roles as rescue workers or body handlers, or preventing unwarranted separations for preschool or school-age children during and after the disaster. These recommendations also suggest a fundamental change in how longitudinal postdisaster interventions are organized by proposing a comprehensive school-based program as the most convenient and cost-efficient setting. As the authors indicate, recent studies on disasters have expanded the knowledge base, and additional systematic research is likely to result in improved specificity about intervention efforts.

Krugman, in the final chapter in this section, raises an issue fundamental to all prevention efforts, namely, phenomena that are not recognized or appreciated to be aversive cannot therefore be adequately addressed. In psychiatry and medicine, similar "blind spots" have existed—among adults with regard to alcoholism and other drug abuse, and among children with regard to physical and sexual abuse. Furthermore, because abuse leads to a myriad of clinical presentations, the original psychological insult is often camouflaged. Krugman outlines steps required to ensure recognition, including identifying the at-risk abuser.

In describing special techniques for working with the family, Krugman reiterates a point made by several other authors, that although some demonstrations of preventive intervention strategies have been successful, a societal or professional commitment to accept a more widespread public health approach to problem-solving has been lacking. Rather, the health-care system falls back to the traditional role of waiting for the serious aftermath to develop before intervening. In Krugman's discussion of primary prevention we come full circle to the content of the second section of this book, where Heinicke describes the early postbirth home program for at-risk parents, which is a cost-efficient, effective, and practical intervention to prevent child abuse.

The chapters in this section address aspects of the prevention agenda that deal with the diverging needs of older children and adolescents. The methods of analysis, the tailoring of prevention strategies to longitudinal empirical findings, and the design of innovative interventions detailed in the chapters hold promise for the future of preventive child psychiatry.

CHAPTER 8

Suicide Crisis Centers: A Critical Reappraisal With Special Reference to the Prevention of Youth Suicide

David Shaffer, M.D.
Ann Garland, M.A.
Prudence Fisher, M.S.
Kathleen Bacon, Ph.D.
Veronica Vieland, Ph.D.

Skepticism about being able to prevent suicide is often attributed to the relative rarity of suicidal deaths. In the United States the annual incidence among 15- to 19-year-olds is approximately 9 per 100,000—about 2,000 cases a year, or 14% of all deaths in this age group (National Center for Health Statistics 1988). Rarity is not the issue. Far more young people are affected by suicide than by the rare inherited metabolic diseases for which routine preventive screening is accepted without question because the screens used to predict the conditions are both specific and sensitive. By contrast, the known risk factors for suicide, although sensitive (i.e., they can accurately define and identify most suicide victims before their death), are very nonspecific, that is, they include too many people who will not actually suicide. These risk factors include such common conditions as antisocial behavior (with an estimated prevalence of approximately 10%), substance abuse (with a prevalence of 5%), and depression (which in adolescence has an estimated prevalence of about 2%) (Kandel et al., in press; Offord et al. 1987). Even though there is considerable diagnostic overlap among these conditions, applying effective suicide prevention methods—assuming that we knew what these

135

were—to such large groups would involve an overwhelming proportion of individuals who would never commit suicide (Rosen 1954; Temoche et al. 1964).

Suicide crisis centers circumvent the low specificity problem. They serve self-identified suicidal individuals who are motivated to receive help, and their impact is potentially efficient. These centers are in marked contrast to the increasingly school-based suicide prevention programs and television shows that heighten awareness of the problem of youth suicide (Garland et al. 1989). We have shown that school-based programs not only are ineffective but may be harmful to some vulnerable participants (Shaffer et al. 1987; Gould and Shaffer 1986). Furthermore, we also have found that suicide hotlines, which were often described during the educational programs that we evaluated, seem attractive to teenagers. One of the few desired changes noted in our evaluation was the teenagers' willingness to use a hotline if they were experiencing significant emotional distress.

However, because evaluations have shown little impact in the adolescent population on suicide morbidity and mortality, hotlines have gone out of fashion, and they are regarded skeptically by many persons in the professional, academic, and scientific communities. This chapter examines whether lessons can be drawn from the extensive research on hotline services that would permit the reformulation and application of hotlines in the task of preventing youth suicide. Because hotline use and suicide attempts are closely linked, and because there is much debate about whether suicide attempts are a distinct entity that only occasionally overlaps with suicide completions, this review is prefaced with a reconsideration of that relationship. Other general reviews of the suicide prevention literature are as follows: Motto et al. 1974; McGee 1974; Stelmachers 1976; Auerbach and Kilmann 1977; Stein and Lambert 1984.

RELATIONSHIPS BETWEEN ATTEMPTED AND COMPLETED SUICIDE

Suicidal behavior has been classified, especially among British psychiatrists, into completed suicide and "parasuicide," the latter being an essentially benign behavior shown by predominantly young females who take nonlethal overdoses of potentially poisonous substances (Stengel and Cook 1958; Neuringer 1962). Assumedly, the parasuicide does not wish to die, but uses a behavior that produces anxiety or distress in others to bring about some immediate change in his or her circumstances.

This classification has important implications for suicide prevention. If suicidal thoughts, threats, attempts, and completions are separate, albeit overlapping, entities characterized by different types of psychopathology, and if only a very small minority of those who threaten or attempt suicide intend to die, then the focus of suicide prevention should be limited to the minority of attempters or threateners who are judged to be potential suicide completers. Clearly, this screening activity would throw a major burden on the suicide crisis hotline. On the other hand, if ideators, attempters, and completers differ only in how effectively they have acted, and not in their intentions, then efforts that are broadly directed to anyone who self-identifies as suicidal would be appropriate.

The argument for suicide and attempted suicide being distinct diagnostic entities is based mainly on apparent demographic differences between the two groups. Most suicide attempters are young females (Bergstrand and Otto 1962; Morgan et al. 1975; Goldacre and Hawton 1985), whereas death certificate data (Shaffer and Fisher 1981; Centers for Disease Control 1986) indicate that, at least in the United States and Western Europe, the incidence of completed suicide increases with age and is higher in males. These sex differences are unlikely to be a result of reporting bias, for more aggressive case-finding methods do not materially alter sex ratios (Kennedy et al. 1974). However, we argue here that there is abundant evidence that ideators, attempters, and completers share many characteristics, and that it is possible, as described below, that choice of method is confounded both by sex and by the degree of intent to die.

POSSIBLE CONFOUNDING OF SEX, AGE, METHOD, AND OUTCOME

Sex and Method

Although most suicides in the United States are committed with firearms, sizeable sex differences can be found for any given method. Ingestion deaths are significantly more common among females; shooting and hanging are used more often by males (Centers for Disease Control 1986). However, overdoses are frequently ineffective because they take effect relatively slowly and thus afford time for second thoughts and effective treatment. It could be argued (and usually is) that these differences in outcome must be known to those individuals who choose them, so that method preference reflects a difference in intentionality. It is believed that females who overdose are at best ambivalent about wanting to die and are therefore assumed to suffer from less severe psychiatric problems; men, on the other hand, as evidenced by their more frequent use of highly lethal methods, are generally thought to be more likely to want to die because of more serious underlying psychiatric conditions.

However, it may be that the sexes do not differ in their (generally ambivalent) motivation to die. Perhaps choice of method is a sex-typed behavior, so that when suicidal males and females respond to an extreme affect, they do so in different ways, which, at least in North America and Western Europe, is likely to lead to death in males but is unlikely to do so in females.

This explanation would be compatible with the finding that sex differences in the suicide rate are not universal, and vary in different countries (World Health Organization 1974). For example, a survey of consecutive youth suicides in India (Sathyavathi 1975) showed no sex differences in the suicide rate in teenagers. This finding may be attributed to the fact that resuscitation methods are less effective in that country, even if the victim has second thoughts, because the preferred ingestant is an insecticide (paraquat) for which no treatment is available, and because jumping from a height—a lethal, female-preferred method—is more readily available in a country where backyard wells are ubiquitous.

However, the possibility exists that there are sex-related differences in psychopathology among completers, since the relationship among sex, psychopathology, and intent may be quite complex. In our New York study (Shaffer et al. 1988), depression was more common in female than in male completers, perhaps reflecting the differential prevalence of depression in adolescent males and females. Many of the male completers had a history of poor impulse control, committing suicide shortly after an acute precipitant at a time when their intentionality was high but could have been predicted to diminish had they survived. At these times the males acted in a highly lethal fashion (usually by hanging or shooting themselves), whereas we guess that many females who felt similarly acted on their suicidal impulses by taking what turned out to be an ineffective overdose.

Age and Method

Representative attempt data are hard to come by, but in a survey of all suicide attempts in the county of Oxford in Great Britain, Goldacre and Hawton (1985) found that attempts were somewhat more common in the early than in the later teen years, whereas the reverse held true for completions. Completions are uncommon in the early teens and peak at around age 24 (Shaffer and Fisher 1981). This picture of reciprocal trends must be interpreted carefully because attempts are more common than completions. However, these findings are compatible with the notion that as teenagers mature, they become more astute in deciding on a choice of methods.

Age-related method preference in youth is not well documented, although there is evidence that younger children and teenagers are more likely to make suicide attempts with over-the-counter (less lethal) analgesics, whereas older adults most often use more dangerous, legitimately prescribed psychoactive drugs (Morgan et al. 1975). This difference could be due to the greater ease with which adults can access physicians for prescribed drugs or to differences in intentionality. If the former hypothesis is the case, and if intent is the same in the two groups, the use of more lethal drugs by older patients and less lethal drugs by younger ones would be expected to result in (a) more failed suicide initiatives and thus a larger number of attempts, and (b) a smaller proportion of completed suicides attributable to overdose in the young, and the reverse in older individuals, precisely what is found (Centers for Disease Control 1986).

Sex Differences and Secular Trends

Suicide completion rates have increased during the past three decades. If attempts and completions reflect the same underlying phenomena, one would expect to see somewhat different sex-related secular trends. Attempts, being a more direct index of suicidal behaviors, should show an increasing trend in both sexes. However, if completion depends on the sex-linked selection of more lethal methods, the increase should be confined to males. Both seem to be happening, with attempts increasing during the past three decades in both sexes (Weissman 1974) and deaths increasing only among males (Shaffer and Fisher 1981).

SIMILARITIES BETWEEN SUICIDAL IDEATION AND BEHAVIOR

In a general population study of adults, responses to a range of questions about suicidal ideation and behavior were strongly interrelated in a hierarchical fashion (Paykel et al. 1974). Not surprisingly, almost all subjects who admitted to having made a previous suicide attempt had experienced suicidal ideation. More interesting, the age and symptom profiles of ideators who had not made a prior attempt resembled those of the attempters and differed from those of the attempters who had not had suicidal ideation. Pfeffer et al. (1984) similarly found that symptom profiles of child ideators resembled those of child attempters, with both differing significantly from profiles of nonideator/nonattempter individuals. This evidence of overlap supports the idea of suicide as a unitary phenomenon.

SIMILARITIES BETWEEN SUICIDE ATTEMPTERS AND COMPLETERS

Similar Diagnostic Profiles and Other Correlates

A preliminary comparison of teenage completers and age-, race-, and sex-matched attempters (who were judged to need hospital admission) in our New York study (see below) reveals no differences in diagnostic profile, previous attempt history, or familial incidence of suicide and suicide attempts between attempters and completers. The only difference noted so far is a low prevalence of substance abuse in female completers (no different from that in control subjects), whereas female attempters had high rates of substance abuse, comparable to those found in male attempters and completers. The rates for substance abuse did not differ between male attempters and completers. In a smaller study (Brent et al. 1987) there were similarly no significant differences in diagnosis and prior attempt history after age and sex differences were taken into account.

Continuity Between Attempts and Completions

Follow-up studies of teenage attempters show that even though only a small proportion of suicide attempters will go on to commit suicide, the rate of completed suicides in these individuals is many times higher than that found in the general population (see below). A suicide rate of approximately 10% has been reported among boys who had previously been admitted to a psychiatric inpatient unit following a severe attempt or because of depression (Otto 1972; Motto 1984). A rate of just under 1% was found in a 3-year average follow-up of boys who presented at an emergency room after an overdose but who were not admitted to a psychiatric hospital (Goldacre and Hawton 1985). These rates are between 16 and 160 times greater than the expected 5-year incidence in the general population (approximately 0.06%). Similar proportions for girls range from 1% for former inpatients to approximately 0.1% for those who received medical outpatient care only, an incidence between 10 and 100 times greater than the expected 5-year incidence of approximately 0.015% for the general population.

Effect of Suicidogenic Stimuli on Attempts and Completions

If completed and attempted suicide are closely related, factors that potentiate or inhibit suicide should have a similar effect on both phenomena. Regrettably, there are no readily available techniques for inhibiting suicide, but there is extensive evidence that attention and publicity given to a suicidal death will lead to an increase in suicides. In the only study that has examined the effect of media on both deaths and attempts, Gould and Shaffer (1986), studying the impact of television programs that dramatized the plight of suicidal teenagers or the impact of their death on survivors, found that a majority of the programs were followed by an increase in suicide attempts.

CONCLUSIONS

Suicide attempters and completers are more similar than different. While there are undoubtedly some suicide "attempts" in which death is not intended, there are many in which it is, just as there are some suicides in which death was inadvertent. However, it is a bold—or foolish— clinician who can declare with certainty that a particular instance of suicidal behavior or declaration of suicidal intent is only an empty gesture. The time-honored ways of assessing suicidal intent, such as evaluating the medical seriousness of the behavior or determining the detail with which suicide planning has been undertaken, have been shown to have poor predictive power, and the specificity and sensitivity of the several suicide intent scales that have been developed either are poor or have never been established. Furthermore, many nonlethal attempts result in serious or even permanent injury. Given this state of affairs, it is safest to assume that all suicide acts have a lethal or at least harmful potential, and that the term suicide gesture may serve more to reassure the professional or the relative than to accurately describe the victim. Thus, for the purpose of this review, preventive endeavors are appropriately directed to those who threaten or contemplate suicide.

EVALUATING PREVENTION PROGRAMS

Evaluating a program's efficacy requires some comparison, either among individuals before and after they have received the intervention, or between individuals or communities who have versus have not received the intervention, or both.

Before-and-after comparisons require that the outcome to be measured has been systematically recorded before the start of the intervention. When a before-and-after study has been planned in advance, this presents no problem; but sometimes it would be useful to evaluate programs that came into existence without any a priori plans to evaluate efficacy. In these instances the base ratio must be inferred from reliable data obtained from contemporary records, such as the number of suicidal deaths recorded within a community, the number of visits to local emergency rooms for suicide attempts, or the number of suicide hotline calls.

However, unless it can be specifically demonstrated that higher morbidity is linked to nonexposure to the intervention, such studies are prone to ecological confounds, i.e., some other shift in the community may have accounted for the change. For example, because suicide is more common in the elderly and is less common among blacks, an increase or reduction in the proportion of the elderly or blacks in a community can therefore be expected to alter the local suicide rate. Or, changes may be due to some other, more specific factor, such as a change in the availability of a method for committing suicide. To reduce the likelihood of such confounds it is helpful to include comparisons between the target population and an appropriately matched control community that lacks a prevention program but in which any general effects would still be expected to operate.

The probability also arises that a given observed change results from some general influence other than the introduction of the prevention service. Here, any factor that may link the changes in question to exposure versus nonexposure to the service would be helpful. For example, Miller et al. (1984), in their study referred to below, demonstrated a reduction in suicidal deaths among young white women in communities after the introduction of a suicide prevention hotline. This finding is consonant with the observation that hotline usage was greatest among young white females, i.e., the group that showed the reduction in suicide rate.

The timing of the evaluation is important. A program may have important short-term effects that are best picked up by an evaluation carried out within days following the intervention (e.g., an advertising campaign for a hotline may induce calls from teenagers who are troubled at the time of the campaign). However, the intervention may have longer-term effects that might be demonstrable only by a longer-term evaluation (e.g., a crisis service could lead to effective interventions that abort suicide attempt repetitions).

Finally, it is important to evaluate the fundamental goal of the program. For example, the proponents of a program may feel that improved community knowledge about certain aspects of suicide is important to the program's success. They may devise a before-and-after measure to show improvement in depression scores among youngsters who are exposed to the service. However, this improvement may have no effect at all on subsequent suicidal behavior, a fact that would become apparent only if the evaluators studied both mood changes and suicide attempt and/or completion rates. Because the number of teen suicides will be small in most administrative areas, there will rarely be sufficient statistical power to demonstrate a program's efficacy (or the reverse) by examining deaths before and after a program's introduction. This problem can be circumvented if either (1) several programs with broadly similar characteristics pool their data, or (2) a more prevalent index of suicidality (e.g., suicide attempts) is used as the dependent variable rather than completed suicides.

SUICIDE CRISIS SERVICES

RATIONALE

Although some suicide crisis services provide walk-in facilities where suicide patients may have a face-to-face encounter with a counselor, such services are uncommon, and this section refers to telephone services unless otherwise specified.

The rationale for suicide crisis care has been articulated by Shneidman and Farberow (1957):

1. Suicide behavior is often associated with a crisis.
2. Suicide is contemplated with psychological ambivalence; that is, wishes to die exist simultaneously with wishes to be rescued and saved.
3. There is a basic need for humans to express themselves and to communicate with others.
4. The suicidal individual's ambivalence about dying stems from a psychiatric illness in which the suicide represents an unsatisfactory means of attaining a variety of psychic goals. This ambivalence leads to an oblique communication, signal, or "cry for help" that can be identified and understood by those with special training (Litman et al. 1965).

ADVANTAGES AND DISADVANTAGES

Telephone crisis services offer several advantages: (a) They are available outside usual office hours. (b) They are convenient and obviate the need for a trip to the clinic or professional office. (c) They offer the caller in crisis an opportunity for immediate support, without the individual having to travel or wait for an appointment. (d) They are anonymous, allowing callers to say shocking or embarrassing things that the callers might find difficult in a face-to-face interview. (e) They give those who are concerned with control and power the freedom to hang up. (f) When linked to a well-coordinated service network, they may provide highly efficient case management services, directing the caller to appropriate professional services and providing appropriate follow-up to optimize compliance.

It has been argued that one disadvantage created by readily accessible crisis services is the potential complication of other therapeutic interventions. Certainly, many callers are receiving concurrent psychiatric treatment elsewhere. In a study of college student crisis service users, King (1977) found that 8% of callers were currently in some form of therapy. Litman et al. (1965) noted that about 45% of 1,607 consecutive callers to the Los Angeles Suicide Prevention Center were currently receiving some form of therapy. Hirsch (1981) noted that many of the calls to the Los Angeles Suicide Prevention Center actually dealt with complaints about therapists. The undermining of other effective forms of treatment is likely to be a problem if the skills of the responders are limited, if "professional" opinions are offered without an adequate evaluation being completed, or if the center has a strong, dogmatic theoretical bias. However, it could also be argued that, other factors being equal, hotlines can serve as a useful way for patients in therapy to obtain a "second opinion."

HISTORY

The first crisis center, "The Antisuicide Bureau," was started in 1906 in London by the Salvation Army. In the same year the National Save a Life League was established in New York City. Shortly after World War II, the Neuropsychiatric Institute in Vienna established a counseling center run by volunteers. Six years later in London, the Samaritan organization was started by the Reverend Chad Varah (see Varah 1973 and Fox 1976 for full descriptions). Twenty-two years after its establishment, the Samaritans had 165 branches in Great Britain alone and received over one million calls a year. The branches are staffed by volunteer "listeners," and the program insists on strict confidentiality. Their interactions, characterized as acts of "befriending," are predominantly nondirective.

The Los Angeles Suicide Prevention Center, established in 1958, initially was concerned with evaluation and rehabilitation of hospitalized suicide attempters (Litman et al. 1961). In 1961, its activities were broadened to include community outreach, and a short while later a 24-hour telephone hotline was added, the Center thus becoming the prototype of American crisis centers (Heilig et al. 1968; Litman 1971). Crisis services modeled on this program rapidly proliferated during the late 1960s and early 1970s. By 1974, nearly all metropolitan areas in the United States had such a center, and many had two or more (Miller et al. 1979).

DIFFERENCES AND SIMILARITIES AMONG CRISIS CENTERS

Telephone crisis services have certain characteristics in common: (a) They are most often staffed by volunteers. (b) The assistance they offer is often problem- rather than "diagnosis"-specific. (c) The services are always short-term, with an emphasis on reducing the anxiety or agitation of the person in crisis.

Within these similarities there exist differences in emphasis. Some services function predominantly as information or referral providers, rapidly ascertaining the problem and then referring the caller to an appropriate treatment center. This type of service sometimes extends to having the volunteer make the appointment and check that it has been kept. Sometimes this type of case management is offered by multiservice agencies that link the callers with the most appropriate units of the service. When appropriate, calls may be passed directly to an on-duty psychiatrist or social worker. At the extreme of the intervention spectrum, some crisis services function predominantly to offer a supporting psychological environment that encourages callers to drop in.

Centers vary in the emphasis placed on confidentiality and a therapeutic approach. The Samaritans generally offer total confidentiality (Hirsch 1981), whereas many services in the United States are willing to intervene very actively in order to avert a suicide (including summoning the police). The "befriending" process of the Samaritans has been likened to Rogerian psychotherapy, with its emphasis on acceptance and warmth. This approach is shared by many centers in the United States. Ross (1980, p. 240) states that the "most important objective in responding to suicidal youth is to open the lines of communication. ... [This is] accomplished by showing concern, interest and understanding in a nonjudgmental manner." The anonymity provided by a telephone crisis center is likely to be helpful to callers who find a face-to-face discussion of their problems embarrassing.

Volunteer responders are often supervised by social workers or other mental health professionals who are also available for consultation. This is not generally the case with Samaritan services. Some programs target a specific population such as college students (Ottens 1984), and at least one program (Glatt et al. 1986) has situated a telephone on a bridge that is renowned as a place for fatal suicide leaps.

The differences between centers are sometimes subtle and implicit rather than obvious, making research difficult and requiring researchers to use rather general operational criteria. For example, Bridge et al. (1977) designated any entity a suicide prevention center if (1) there was an identifiable person in the community responsible for the service, (2) it provided 24-hour telephone or emergency service coverage, and (3) it advertised its existence.

IMPACT OF CRISIS CENTERS ON MORTALITY

Several cross-sectional studies have compared the suicide rates in areas with and without crisis centers, or in areas before and after the introduction of a crisis center. Two early studies (Litman and Farberow 1969; Ringel 1968) reported a fall in the suicide rate (in Los Angeles and Vienna, respectively) after a service was introduced at a time when the rates in California and in the rest of Austria were reported to be increasing. However, these studies were not controlled, and the findings could have been due to other confounding changes in the communities that were studied.

One of the first studies to use a control population was carried out by Weiner (1969) to assess the impact of the Los Angeles Suicide Prevention Center. Comparisons were made between the suicide rates during the 6 years before versus after the introduction of hotline services at the Los Angeles Suicide Prevention Center and between two major California metropolitan areas that had services (Los Angeles and San Francisco) versus two that did not (San Diego and San Bernardino County). However, changes in these rates were not corrected for demographic changes in the areas under study. The study noted a significant increase in the suicide rate after the introduction of the hotline service in Los Angeles. However, this increase does not seem to have been systematically related to the presence of suicide prevention centers, because there were similar increases in San Francisco, which had a service, and San Diego, which did not, while the rate fell in San Bernardino County, which also did not have a service. These fluctuations in rate are common and cannot be interpreted without corrections for changing sociodemographic profiles. As an additional confounding factor in this study, the study period coincided with the development of a close collaboration between the Center and the medical examiner; this working relationship may have resulted in a broader definition of suicide and a concomitant increase in the coroner's determinations (Litman and Farberow 1969).

Lester (1973) examined the suicide rate in a number of major metropolitan areas in the United States, comparing rates in cities before 1967 and after 1969. He compared cities where a suicide prevention center had been established with rates in cities where no center existed. An analysis of covariance was used to control for the size of the city. No differences were found, but the study did not control for changes in reporting procedure or for differences in demographic makeup. Given the low incidence of suicide, the sample of cities was small and the duration of surveillance short.

In a methodologically rigorous study, Bridge and his colleagues at Duke University (1977) compared the incidence of suicide in counties with versus without suicide prevention centers in all 100 counties of North Carolina. They used a multivariate approach to account for a number of possibly confounding variables, including how long a center had been present in the community, as well as a variety of sociodemographic variables. The mean duration of establishment of a center was 2.8 years. No changes in reporting procedures occurred during the time under study. Their results suggested that compared to the influence of demographic variables, suicide centers have a minimal effect on suicide rate. They also found only trivial interactions between the presence of a center and community characteristics such as age distribution, method of determining "cause of death," and population density of an area; that is, there was no evidence that hotlines were more effective in certain communities than in others. An interesting finding was that although the highest suicide incidence was in communities that had a high proportion of older, white, married persons, suicide centers were more often located in areas with very different demographic characteristics.

A British study by Bagley (1968) is widely quoted as supporting the efficacy of suicide prevention centers. It noted that suicide rates in the United Kingdom were in decline and that the period of decline coincided with the growth of the Samaritan movement. In fact, this was inaccurate. The decline in British suicide rates (which was almost certainly due to the introduction of nonlethal domestic cooking gas as a substitute for coal gas) halted in 1971, although the number of Samaritan branches and clients continued to rise until 1975 (Brown 1975). Bagley used both empirical and a priori techniques to identify control communities. The empirical match was based on two factors that correlated most highly with the suicide rate. (These factors accounted for 35% of the variance.) The a priori match was for population aged over 65, percentage of females, and socioeconomic class index. He compared index communities with centers to control communities without centers matched through both empirical and a priori methods. Bagley found that 15 communities served by the Samaritans experienced a fall in the suicide rate of 6%, whereas control boroughs experienced a rise of 20% (empirical match) or 7% (a priori match).

Research scientists from the Medical Research Council Suicide Research Unit attempted to replicate Bagley's findings (Barraclough et al. 1977; Jennings et al. 1978). They employed methodological improvements, using a wider variety of matches, more geographical areas, and a matching technique that accounted for more of the suicide rate variance. On the same target communities they used four coordinates to do the empirical matching instead of two, thus accounting for 65% of the variance instead of Bagley's 43%. Further, they broadened the search for matchable communities and derived a different predicted rate by choosing communities with similar rates before the establishment of a center and also by matching for the proportion of single-person households. These additional matches accounted for significantly more of the variance than those adopted by Bagley. The Unit researchers examined suicide rates for 6 years prior to the establishment of a center, and for 6 years after its opening. They were unable to replicate Bagley's findings; no difference was found between Samaritan and control towns. They also noted that the rates of suicide decline did not parallel the increase in Samaritan usage (Barraclough et al. 1977). Bagley (1977) responded to this exercise at replication by stating that the difficulties in evaluating the impact of services were too great and that there was no reasonable way to demonstrate the efficacy of the services.

Most recently, in the United States, Miller et al. (1984) compared communities with and without a center between 1968, when few cities had a suicide prevention center, and 1973, when these centers were widely available. This study was unique because it examined the effects of suicide prevention services on individual age-, race-, and sex-specific population groups. After going through a lengthy series of procedures to verify the date of a center's introduction, Miller et al. compared suicide rates in 25 locations that had no center prior to 1969 but in which one was then introduced and maintained until at least 1973, with rates in 50 counties that experienced no change in the number of crisis centers during that time. Age-, race-, and sex-specific rates were examined for all years for all centers. Difference scores were calculated by covarying on the base rate. It was reasoned that if crisis centers serve predominantly younger women, then any impact of services should be demonstrable in that group. This was found to be true. A small but significant reduction in suicide rate (1.75 per 100,000) occurred in white females after the introduction of a service, but no evidence of an impact was seen in other population groups. The analysis was repeated on a second data set drawn from a different time period, and these findings were replicated.

REASONS FOR THE LOW IMPACT OF SUICIDE CRISIS CENTERS

Miller's study suggests that the failure to identify any general benefit from suicide crisis centers may result from the restricted groups that have made use of them. By extension, there may be specific identifiable and alterable faults that, if addressed, could result in greater efficacy. To explore this possibility further we have analyzed the literature on who uses crisis centers, assessing whether or not utilizers are actually suicidal, whether any particular types of cases seem resistant to the impact of these services, and whether any features of the services provided could account for their low impact.

Who Uses Crisis Centers?

Descriptions of both adult (Sawyer et al. 1972; Murphy et al. 1969) and teen (King 1977; Slem and Cotler 1973; Morgan and King 1975) callers of suicide prevention and counseling services centers indicate that these centers are used predominantly by young females with the same ethnic distribution as the area in which the center is based. They do not, therefore, reflect the special demographic characteristics of suicide completers who are predominantly white males.

What Proportion of Users Are Suicidal?

Litman et al. (1965), in an early report from the Los Angeles Suicide Prevention Center, noted that 45% of the callers were either currently receiving or had previously received psychiatric treatment, 50% talked about suicide during their call, and 40% had made a previous suicide attempt (of whom 22% had done so within the preceding week). Only 10% of calls were unrelated to "suicide potentiality." Usage patterns may have subsequently changed, because in a survey of 100 calls each at the Los Angeles Suicide Prevention Center and at the London branch of the Samaritans, Hirsch (1981) found a still impressive 60% of both the British and the Los Angeles centers' calls to be suicide-related. Many of the nonsuicidal calls to the Samaritans were characterized as "sex" calls.

Other evidence for the suicide potential of hotline users has been derived from studies that have examined the subsequent suicide rates of callers. In interpreting studies of this kind it should be remembered that the following factors lead to an underestimate of later suicide rates among users:

1. Many studies match callers' names with death certificate data collected only from the same administrative area (e.g., county) as the service, and therefore miss those cases in which the individuals have died in other locations.
2. A sizable proportion of calls are made anonymously and cannot be linked to death certificate or clinic records. There is some evidence that anonymous callers are more likely to be living on their own, thus placing them in an especially high-risk group (Tabachnick and Klugman 1965; Nelson et al. 1975).
3. The suicide rates among crisis center callers cannot be used to infer information about the efficacy of a center because no comparison can be made to the rates among suicidal individuals who do not call the center.

With these limitations in mind, research has shown the following:

1. In an uncontrolled follow-up of a random sample of Los Angeles Suicide Prevention Center callers (Litman 1970; Wold and Litman 1973), it was noted that between 1% and 2% of callers committed suicide within 2 years of their initial contact.
2. Sawyer et al. (1972) compared the later suicide rate of callers to the rate in the community but did not correct for age and sex. Of the approximately 11,000 callers to the Cleveland Suicide Prevention Center, 0.6% had committed suicide within 4 years of calling, a rate of 288 per 100,000 or approximately 25 times the expected death rate (uncorrected for age and sex). Three-quarters of the suicides had been referred to the Center by others, compared with one-quarter of all callers so referred. The median interval between time of contact and suicide was 4 months.

3. In six British counties, Barraclough and Shea (1970) examined death rates (suicide and other causes) and corrected them for age, sex, location of call, and death rate of callers to the Samaritans. They found the callers' death rate to be 32 times the expected rate during the first year after the call. This rate fell to seven times the expected rate 3 years after the call. Thirty percent of the deaths occurred within the first month, 71% within a year, and 90% within 2 years after the call. These death rates were intermediate between those of former mental hospital patients and those of currently depressed patients, but were considerably lower than the rate among former psychiatric inpatients admitted following a previous suicide attempt (Temoche et al. 1964). There were marked differences between centers: Some had a lower than expected death rate, and others had a lower initial (first-year) rate but a comparable or higher second-year rate (giving no support to the notion that suicide was simply deferred after a contact). While these differences could reflect differences in the quality of interventions, they might also reflect differences in severity among attempters using different clinics.

CONCLUSIONS

There seems little doubt that suicide crisis centers serve many potentially suicidal individuals, although, as discussed below, even in areas where a service is well publicized, only a small proportion of ultimate suicide completers or attempters make contact. Given this finding, it is important to examine characteristics of the users who do not respond to conventional services.

WHICH USERS WILL GO ON TO SUICIDE?

Several studies (Ovenstone and Kreitman 1974; Wold and Litman 1973; Wilkins 1970; McKenna et al. 1975) have found that suicidal patients who make use of crisis telephone services fall into two groups: (a) a chronically suicidal group and (b) an acutely stressed group without prior attempt history. Litman et al. (1965) predicted that crisis centers would be most helpful to the suicidal individual who is isolated and friendless, or to one who has suffered the loss of an important person through death or rejection. Crisis centers were predicted to be least helpful to suicidal subjects with chronically disorganized behavior or long-standing dysphoric or psychotic states. These predictions were confirmed by Wold and Litman (1973) in a detailed follow-up of a random 1:10 sample of Los Angeles Suicide Prevention Center callers. Among those callers who subsequently committed suicide, most had a chronic history of psychiatric disturbance and several previous episodes of suicidal behavior. The crises that had led to their original call were different than those that ultimately preceded their death. They had gone on to experience, and in all likelihood generate, additional crises. These findings were supported by Wilkins (1970) in a death certificate match of approximately 1,300 callers in Chicago. Suicides were more likely than nonsuicides to be unmarried, to have made a previous suicide attempt, and to have received previous psychiatric treatment.

Because chronically disturbed callers who have made previous attempts and had previous psychiatric treatment are an especially high-risk group for later suicide, and because crisis management is inappropriate for them, alternative strategies such as aggressive active case management should be considered, and questions to identify this subgroup should be part of routine caller screening.

HOW DO SUICIDAL USERS COMPARE TO SUICIDAL NONUSERS?

Only a small minority of suicide attempters or completers call suicide prevention centers. Sawyer et al. (1972) noted that callers accounted for only 6% of all suicides in the city of Cleveland. Barraclough and Shea (1970) found that 4% of a consecutive series of British adult suicides had used the Samaritans. It would be helpful to know more about those who commit suicide without making use of crisis services, because such information could provide guidance regarding how to redirect promotion and publicity for the services.

Differences between attempters who have versus those who have not used hotlines previously have been reported. Wold (1970) compared the characteristics of 26,000 Los Angeles Suicide Prevention Center contacts with a group of 42 suicides. Seventy-five percent of the Center contacts were female, compared with 36% of the completers. Center contacts were on average 9 years younger than completers, and a disproportionate number were less than 30 years of age.

In a study of 575 patients consecutively admitted to a psychiatric inpatient unit for treatment of either a depressive or a suicidal state, Motto (1976) found that 11% had used suicide prevention centers. Over 50% of these patients felt that they had been helped by the contact; 10% said they had been made worse. Among the 89% who had not called, the most commonly stated reason was that the patient had been unaware of the center's existence.

Greer and Anderson (1979) interviewed 90% of 364 consecutive cases of attempted suicide in a hospital in South London, 19% of whom were under age 19. Approximately 14% of these attempters had some contact with the Samaritans in the past, but very few had done so just prior to their recent suicide attempt. Overall, just over 70% of the group knew of the Samaritans; the proportion was far smaller among teenagers. Among those of all ages who knew of the crisis service, the most commonly stated reasons for not calling were (1) it did not occur to the caller, (2) the caller wanted relief from distress or wanted to die, and (3) the caller thought the center would be unable to help (half of this group had prior contact with the Samaritans).

Greer and Strasberg-Weinstein (1979) studied suicidal patients receiving mental health treatment, comparing those who first made contact through a hotline with those initially identified by a mobile emergency outreach team responding to notifications by relatives and friends. Hotline patients were judged to have a lower suicide potential and to be less likely to require inpatient admission.

CONCLUSIONS

Some of the reasons why hotline services have limited impact can be inferred from the literature quoted above. Although a significant proportion of callers state that they are suicidal, most suicidal individuals, particularly teenagers (see below) and males, do not call hotlines. One reason, especially among teenagers, appears to be ignorance about the availability of hotlines—a readily remediable problem—but other resistances to this form of help need to be researched. Second, hotlines appear to be ineffective with high-suicide-potential groups, those individuals with chronic suicidal preoccupations and psychiatric disability. Perhaps an emphasis on case management in addition to crisis relief would serve these callers best.

SOME SPECIFIC PROBLEMS

LOW COMPLIANCE RATES AMONG CALLERS

Several studies of attempters who attended emergency rooms after making suicide attempts have reported low rates of compliance with suggestions these attempters received from hotlines. Chameides and Yamamoto (1973) and Paykel et al. (1974) reported compliance rates of approximately 40% among patients who self-referred to an emergency room. Compliers did not differ clinically from noncompliers with respect to various clinical characteristics, including the seriousness of their attempts. Factors contributing to emergency room referral failure were studied by Knesper (1982) in 300 patients managed by 15 different clinicians. Failure was found to be independent of most patient characteristics, including intentionality. However, there was some evidence for a significant clinician effect. The same appears to hold true among hotline callers. Lester (1970) found that the percentage of service attendees after a telephone call to a crisis service ranged from 29% to 56%, with some seasonal variation and considerable variation among individual volunteer answerers. Approximately half of the personnel involved had success rates of less than 40%, whereas the other half had success rates of between 50% and 80%.

What leads to answerer variation? Slaiku et al. (1975) found no significant relationships between compliance and hotline volunteers' conversational characteristics or whether they made specific reference to words like suicide instead of a euphemism. However, research suggests that compliance is greater when volunteers make the appointment for the patients-callers rather than simply providing them with a name and number to call. Rogawski and Edmundson (1971), using a more stringent index of compliance (two kept appointments), found that only 30% of those given only a name and number kept their appointment, whereas 55% did so when an appointment was made for them. However, neither of the above studies was a random assignment study, and other selection factors may have contributed both to being chosen for the more active intervention and to later compliance. Sudak et al. (1977) reported an overall compliance rate of 60% at the Cleveland Suicide Prevention Center, a facility that routinely makes appointments for hotline callers and then follows up to ensure that the appointments have been kept.

Evidence indicates that compliance is greater when a referral is made to a specific clinic rather than to a general service. Welu (1977) found that 90% of the cases referred to a specific outreach program kept their appointment as compared with 54% of cases referred to a general community mental health service. No details were given about whether elements other than the specific nature of the program played any part in attaining this unusually high compliance rate. However, callers who attended the special program made significantly fewer suicide attempts.

The low compliance of callers with the recommendations made to them clearly limits service impact. It seems sensible that compliance should be monitored routinely and that some of the procedures associated with high compliance rates, such as an active appointment scheduling approach, also should be implemented routinely. There may be some variation among answerers, but there is insufficient research to know what answerer characteristics will lessen the problem.

RESPONDER SKILLS AND THE IMPACT OF TRAINING

Bleach and Claiborn (1974) and Genthner (1974) used students to simulate clients in order to rate empathy among volunteers working in crisis centers. Using standardized rating scales, both groups concluded that most volunteers function with low levels of warmth and empathy. Hirsch

(1981), in an essentially anecdotal comparison of volunteers and professionals, suggested that volunteers showed more warmth, empathy, and
patience, but were less skilled than professionals in eliciting relevant past
history and in integrating information given by the caller. This finding
has been partly confirmed by comparisons between trained and untrained
volunteers. Knickerbocker and McGee (1973) found greater warmth and
empathy in untrained volunteers. However, it is not clear whether the
trained volunteers had received specific training in empathy and warmth.
When such training has been provided, improvements appear to continue
over time (France 1975; Kalafat et al. 1979). Knowledge about suicide
risk may be present without appropriate empathic or communication
skills. Inman et al. (1984), studying a group of nursing students, found
little relationship between their knowledge of potential lethality (which
was uniformly good) and the communication skills that were judged to
be valuable in the effective management of suicidal subjects.

The permissive-directive dimension and its relationship to responder
training has also been studied. Knowles (1979) and McCarthy and Berman (1979) have noted a tendency for untrained volunteers to be very
directive and to offer advice, often prematurely and on the basis of
inadequate information. Elkins and Cohen (1982) found little improvement in hotline volunteers on this dimension after 5 months of training;
however, those who received pre-job training were appreciably less dogmatic and more sensitive.

Volunteers are also apt to give poor quality information. Bleach and
Claiborn (1974) and Apsler and Hodas (1975) simulated real callers and
found that about 15 of 96 volunteer answering calls generated inappropriate information: Callers were given a range of referral sites without
any consideration as to the best fit for the callers' problems.

CRISIS SERVICES FOR TEENAGERS

There are few published evaluations of hotline or crisis services developed specifically for teenagers. Early reports suggested that relatively
few teens make use of hotline services. In 1965, Litman et al. reported
that only 5% of 1,607 consecutive telephone calls to the Los Angeles
Suicide Prevention Center were from teenage callers. Greer and Anderson
(1979), in an interview study of 324 consecutive cases of attempted
suicide in a South London hospital, of whom 19% were aged under 19,
found that teenagers were far less likely than older attempters to know
about or to have used Samaritan services.

Are Teens Interested in Hotline Services?

An opportunity to examine the extent to which teens are interested in
hotline services arose during the course of a survey of 2,806 New Jersey

high school students. An experimental group of 1,317 students were exposed to in-school suicide prevention programs, which varied in length from 1½ to 4 hours; 1,489 were control students, not given suicide prevention programs, who were attending schools matched with the exposed schools on location, size of the student body, ethnic distribution, and special educational features. One of the exposed and one of the control schools were special schools for gifted children. All students were assessed for knowledge and attitudes about suicide on two occasions: shortly before exposure to the program, and again approximately 1 month afterward, in the case of the exposed group, and at comparable intervals for the unexposed controls. The discussion that follows examines only the 763 exposed students and 683 control students who completed forms both before and after exposure to the program (for those exposed), yielding a total sample size of 1,446. The forms were designed to assess the student knowledge of the clinical features of suicidal teenagers to determine their attitudes toward assisting peers who might be suicidal and toward help-seeking in general. The mean age of the students in the sample was 14.7 years; 45% were white, 27% were black, and 22% were Hispanic.

Three items on the assessment instrument solicited information regarding hotlines. The first asked: "If you needed to contact a mental health professional outside of school how would you find out where to go or who to call?" One of the options listed on this question was "Call a hotline or emergency number." The second hotline item asked: "What should you do if a friend tells you he/she is thinking about killing himself/herself?" One of the listed options for this question was "Tell my friend to call a hotline or mental health center." The third item asked: "Have you ever called a hotline or telephone crisis/counseling service?"

A positive response on any one of these three items was considered indicative of a willingness to use a hotline. Students were placed into one of four categories based on their willingness to use a hotline before program exposure versus after exposure (or at comparable times for the controls): (1) those who were unwilling to use a hotline both before and after; (2) those who were unwilling before but willing after; (3) those who were willing both before and after; and (4) those who were willing before but unwilling after.

An additional item asked: "If you have a bad emotional or personal problem, do you talk it over with a teacher; high school counselor; mental health professional; family doctor; nurse; minister, priest, rabbi; friend; parent; brother or sister; other family member; other adult; no one?" This item was used to assess general help-seeking attitudes. Five categories of help-seeking attitudes were defined: (1) isolates (those who would turn to no one); (2) those who would talk to a peer only; (3) those who would talk to a peer or family member; (4) those who would talk to a peer, family member, or other adult; and (5) those who would talk only to another adult. Another item read: "If I felt like I wanted to kill myself, I would . . ." One of the options listed was "Not tell anyone how I felt." Any student who checked this option was considered to be an "isolate."

Just over half of the teenagers surveyed (including controls) before exposure to the suicide prevention program indicated that they would use a hotline. With respect to sex, 54% of girls and 47% of boys were positively predisposed to contact a hotline. Potential hotline users were as likely to be under age 15 as they were to be age 15 and over. Sixty percent of blacks, 50% of Hispanics, and 48% of whites were disposed to use a hotline. Also, 58% of those attending a school for gifted youngsters were disposed to use a hotline, as compared to 50% of regular high school students. Youngsters from outside help-oriented groups were more likely to say they would use a hotline (59%) than self-reliant or reliant-on-peers-only youngsters (42%). There was no difference between youngsters with or without a prior attempt history.

Can Programs Be Devised to Increase Teen Interest in Hotlines?

There were baseline differences between the exposed and the control groups, with a higher proportion of those individuals subsequently exposed being positively disposed to hotline use at the start than the controls. Taking these differences into account we found evidence that exposure to a program had a slight effect on increasing preparedness to use hotlines. Forty percent of those who were initially negatively disposed to hotline use changed their mind in a positive direction after participating in a suicide prevention program, compared with 34% in the control group. There was no evidence that exposure to a program decreased the predisposition to use a hotline: 27% of the youngsters who had originally favored the use of a hotline became negative after participating in a program, compared with 26% in the control group. However, the magnitude of the rate of change in a negative direction in both groups, together with the rate of change for the controls considered alone, suggests that some of the positive change following the program may have been due to random fluctuation.

We further examined the characteristics of those youngsters who changed their mind from initially saying they that would not use a hotline to saying that they would after exposure to the suicide prevention program. Of females in the exposed group who initially responded negatively, 40% changed their minds in a positive direction, while 34% of males did so. Forty-seven percent of those individuals age 15 or over who were initially not disposed to hotline use changed their minds in a positive direction following the program, whereas only 35% of those under age

15 did so. Of Hispanics who were originally not disposed to hotline use, 53% changed their minds after the program, compared to 38% of whites and 32% of blacks. Forty-four percent of youngsters attending a school for gifted children who initially responded negatively became favorably disposed to hotline use following the program, as did 40% of students in the rest of the schools. Of the self-reliant or reliant-on-peers-only group who initially responded negatively, 37% became favorably disposed to hotline use, while 44% of the initially outside help-oriented group did so. Finally, of previous attempters, 44% of those individuals who were initially not disposed to hotline use became favorably disposed following the program, while only 36% of nonattempters became favorably disposed.

In summary, a high proportion of teenagers are favorably disposed toward using hotlines, and there is evidence that this proportion can be increased, especially among blacks, females, and older teenagers, by informational programs. We did not find the same sex bias among those interested in using hotlines that had been reported among actual hotline users—who are predominantly females. Although most of the youngsters who were prepared to use a hotline either before or after exposure to a program declared themselves prepared to obtain assistance from an adult, a sizable proportion also came from a group who said that they would normally not seek help from others or would seek help only from another peer. Finally, there is some evidence to suggest that compared to the effects of programs on those individuals with no attempt history, the programs may be particularly effective in convincing previously suicidal youngsters who are initially not inclined to use a hotline to do so.

Evidence to support the findings that hotlines may appeal to teenagers is consistent with King's (1977) findings among 3,000 college students. Two percent had called a hotline that was developed for students for personal counseling during their freshman year—a significantly higher proportion than the proportion of students who had used the student mental health service. Only 8% of the callers were currently receiving some other form of therapy, indicating that the hotline was reaching a population not served by other community agencies.

How Do Teenagers Evaluate Hotline Services?

Slem and Cotler (1973) studied the impact of a hotline service for teenagers (not specifically oriented toward suicide prevention) in an upper-middle-class community in suburban Detroit. The service had been introduced through advertising in newspapers, on school and community bulletin boards, and by a wide distribution of business cards. An unspecified time later, 1,763 students in a local high school were surveyed to determine whether they knew of or had used the service. In answer to an open-ended question, the same proportion of students indicated knowledge of the hotline as acknowledged other community services such as the YMCA and high school counseling service. Ninety-eight percent recognized the name of the service from a list of community services, and 5.6% stated that they had called it. When asked to rank preferred sources of help for problems, users ranked the service higher than nonusers.

Acceptability to Teenage Users

Slem and Cotler (1973), in their assessment of high school users, reported that 68% had had a good experience with the hotline service. The findings from this study must be interpreted cautiously because the follow-up rate was relatively low (58%) and the number of suicidal users was not specified. This study also provided some information about users. Approximately two-thirds were female, and, as a group, callers ranked help from parents as being potentially less helpful than did nonusers, perhaps indicating that the callers came from less satisfactory home backgrounds. There was a relatively low response rate among former hotline users to a question on whether they had found the service useful; but among responders, two-thirds confirmed that their contact had been useful. King's (1977) study among college student users reported that most of the girls found the counseling services helpful but that fewer than half of the male students did so; the differences between the sexes were statistically significant. About a third of the males and a fifth of the females reported that using the hotline had made their problem worse, but the males who called because of suicidal ideation or after a suicide attempt were significantly less likely to report being helped by the service than suicidal females. Users of both sexes were more likely to report having been helped if they had been in touch with a listener of the opposite sex.

CONCLUSIONS

Although substantial evidence exists that suicide crisis services are used by individuals with a high suicide potential, the impact of these services on the number of suicides within a community has been negligible. It has been the purpose of this review to ask why, and also to suggest that crisis centers, perhaps in a modified form, should be reconsidered as an appropriate element in the armamentarium to reduce the problem of suicide in the young.

To what extent is the low impact of suicide crisis centers a function of inadequate use by potential suicides? The literature suggests that only a small minority of attempters and completers make use of hotlines. There are several possible reasons:

1. The mental state of a substantial number of individuals who are close to suicide (i.e., the affective extremes of fear, jealousy, and rage) and frequent intoxication by this group with alcohol or drugs are probably factors. The distortions from underlying mental illness are incompatible with such logical behaviors as calling a hotline. Paradoxically, it is precisely among such highly aroused individuals that one would expect a crisis call to be most effective, to engage the caller and interrupt the affect. It is unlikely that any manipulation of hotline programs could effectively alter their usefulness with potential suicides in this situation.
2. Lack of knowledge about the availability or usefulness of crisis centers has been shown to be present in a substantial minority of attempters, and in Great Britain, in most teenage attempters. This factor may account for the very small proportion of teenagers who call established hotline services. This problem could be remedied by appropriate advertising in high-incidence areas.
3. Limited appeal, or perhaps selective resistance by important groups, is likely a factor. The literature suggests that the impact of suicide crisis centers is restricted to their predominant user group, i.e., young adult females. Why are the elderly, teenagers, and males reluctant to use hotlines? We do not know, but more research among these subgroups of attempters might be informative. We also need to ask to what extent the problem is inherent in the method of brief crisis intervention without face-to-face contact with the helping agent, in contrast to potentially remediable deficiencies.

There is some evidence for the latter, specifically:

1. Research among callers who subsequently suicide suggests that hotlines are ineffective with callers who are chronically dysphoric and who make repeated suicide attempts. Finding ways to screen, identify, and case-manage this group is an important challenge.
2. Many suicidal callers do not have the psychological resources to make and maintain appointments. Hotlines that offer only information services will fail these callers, and only a small proportion of callers who receive resource information alone will use it. More aggressive case management is needed for these cases, including setting appointments with an appropriate agency, following up to ensure appointments are kept, and then taking appropriate measures. Such management requires efficient record keeping and back-up assistance, and is perhaps

most effectively done by a hotline that is well integrated with other clinical services.

3. Responder techniques present a barely researched challenge. The literature we have reviewed indicates that caller compliance rates vary significantly with different responders. Responder differences in empathy, resource knowledge, and ability to make diagnostic decisions have all been demonstrated. Knowledge is clearly an important factor and should be the focus of appropriate training and subsequent routine assessment using "dummy" callers. However, in psychotherapy research the significance of more subtle variations in empathic and other styles in a hotline situation is uncertain (Shaffer 1984). Better research is needed to elucidate the correlates of responder impact.

One of our purposes in this chapter has been to review the potential value of hotlines for disturbed teenagers. The review shows that we know little about why teenagers do not use the services more frequently. Among those who do call, we know virtually nothing about their demographic and diagnostic characteristics, their reasons for calling, their reactions to services, and the impact of services. We also need to know whether the findings relating suicide completions to adult callers also apply to adolescents. The absence of knowledge about hotline use among adolescents should not be confused with the belief that hotlines are ineffective.

This review has identified several factors that could result in more effective services that might reduce suicide morbidity and mortality, particularly among teenagers. Our research has demonstrated teenager interest in these types of services. This interest must be matched with effective and appropriate services, and we need to carefully evaluate these services to better improve them in the future.

REFERENCES

Apsler R, Hodas M: Evaluating hotlines with simulated calls. Crisis Intervention 6:14–21, 1975

Auerbach SM, Kilmann PR: Crisis intervention: a review of outcome research. Psychol Bull 84:1189–1217, 1977

Bagley C: The evaluation of a suicide prevention scheme by an ecological method. Soc Sci Med 2:1–14, 1968

Bagley CR: Suicide prevention by the Samaritans. Lancet, Aug 13, 1977, pp 348–349

Barraclough B, Shea M: Suicide and Samaritan clients. Lancet, Oct 24, 1970, pp 868–870

Barraclough BM, Jennings C, Moss JR: Suicide prevention by the Samaritans. Lancet, July 30, 1977, pp 237–239

Bergstrand CG, Otto U: Suicidal attempts in adolescence and childhood. Acta Paediatr Scand 51:17–26, 1962

Bleach G, Claiborn WL: Initial evaluation of hot-line telephone crisis centers. Community Ment Health J 10:387–394, 1974

Brent DA, Perper JA, Allman CJ: Alcohol, firearms and suicide among youth. JAMA 257:3369–3372, 1987

Bridge TP, Potkin SG, Zung WW, et al: Suicide prevention centers: ecological study of effectiveness. J Nerv Ment Dis 164:18–24, 1977

Brown JH: Reporting of suicide: Canadian statistics. Suicide 5:21–28, 1975

Centers for Disease Control: Youth Suicide in the United States, 1970–1980. Atlanta, GA, U.S. Department of Health and Human Services, 1986

Chameides WA, Yamamoto MD: Referral failures: a one-year follow-up. Am J Psychiatry 130:1157–1158, 1973

Elkins RL Jr, Cohen CR: A comparison of the effects of prejob training and job experiences on nonprofessional telephone crisis counselors. Suicide Life Threat Behav 12(2):84–89, 1982

Fox R: Suicidology: Contemporary Developments. New York, Grune & Stratton, 1976

France K: Evaluation of lay volunteer crisis telephone workers. Am J Community Psychol 3:197–220, 1975

Garland A, Shaffer D, Whittle B: A national survey of adolescent suicide prevention programs. J Am Acad Child Adolesc Psychiatry 28:931–934, 1989

Genthner R: Evaluating the functioning of community-based hotlines. Professional Psychol 5:409–414, 1974

Glatt KM, Sherwood DW, Amisson TJ: Telephone helplines at a suicide site. Hosp Community Psychiatry 37:178–180, 1986

Goldacre M, Hawton K: Reception of self-poisoning and subsequent death in adolescents who take overdoses. Br J Psychiatry 146:395–398, 1985

Gould MS, Shaffer D: The impact of suicide in television movies: evidence of imitation. N Engl J Med 315:690–694, 1986

Greer FL, Strasberg-Weinstein R: Suicide prevention center outreach: callers and noncallers compared. Psychol Rep 44:387–393, 1979

Greer S, Anderson M: Samaritan contact among 325 parasuicide patients. Br J Psychiatry 135:263–268, 1979

Heilig SM, Farberow NL, Litman RE, et al: The role of nonprofessional volunteers in a suicide prevention center. Community Ment Health J 4:287–295, 1968

Hirsch S: A critique of volunteer-staffed suicide prevention centres. Can J Psychiatry 26:406–410, 1981

Inman DJ, Basque LO, Kahn WJ, et al: The relationship between knowledge and suicide interviewing skill. Death Educ 8:179–184, 1984

Jennings C, Barraclough BM, Moss JR: Have the Samaritans lowered the suicide rate? A controlled study. Psychol Med 8:413–422, 1978

Kalafat J, Boroto DR, France K: Relationships among experience level and value orientation and the performance of paraprofessional telephone counselors. Am J Community Psychol 5:167–179, 1979

Kandel D, Raven V, Davies M: Suicide ideation in adolescence: depression, substance abuse and other risk factors. J Youth Adolesc (in press)

Kennedy P, Kreitman N, Ovenstone IMK: The prevalence of suicide and parasuicide (attempted suicide) in Edinburgh. Br J Psychiatry 124:36–41, 1974

King GD: An evaluation of the effectiveness of a telephone counselling center. Am J Community Psychol 5:75–83, 1977

Knesper DJ: A study of referral failures for potentially suicidal patients: a method of medical care evaluation. Hosp Community Psychiatry 33:49–52, 1982

Knickerbocker DA, McGee RK: Clinical effectiveness of nonprofessional and professional telephone workers in a crisis intervention center, in Crisis Intervention and Counseling by Telephone. Edited by Lester D, Brockop GW. Springfield, IL, Charles C Thomas, 1973, pp 298–309

Knowles D: On the tendency for volunteer helpers to give advice. J Counseling Psychol 26:352–354, 1979

Lester D: Attempts to predict suicidal risk using psychological tests. Psychol Bull 74:1–7, 1970

Lester D: Prevention of suicide. JAMA 225:992, 1973

Litman RE: Suicide prevention center patients: a follow-up study. Bull Suicidol, Spring 1970, pp 12–17

Litman RE: Suicide prevention: evaluating effectiveness. Suicide Life Threat Behav 1:155–162, 1971

Litman RE, Farberow NL: Evaluating the effectiveness of suicide prevention, in Proceedings of the Fifth International Conference for Suicide Prevention, London, 1969, pp 246–250

Litman RE, Shneidman ES, Farberow NL: Suicide prevention centers. Am J Psychiatry 117:1084–1087, 1961

Litman RE, Farberow NL, Shneidman ES, et al: Suicide prevention telephone service. JAMA 192:107–111, 1965

McCarthy BW, Berman AL: A student operated crisis center. Personnel and Guidance 49:523–528, 1979

McGee RK: Crisis Intervention in the Community. Baltimore, MD, University Park Press, 1974

McKenna J, Nelson G, Chatterson J, et al: Chronically and acutely suicidal persons one month after contact with a crisis intervention center. Can Psychiatr Assoc J 26:451–454, 1975

Miller HL, Coombs DW, Mukherjee D, et al: Suicide prevention services in America. Ala J Med Sci 16:26–31, 1979

Miller HL, Coombs DW, Leeper JD, et al: An analysis of the effects of suicide prevention facilities on suicide rates in the United States. Am J Public Health 74:340–343, 1984

Morgan HG, Burns-Cox CJ, Pocock H, et al: Deliberate self-harm: clinical and socioeconomic characteristics of 368 patients. Br J Psychiatry 127:564–574, 1975

Morgan JP, King GD: The selection and evaluation of the volunteer paraprofessional telephone counselor: a validity study. Am J Community Psychol 3:237–249, 1975

Motto JA, Brooks RM, Ross CP, et al: Standards for Suicide Prevention and Crisis Centers. New York, Behavioral Publications, 1974

Motto JA: Suicide prevention for high-risk persons who refuse treatment. Suicide Life Threat Behav 6:223–230, 1976

Motto JA: Suicide in male adolescents, in Suicide in the Young. Edited by Sudak HS, Ford AB, Rushforth NB. Boston, MA, John Wright PSG, 1984, pp 227–244

Murphy GE, Wetzel RD, Swallow CS, et al: Who calls the suicide prevention center?: a study of 55 persons calling on their own behalf. Am J Psychiatry 126:314–324, 1969

National Center for Health Statistics: Vital Statistics of the United States, 1986, Vol 2, Mortality, Part A. (DHHS Publ No [PHS] 88-1122). Washington, DC, U.S. Government Printing Office, 1988, p. 298

Nelson G, McKenna J, Koperno M, et al: The role of anonymity in suicidal contacts with a crisis intervention centre. Can Psychiatr Assoc J 20:455–459, 1975

Neuringer C: Methodological problems in suicide research. J Consult Clin Psychol 26:273–278, 1962

Offord D, et al: Ontario Child Health Study. Arch Gen Psychiatry 44:832–836, 1987

Ottens AJ: Evaluation of a crisis training program in suicide prevention for the campus community. Crisis Intervention 13:25–40, 1984

Otto O: Suicidal acts by children and adolescents: a follow-up study. Acta Psychiatr Scand (suppl), Vol 233, 1972

Ovenstone IMK, Kreitman N: Two syndromes of suicide. Br J Psychiatry 124:336–345, 1974

Paykel ES, Meyer JK, Lindenthal JJ, et al: Suicidal feelings in the general population: a prevalence study. Br J Psychiatry 124:460–469, 1974

Pfeffer CR, Zuckerman S, Plutchik R, et al: Suicidal behavior in normal school children: a comparison with child psychiatric inpatients. J Am Acad Child Psychiatry 23:416–423, 1984

Ringel E: Suicide prevention in Vienna, in Suicidal Behaviors: Diagnosis and Management. Edited by Resnick HLP. Boston, MA, Little, Brown, 1968, pp 381–390

Rogawski AB, Edmundson B: Factors affecting the outcome of psychiatric inter-agency referral. Am J Psychiatry 127:925–934, 1971

Rosen A: Detection of suicidal patients: an example of some limitations in the prediction of infrequent events. J Consult Psychol 18:397–403, 1954

Ross CP: Mobilizing schools for suicide prevention. Suicide Life Threat Behav 10:239–243, 1980

Sathyavathi K: Suicide among children in Bangalore. Indian J Pediatr 42:149–157, 1975

Sawyer JB, Sudak HS, Hall RS: A follow-up study of 53 suicides known to a suicide prevention center. Suicide Life Threat Behav 2:228–238, 1972

Shaffer D: Notes on psychotherapy research among children and adolescents. J Am Acad Child Psychiatry 23:552–561, 1984

Shaffer D, Fisher P: The epidemiology of suicide in children and young adolescents. J Am Acad Child Psychiatry 20:545–565, 1981

Shaffer D, Garland A, Underwood M, et al: An evaluation of three youth suicide prevention programs in New Jersey. Report prepared for the New Jersey State Department of Health and Human Services. New York, Shaffer, Garland, and Underwood, 1987

Shaffer D, Garland A, Gould M, et al: Preventing teenage suicide: a critical review. J Am Acad Child Adolesc Psychiatry 27:675–687, 1988

Shneidman ES, Farberow NL (eds): Clues to Suicide. New York, McGraw-Hill, 1957

Slaiku KA, Tulkin SR, Speer DC: Process and outcome in the evaluation of tele-phone counseling referrals. J Consult Clin Psychol 43:700–707, 1975

Slem CM, Cotler S: Crisis phone services: evaluation of hotline program. Am J Community Psychol 1:219–227, 1973

Stein DM, Lambert MJ: Telephone counseling and crisis intervention: a review. Am J Community Psychol 12:101–126, 1984

Stelmachers ZT: Current status of program evaluation efforts. Suicide Life Threat Behav 6:67–78, 1976

Stengel E, Cook NG: Attempted Suicide. London, Oxford University Press, 1958

Sudak HS, Sawyer JB, Spring GK, et al: High referral success rates in a crisis center. Hosp Community Psychiatry 28:530–532, 1977

Tabachnick N, Klugman DJ: No-name—a study of anonymous suicidal telephone calls. Psychiatry 28:70–78, 1965

Temoche A, Pugh TF, McMahon B: Suicide rates among current and former mental institution patients. J Nerv Ment Dis 138:124–130, 1964

Varah C: The Samaritans in the 70's. London, Constable, 1973

Weiner IW: The effectiveness of a suicide prevention program. Ment Hygiene 53:357–363, 1969

Weissman MM: The epidemiology of suicide attempts, 1960 to 1971. Arch Gen Psychiatry 30:737–746, 1974

Welu TC: A follow-up program for suicide attempters: evaluation of effectiveness. Suicide Life Threat Behav 7:17–30, 1977

Wilkins J: A follow-up study of those who called suicide prevention center. Am J Psychiatry 127:155–161, 1970

Wold CI: Characteristics of 26,000 suicide prevention center patients. Bull Suicidol 6:24–48, 1970

Wold CI, Litman RE: Suicide after contact with a suicide prevention center. Arch Gen Psychiatry 28:735–739, 1973

World Health Organization: Suicide and Attempted Suicide. Public Health Papers, No 58. Geneva, World Health Organization, 1974

CHAPTER 9

Preventive Interventions With Divorcing Families: A Reconceptualization

Judith S. Wallerstein, Ph.D.

Families who have separated or divorced represent a large, relatively new, distinct client population who differ considerably from those who customarily seek psychological help. Young children and adolescents from divorced families are significantly overrepresented in psychiatric facilities, family agencies, and private practice populations compared with their numbers within the general population (Furstenberg et al. 1983; Kalter 1977). Divorced adults use mental health services at a significantly higher rate than adults in intact marriages (Bloom et al. 1979). Within the past decade, a significant body of knowledge has been accumulated about the nature of the divorce process and its grave psychological and social impact on adults and children (Emery 1988; Wallerstein and Blakeslee 1989). These findings await translation into improved economic and social programs and psychological measures that will ease the acute distress and ameliorate or substantially prevent the long-lasting detrimental effects that have been reported (Hetherington et al. 1985; Wallerstein 1985a, 1985b).

DIVORCE ISSUES

Divorcing families confront two sets of issues that fall within the domain of the clinician: (a) those associated with the acute crisis engendered by the marital rupture, and (b) those associated with rebuilding the family, or families, which will provide a "holding environment" for children and adults during the postdivorce years. These two sets of issues translate into a series of immediate and long-term psychological and social tasks for adults and children (Wallerstein 1983, 1986b). They translate as well into two separate but complexly linked preventive agendas: one addressed primarily to the amelioration of the psychological disequilibria of the separation crisis and its immediate aftermath, and a second addressed to building or restoring structure and parent-child relationships within the postdivorce family.

We have learned that marital breakdown is a wrenching experience that can have a severely disorganizing impact on children and adults. Their acute, initial responses may endure over several months or years following the marital rupture. Nevertheless, current research suggests that it is the overall quality of life and the patterning of parent-child relationships that are created or recreated within the postdivorce family that are ultimately linked to long-term psychological outcome among children and adults (Hess and Camara 1979; Hetherington et al. 1982; Wallerstein and Kelly 1980). The significance of these long-term issues for the overall psychological and social functioning of the child outweighs the importance of resolving the crisis-related distress. Even the extent to which immediate, acute responses are likely to become chronic symptoms incorporated within the child's developing psychic structure and attitudes appears to be related more to experiences that span the postdivorce years than to the intensity or pervasiveness of initial reactions to the divorce (Wallerstein and Blakeslee 1989).

In addition to the distinctive attributes of the divorce process and its extended time trajectory, the fact that there are many subgroups within the divorce population that differ along a range of dimensions has important implications for preventive intervention theory and strategy. Our increasing knowledge of divorce-specific problems and their sequelae has underscored the limitations of conventional intervention methods as they have been conceptualized in the past.

CONVENTIONAL INTERVENTION MODELS

CRISIS INTERVENTION

Typically, clinicians have drawn upon crisis theory for their work with families at the time of the decisive separation and during its immediate aftermath. As a consequence, the period of crisis and the initial crisis-engendered responses have received major attention. Because the crisis intervention model (which is based primarily on the experience of loss and bereavement) has provided the paradigm for many divorce intervention programs, the major strategies employed to achieve resolution and recovery have encouraged the expression of feelings and, more particularly, have facilitated mourning of the multiple losses associated with the failed marriage. This model, which has emphasized the centrality of mourning in the recovery process, has failed to encompass the many feelings associated with divorce that have little place in bereavement. Coexistent with feelings of loss and grief stirred by the marital breakdown are the passions of love and hate, sexual jealousy triggered or reinforced by a sense of betrayal, relief (sometimes overlaid with guilt for having left a dependent or loving partner), narcissistic rage precipitated by humiliation, acute depression precipitated by rejection, and in long-lasting marriages, an impaired sense of oneself as an adult and parent, because these identities had been shaped and confirmed within the collapsing marital relationship. These feelings and their associated internal conflicts do not lend themselves to significant relief or resolution within the brief time period postulated by crisis intervention theory and practice. Moreover, reliance on the crisis intervention model has failed to address the critical long-term issue of the shape of relationships within the postdivorce family. We may have been led astray by the compelling bereavement paradigm into a misguided search for general methods of preventive intervention, failing to recognize the distinguishing characteristics of different crisis populations and the specific psychological and social impact of each crisis.

FORMAL MEDIATION

Mediation has been developed specifically as a preventive measure with particular subgroups within the divorce population, in which the relationship between the parents has been marked by conflict (Haynes 1981). This process was designed to facilitate the mutual decision making about children and property that the legal process requires, and to forestall litigation that can deplete family resources and emotionally devastate adults and children alike (Johnston and Campbell 1988). The use of mediation reflects the recognition that ego-syntonic anger represents a hallmark of divorce that requires special intervention techniques; however, because mediation is a highly focused, task-oriented method that does not directly attempt to diminish angers or deal with issues that are not germane to the courts or to the parents' agreed-upon agenda, it fails to address the many subtle psychological issues in the postdivorce family that fall outside its purview. Nor is it suited to the many interparental conflict situations in which the issues remain entirely unresolved, or to those instances when one parent withdraws from engagement in the children's lives, often to their detriment.

SUPPORT GROUPS

One major research finding has been that customary social supports fall away in the wake of divorce (Wallerstein and Kelly 1980). As a result, despite the pervasive incidence of divorce in this society, adults and children at the height of the family crisis feel lonely and isolated. One model that has been widely adapted for use with this population is the social support group. Agency or school-based groups for children, adolescents, and adults have been established in many localities in the voluntary and private sectors. Some of the programs emphasize cognitive mastery of the divorce experience and its sequelae; others permit or encourage the expression of suppressed feelings; while still others advocate returning to customary activities and building friendship groups to offset the loss of family and other supports. There is persuasive evidence that these groups do provide comfort and that they can alleviate the loneliness of the child or adult, along with the anxiety of being burdened with thoughts and feelings that cannot be shared (Kalter et al. 1984). Support groups, however, do not address family issues that are not within the immediate awareness of the participants. Child support groups without collateral work with parents are limited in their scope. Although the child's self-concept can be improved temporarily, or even more lastingly, and his or her courage and social skills can be strengthened by the group experience, the fact that many groups for children do not engage the parents' participation restricts the ability of such groups to bring about needed changes in family relationships.

Support groups for adults as well as individual treatment have also been instituted widely throughout the country in the expectation that the benefits of the adults' experiences would "trickle down" to the children. In this way, it was thought, direct intervention with the parents would indirectly provide adequate preventive intervention for the children. Our finding is that the trickle-down effect, which has guided many intervention efforts with parents, including individual psychotherapy and psychoanalysis, is not an expectable phenomenon. Although parents who are in distress often have difficulty providing appropriately for their children, it does not follow that when the parent feels better, the parenting of the child will necessarily improve, or that the child will share the benefits of the parent's greater happiness resulting from a new love affair or an exciting career advance.

ASSESSING THE CHILD'S EXPERIENCE

In all our thinking about preventive intervention, and this is equally true in divorce, there has been a tendency to generalize too quickly from adults to children without sufficient recognition of the wide psychological dissimilarities that are reflected in the changing perceptions at each stage of life, as well as in the different modes of mastery at different stages. Time and again, traumatic events reported by older family members have proved not to be stressful to the child. On the other hand, the child might well react with terror to an affective experience that eluded the parents entirely. Similarly, we have sometimes generalized too readily from our clinical experiences with adults. For example, we have been too quick to dismiss the usefulness of denial or avoidance among children. Yet, longitudinal findings from our 10-year study of children following divorce demonstrated that young children who were reluctant to speak of their distress or their anger at their parents during the height of the crisis, did not differ significantly in their psychological adjustment, 5 and 10 years later, from those who were better able to articulate their feelings (Wallerstein 1987). There was, in fact, no significant link between a child's ability to express feelings at the outset and his or her psychological adjustment at a later time. This was not the finding, however, for preadolescents or adolescents in the same study.

Moreover, there is a continuing reliance on parents for assessment of their children's behavior and functioning. Although it has been well established that parents in the process of divorce are often poor observers of their children (Hetherington et al. 1982), and that the phenomenon that has been characterized as "the diminished capacity to parent" is widespread at the time of the marital breakdown and during its sometimes extended aftermath, and should be considered an expectable divorce-specific change (Wallerstein 1985b; Wallerstein and Kelly 1980), nevertheless, it is not yet common practice to assess children, especially small children, directly.

All of these considerations governed our decision to develop models of preventive intervention for divorcing families, and specifically for the children, that had not been essayed before. The propositions governing the structure and direction of the preventive intervention program we developed included the following:

1. Divorce is distinguishable from bereavement and other crises along a range of dimensions that are relevant to preventive and clinical intervention.
2. The acute responses to marital breakdown, although frequently grave, represent only one focal point of the intervention.

3. Parental dysfunction and the continuing quality of relationships within the postdivorce family are critical in the psychological and social outcomes of children over the postdivorce years.
4. The divorce population is far from unitary and contains a range of subgroups that require a diversity of intervention models.
5. Many of these subgroups are relatively new to the mental health professions, although they are surely not new within a general population (e.g., those who present with ego-syntonic anger).
6. Children and adolescents of divorce represent a particularly high-risk group who need to be addressed directly and assessed individually as well as together with their parents.

A NEW MODEL FOR PREVENTIVE INTERVENTION

The preventive intervention program presented in this chapter is drawn from an ongoing experimental service and research project at the Center for the Family in Transition in northern California. The Center was established in 1980 to undertake research, develop training programs, and establish and provide services that would safeguard children and parents in separated, divorced, and remarried families. The overarching goals have been to generate new knowledge about marital breakdown and related family changes and their impact on parents and children, and to develop and assess preventive intervention programs that could be adapted to other communities and within other settings. A range of preventive intervention models were developed, tested, and compared for their efficacy and suitability in addressing the different subgroups within the divorced population: (a) a family-centered model, (b) a group model, (c) a brief educational/consultation model, and (d) a counseling-mediation model. This chapter discusses the family-centered model, which formed the core of our reconceptualization of preventive intervention.

OUTREACH PROGRAM

At the outset of the research project, a vigorous and multilayered outreach program was targeted at the entire county. Professionals (e.g., attorneys, teachers, pediatricians, and clergy) whose daily work brings them into contact with adults and children from divorcing families and who serve as advisors to these families, were contacted in person and by mail. Local newspapers and television stations were contacted and proved interested in describing new research about divorced families and the particulars of our program. Liaison with the school districts was established with an active program within the schools that included groups for children as well as consultation and training for teachers, counselors, and school administrators. Liaison with the courts was established and maintained. In sum, a visible presence was achieved in the community and sustained over the years.

Most importantly, a letter was sent each month to all families with minor children who had newly filed for marital dissolution. The letter, which went separately to each parent, invited their participation, noting that divorce is stressful for adults and children, a time of decision making under pressure, and offering counseling and help in making family plans.

In these ways information about the service reached every legally separating family within the county as well as the professionals whom the parents were most likely to consult. As an inducement the service was offered without charge if filing for divorce had occurred within a year of the family's participation and if both parents agreed to cooperate, along with their children, in the assessment procedures of the project, as well as in the follow-up interviews scheduled at 1 and 2 years after the initial intervention.

THE SAMPLE

The population served in this part of the research study comprised 184 families with a total of 351 children, from a suburban county in the San Francisco Bay area. At the outset, 104 families were in individual family-centered interventions, 40 families were in group interventions, and 40 families were seen in brief educational/consultation sessions. At the 2-year mark, 85% of the individually seen families, 82% of those in the group model, and 68% of those in the educational model returned for follow-up interviews. The children ranged in age from 1 to 18 years at the time they were first seen. The families were representative of the county population ethnically, socioeconomically, and educationally. They were mostly Caucasian (93%), predominantly white-collar or professional (median income = $35,000), and well educated, with 88% having at least some college education.

DIVORCE-SPECIFIC ASSESSMENT

Clinical Considerations

The first step in each of the intervention models was a divorce-specific assessment of the family. Assessment takes on special importance in work with this population, particularly in a preventive program, because a significant measure of responsibility for selection of the agenda of the intervention falls on the clinician. In the ordinary course of psychotherapy, the client, whether a family or an individual, presents the symptoms, complaints, and hoped-for goals to the clinician. In child-centered work the parents present their concerns regarding the child. These concerns provide the starting point for the therapeutic alliance. By contrast, divorcing families, especially those who come in response to an outreach program, bring multiple and conflicting, overt and covert agendas, each of which is likely to cancel out the others. These agendas range from the wish to reconcile the marriage to fantasies of Medea-like revenge; from the need to hear that the children are untroubled to well-founded, serious concerns about their welfare. Additionally, the agendas of the children are usually very different from that of either parent. Nowhere is the difference between an intact family, however conflict ridden, and a disrupted family more evident than in the difficulty in arriving at a shared set of interests or a common agenda.

An additional consideration in the clinician's greater responsibility for the agenda of the intervention is that often parents are unaware of what may be the grave psychological condition of the children, or of one partner in the failing marriage. Time and again, we have observed children in serious trouble, even in dire emergencies, whose parents (who under ordinary circumstances would have surely taken appropriate measures) seem oblivious to the danger, caught up as they are in their own concerns at this critical time in their lives. This is true not only of threats to the psychological health of the child; we have observed as well a decline in attention to the physical health of the child. For this reason, also, the clinician cannot depend on parental reports but needs direct observation together with the freedom to set the agenda of the intervention.

Psychological assessment is complicated at this time of family crisis. It is difficult to differentiate acute stress-engendered responses of ordinarily stable persons from those that reflect long-standing psychiatric illness, or from those that reflect persons in the process of becoming seriously ill immediately prior to or during the marital dissolution. This is especially relevant because divorce correlates with mental illness and various indices of social pathology (Bloom et al. 1979). Our customary clinical nosology is far less useful when applied to a general divorcing population at the height of the crisis. Moreover, there are subgroups within the divorce population that rarely, if ever, apply for psychological help, and about whom our understanding is limited, such as those people who function well in many domains of their lives but who remain obsessed with the failed marital relationship, unable either to integrate or encapsulate the trauma.

Diagnostic Process

We constructed, therefore, an abbreviated divorce-specific diagnostic process that yielded the information required to develop a strategy that would address the salient issues within each family. This included divorce-specific psychological tests given by the clinician, and client self-report questionnaires of our own devising that were extremely helpful in shortcutting the assessment process. A marital history that began with the courtship, and led sequentially through the vicissitudes of the marriage, its failure, and the specific events of the separation, was not only helpful to the clinician but was also often congenial to the mood and preoccupation of many parents, enabling them to become rapidly engaged in the counseling relationship.

Careful psychological evaluation of the children was also undertaken, with attention given to the child's thoughts, preoccupying fantasies, affects, and behavioral responses to the marital rupture, and the extent to which pain and anxiety were consciously experienced that interfered with or caused a skewing of developmental progress. Young children were examined in the playroom, where we were able to engage them in play with two doll houses and a variety of other specially designed play and art materials. Here, too, standard psychological tests, as well as projective tests of our own devising, augmented clinical interviews with the children and child history questionnaires filled out by the parents. Parent-child relationships were carefully explored, both past and present, as well as with regard to their future expectations. Considering the centrality of custody and visitation issues, we found it especially helpful to observe each child in separate interaction with each parent. Particular attention was paid during the assessment process to depression and suicidal thoughts as well as to aggression and violence.

All members of the family were evaluated. Sometimes the parents were seen together, initially, depending upon the preference of the clinician and, of course, the wishes of the family. Sometimes adolescent siblings were seen together as well. However, in the main, adults and children were assessed individually. We found it especially important to assess the children alone, because their responses were likely to be heavily guarded in the presence of their parents, out of compassion or anxiety, or sometimes out of realistic fear. The average duration of the initial assessment was 1½ hours for each parent and 1 hour for each child.

FORMULATING GOALS AND STRATEGIES: ORDERING THE ASSESSMENT DATA

From the assessments we were able to arrive at four interlocking sets of tentative formulations that could serve as the basis for establishing agendas and priorities within the counseling process. For the adults, these included the following:

1. Assessment of the central psychological impact of the divorce and the defenses and coping measures employed, along with a determination of whether these responses were adaptive or dysfunctional for the psychological health of the child and the parent.
2. General estimate of the customary functioning and character structure of the individual.
3. Assessment of the marital history to determine the motivation and capacity of the adult to resume or continue in the role of parent and to cooperate with the divorcing spouse.
4. Determination of the social isolation or integration of the family, and the availability of supports for child and parent within the extended family or the community.

This overall assessment of each parent and child within the context of available or absent supporting networks facilitated the selection of goals and strategy in the counseling process.

TYPOLOGY OF THE FAILED MARRIAGE

Over and beyond the psychological and social interactions within the family at the time of the crisis, there is clear evidence that the dynamics of the failed marriage and issues surrounding the behaviors of the parents at the separation cast a long shadow over the divorce and its aftermath. For adult and child alike, the roots of their divorce experience extend back into the faltering marriage and the ambience of the separation. The issues of what has been lost and gained with the divorce, who wanted and who opposed it (and why and for how long), the social, economic, psychological, and even the fantasy factors that make up this complex balance sheet—all are likely to have a profound effect on attitudes and expectations toward the other partner and the children that each person brings into the intervention. These issues will play a large part in determining the shape of the emerging postdivorce family. The factors of this balance sheet may also govern the amount of change that each member is willing to accept in himself or herself as well as in the other family members. Often these issues dictate the initial strategy.

Some Dimensions of the Failed Marriage

To mention only a few of the dimensions of the typology that we have employed: The presence or absence of love and intimacy in the failed marriage is important. Divorce is a different experience and will require a different strategy if the marriage had once been satisfying or passionately loving, than if the couple had never achieved intimacy, love, or even friendship. People who have once had a passionate love relationship need to mourn the loss of the real experiences they shared as well as the hopes and fantasies that were invested in the relationship. They need to begin the mourning process before they can plan the postdivorce family realistically or address the needs of their children with any measure of understanding.

The age of the partners, the duration of the marriage, and the age of the children all represent important dimensions in understanding each individual's response and each family's experience. Divorce requires a different intervention strategy if the marriage has lasted the better part of the adult's lifetime and the children are adolescents or young adults, as opposed to the divorce that occurs early on, in a family with infants or young children. People who divorce after spending a major part of their adulthood within the marriage often face an enormous task in redefining themselves. So much of their identity has been shaped and affirmed within a marital relationship that no longer exists; their confidence to take on adult responsibility alone, or even to be alone and make ordinary day-to-day decisions, may be severely shaken.

Issues of identity, separateness, and self-esteem need to be addressed prior to discussion of the child-related issues. The guilt an individual experiences in quitting a long-term marriage may make it impossible for that person to deal realistically with the issues of the future until the internal conflict has been explored and made conscious within the intervention. Similarly, experience has taught us that the ego boundaries between parents and very young children are easily confused, and that during the divorce crisis young children are especially at risk for serving as self-objects for wounded, distressed, and needy parents. These are grave concerns that the clinician must bear in mind; they will point to the need for an especially careful examination of the parent-child relationship.

Divorce is yet another experience if the marriage has been marked by loss of control and verbal or physical violence, or if the unhappy couple have lived side by side in quiet loneliness. The persistence of anger may dictate the use of mediation in lieu of other interventions and may render greater psychological change impossible to achieve during the acute phase.

Nature of the Separation

In addition to the specific history of the marriage, the events and interactions of the separation period have a powerful potential for freezing into position and continuing to cast a chill over the feelings and relationships of the postdivorce years. If the separation was precipitated by a suddenly discovered infidelity, especially with a mutual friend or a family member; or if it was marked by cruelty or abandonment, as when—

and we have reports of several such occasions—a note left on the kitchen table informs the wife or husband without prior warning that the other spouse has left; or if one parent disappears with the children, leaving no forwarding address; such experiences are likely to influence the individual's interaction over many years, sometimes forever. Conversely, the expression of continued trust and concern for the other person during the separation may have a softening effect on parental interactions over the coming years. An understanding of the emotional impact of the separation events can inform the clinician's judgment and influence the strategy and realistic goals of the intervention.

Diagnosis is unquestionably more complex in the preventive intervention models we developed and perhaps in preventive intervention generally as well. For, in ordering observations about each family preparatory to developing the intervention that will be suitable for that family, we have found that the clinician needs to draw on several complex bodies of knowledge. In addition to the clinical assessment of the family and the problems inherent in this process of observing a family at a time of high crisis, the clinician relies also on a broad understanding of the preexisting marriage and the nature of the separation experience, a knowledge of the risks associated with long-term outcome, and an understanding of the psychological tasks of divorce that children and adults must confront during the many years that follow.

Hazards That Children Face

The data on each family's past and present funnel into what becomes the primary formulation for the clinician, namely, what are the critical issues for child and parent at this time? And more precisely, what are the greatest hazards that the children face at this time and in the immediate future?

Children face many new and serious hazards at the marital rupture and during its immediate aftermath. These need to be identified on a case-by-case basis, for the disruption of parenting can take many forms, ranging from open neglect to overburdening the child.

A sudden collapse of the childrearing functions of the family that leaves previously well-cared-for children in emergency circumstances is not uncommon. For example, Mrs. J had been a devoted suburban mother prior to her husband's abrupt departure from the home. Announcing loudly to one and all, "I'm through with mothering," she left the house nightly, leaving three preschool children in the care of an 11-year-old. The father, who had had occasional, serious alcoholic bouts during the marriage, had been drunk continuously since his wife filed for dissolution.

A second hazard is the threatened loss of contact with one parent. Lisa was 6 years old when her father, whom she loved dearly and with whom she had regularly spent three-day weekends since the parental separation, turned his time and attention increasingly to his new girl-friend. As his interest in his daughter waned, he began leaving her with sitters during the entire weekend. The hapless child developed severe night terrors, refused to attend school, and was calling her father daily, in frantic but failing efforts to recapture his interest.

A third set of hazards revolves around the angry battles that rage between the parents, and the child's anguish and terror that one parent will be hurt, perhaps destroyed. Pat, a 7-year-old girl in our sample, had often witnessed her parents' violent battles. She was preoccupied with rescue fantasies. "I wish," said the child, "that I had magic so I could help my mother all the way." "Find me," she challenged the clinician, presenting a drawing of a whirlpool with drowning, fragmented letters that, put together, spelled her name.

One especially grave hazard rarely reported to the clinician is that posed to the youngster's moral development and integrity by the attempted emotional seduction or domination by a morally flawed parent. Jack, aged 15, was enlisted by his father to cooperate in a plan that would turn the depressed and potentially suicidal mother out of the family home. Jack was promised a car if he would state in court that he wished to live with his father in the family home. The boy was racked by conflict over his guilt and compassion for his mother and his admiration for and eagerness to please his powerful and exciting father.

Another serious risk to the child's psychological health that may go undetected is posed by a maladaptive response that can become incorporated into the child's developing personality and character, especially when the response is successful in controlling or masking the young person's anxiety and anger, and at the same time is often fully acceptable, even congenial, to the other family members. Jim's mother left her marriage of many years to live with her lover. Jim, aged 14, reported to us that "it was cool." He proceeded silently and stoically to take over his mother's role—shopping, cooking, cleaning, and caring for the family—while neglecting his school work and turning away from relationships with his peers.

The hazards in these instances derive from three sources: from the temporary or more lasting disruption of the childrearing function that accompanies marital rupture; from the psychopathological solutions adopted by parents and child to control the painful affects and anxieties stirred by the marital rupture; or from the long-standing psychopathology of the parent in the parent-child relationship. All have implications for long-term suffering and psychological maladjustment. All can be magnified when incorporated into a custody or visitation plan, or into a lifestyle that is unsuited to the physical, emotional, or moral needs of the child.

Goals for the Child

The goals of preventive intervention with adults on behalf of the child are to restore the diminished parenting and to undo or prevent the early dysfunctional responses of one or both parents to the marital rupture, which pose severe threats to the child's psychological development. The intention is not only to relieve suffering but also to reduce the possibility of a negative chain reaction of dysfunctional responses that can so easily be set into motion at this vulnerable time (Rutter 1987), and to distance the child from psychopathological parent-child relationships that may have existed during the failing marriage. The overarching goal is to help the parents establish a postdivorce family that will safeguard the child's development in the immediate present and during the years that lie ahead.

The goals for the direct work with the child of divorce are to enable him or her to maintain developmental progress via beginning mastery of a complex series of new psychological tasks, which, as suggested elsewhere, have been added to the expectable psychological tasks of growing up that all children face (Wallerstein 1983). These include, as the immediate tasks, acknowledging the reality of the marital rupture and understanding the family and household changes that ensue, separate from the frightening fantasies that have been evoked in the child's mind. These tasks also include the return to customary activities and relationships at school and play, by establishing and maintaining some measure of psychological distance and separation from the parents. Helping the children to disengage from the parental distress and conflict and to find surcease from profound worries about themselves, and about one or both parents, is often the central agenda of the initial intervention with the child and the adolescent. Expectably, each of these psychological tasks translates into a range of issues depending upon the child's developmental stage and the particular family circumstances.

STRUCTURE OF THE INTERVENTION MODEL

TIME TRAJECTORY

The time line of the family-centered intervention model that we propose is suited to the time trajectory of the divorce process. Over the years we have learned that intervention during the acute phase of the crisis is critical. Our experience suggests that 3 to 6 months postseparation represents the optimum period for the initial intervention. Early denial and disbelief have weakened by then, and the decisions required by the legal system are still not final. Relationships between parents and children are likely to be relatively fluid and more amenable to influence than at a later time. Dysfunctional resolutions to the crisis, especially psychopathological relationships between parents and children, have not yet become consolidated. Ill-advised decisions regarding custodial arrangements and visitation patterns have not yet been reinforced by requirements of the workplace and the court. Abandonment fantasies have not been translated into withdrawal and relocation. Although feelings run high and anger may be at its most intense, conflict has not yet become a fixed mode of interaction that allows no retreat. Perhaps most importantly, the relationship at this time between the child and the visiting parent—usually the father—hangs in the balance (Wallerstein 1986a).

DURATION OF THE INTERVENTION

In our original planning we allowed for an initial intervention of from 6 to 8 weeks in duration. Gradually, this was extended to an average of 3 months. This still brief, time-limited intervention represents, in our experience, the treatment of choice at the time of the marital rupture. It permits the family members and the clinician to select one or two issues for their work together in regard to the children and the evolving family structure, and to set the relationship in place for future contacts. We have found, as have others, that many families do not welcome, perhaps cannot tolerate, long-term interventions at this time of high turmoil in their lives. In the model we propose, however, completion of the initial intervention is not intended to terminate the family's contact with the clinician. Indeed, yet another termination at this point would be very painful for the adults and the children. Instead, continuity is stressed.

FOLLOW-UP

The family is requested to return for follow-ups at regular intervals over a 2-year period, or longer. These follow-up meetings, which usually occur once yearly, provide the opportunity for another brief assessment and additional counseling for issues that are salient at that time. Such meetings can be especially important for those individuals whose defensive anger and denial at the height of the crisis severely limited the original agenda. Often the passage of a year or two will find these defenses somewhat less firmly in place, or less supported by the distracting family-and-friends' chorus of advisors. Perhaps even more importantly, the family is encouraged to feel the continued concern of the community as represented by the clinician and the continuing availability of expert help. Therefore, in the period between the first meeting and the follow-up, the clinician remains on call as needed. Many families use this feature of the service for referrals and assistance during serious emergencies, for advice about returning to work, for the name of a nursery school, for clarification of a child's behavior—for the myriad questions that people have who face a new and frightening situation with a sense of having no experience to rely on and nowhere to turn.

This family-centered preventive intervention, which we have come to regard as the one realistically appropriate to the time trajectory of the divorce process, may in some cases extend over a period of several years. Many families are fragile and weak during this reconstituting phase and are unable to deal with the many changes that are experienced as crises or as emergencies. This model approximates a family-practice model, utilizing an initial intervention period of approximately 3 months' duration, followed by regularly scheduled follow-ups at yearly intervals during the subsequent 2 years, and availability for consultation long beyond the 2-year period.

FLEXIBILITY IN STRUCTURE AND TECHNIQUE

Within this program the clinician employs a wide range of strategies and techniques, drawing freely from a large psychotherapeutic armamentarium that includes supportive treatment modes, expressive and interpretive models, educational and child guidance strategies, as well as mediation techniques.

The goal has been to develop an intervention suited to the central issues and capacities within each family, rather than to predetermine the choice of treatment, or to design a single one that would fit all. Accordingly, after the assessment, during which family members are often seen individually, the structure of the intervention follows from the strategy. Sometimes the family members are seen together; however, individuals may be counseled separately or in various family group combinations. Often mothers or fathers are seen with one or more of the children during several sessions. Sometimes the family is brought together at the termination. On rare occasions we ask to see the grandparents as well. When it is indicated, we invite a lover to participate. We do not hesitate to ask a parent or family member who lives a great distance away to come to the meetings.

MAINTAINING THE FOCUS ON THE CHILD

This brief family-centered model requires that the agenda be strictly limited. The clinician is constrained to focus on a specific set of issues for the central agenda of the intervention, despite the divergent or multiple needs of the family members. There remains the opportunity provided by the follow-up to address issues that were not included in the initial intervention. Additionally, referrals for long-term treatment are made, where indicated, for children and adults.

We have regarded our primary commitment throughout to be to the children and to the restoration of a family structure that will support their growing-up needs. As a result, we often struggle with the ethical dilemma that the needs of the family members cannot be assumed to converge or coincide, and that the obligation that binds an intact family unit—namely, that one or more persons within the family will at various times sacrifice their own interests on behalf of the more compelling needs of the other members—can no longer be taken for granted after divorce. Paradoxically, it is precisely in the partial restoration of this guiding principle that family-centered intervention has its greatest effectiveness. And it is precisely because the parents are aware that the clinician gives priority to the needs of the children and speaks with knowledge of the children, that the intervention acquires the moral leverage to bring about surprising changes in a very brief period of time.

CENTRALITY OF THE CLIENT-CLINICIAN RELATIONSHIP

Finally, it is important to note briefly the distinctive characteristics of the relationship between client and clinician, and the divorce-specific transferences and countertransferences that are relevant to the process and outcome of the treatment. For it is here, also, in the extraordinary power of the client-therapist relationship at this critical time, and the rapidity with which identifications develop and lasting alliances are forged, that this family-centered preventive intervention model finds its greatest strength. It is also because of the intensity of this relationship that develops so quickly, and because the clinician feels closely identified with the client, that this difficult and challenging work differs profoundly from the customary psychotherapeutic undertaking.

SUMMARY

The main building blocks of a preventive intervention program for divorcing families in a largely white, middle-class community have been presented. The program was developed over several years as part of a research and demonstration project in northern California. These interventions differ conceptually from those predicated on crisis theory or social support theory, although elements from each of those perspectives have been incorporated. They depart as well from the view that mediation should regularly be considered the treatment of choice for divorcing families, although the selective use of mediation has been incorporated in the interventions proposed here.

The intervention models have been constructed to accord with the time trajectory of the divorcing process and the expectable stress points of change. A family-centered model in which the relationships of the parents and the children are the focus of the intervention has been presented in some detail. Counseling is designed to occur during the separation period, when children and adults are likely to be most distressed, when family relationships are often in disarray, and when patterns of the postdivorce family are emerging. The initial intervention is succeeded by scheduled follow-up interviews 1 and 2 years later, and it extends, when needed, over many years in its availability and responsiveness to the needs of family members as they build on relationships that were created at the crisis point.

Diagnosis poses complex, unfamiliar problems in preventive work. In the absence of concerns or symptoms that have been predefined by the client, as happens frequently in a population that responds to an outreach program, and because of conflicting agendas in the family, as happens frequently in a divorce population, the major burden of establishing the goals and strategy falls directly on the clinician. In addition to relying on clinical assessment, the clinician draws on several bodies of knowledge that pertain specifically to divorce. These include a typology based on the marriage and the separation, an awareness of risk factors associated with poor outcome and protective factors associated with good outcome over the years, and the psychological tasks that child and adult confront during and after divorce.

The strategy, based on determination of the most serious risk to the child and the resourcefulness and points of access within the family system, is intended to intervene on behalf of the child (as well as directly with the child), to restore parenting, to undo responses to the divorce in adults and children that are dysfunctional, and to facilitate transition to the postdivorce family. Toward this end, the clinician employs a wide range of intervention methods, including expressive psychotherapy, supportive treatment, and mediation. Additionally, the relationship between clinician and client, which often develops with great rapidity, provides a powerful instrument of psychological change.

REFERENCES

Bloom BL, White SW, Asher SJ: Marital disruption as a stressful life event, in Divorce and Separation: Context, Causes, and Consequences. Edited by Levinger G, Moles OC. New York, Basic Books, 1979, pp 184–200

Emery RE: Marriage, Divorce, and Children's Adjustment. Developmental Clinical

Psychology and Psychiatry, Vol 14. Newbury Park, CA, Sage Publications, 1988

Furstenberg FF, Peterson JL, Nord CW, et al: The life course of children of divorce: marital description and parental contact. Am Sociol Rev 48:656–668, 1983

Haynes J: Divorce Mediation: A Practical Guide for Therapists and Counselors. New York, Springer, 1981

Hess RD, Camara KA: Post-divorce relationships as mediating factors in the consequences of divorce for children. J Soc Issues 35:79–96, 1979

Hetherington E, Cox M, Cox R: Effects of divorce on parents and children, in Nontraditional Families: Parenting and Child Development. Edited by Lamb ME. Hillsdale, NJ, Erlbaum, 1982, pp 233–285

Hetherington E, Cox M, Cox R: Long-term effects of divorce and remarriage on the adjustment of children. J Am Acad Child Psychiatry 24:518–530, 1985

Johnston JR, Campbell LEG: Impasses of Divorce: The Dynamics and Resolution of Family Conflict. New York, Free Press, 1988

Kalter N: Children of divorce in an outpatient psychiatric population. Am J Orthopsychiatry 47:40–51, 1977

Kalter N, Pickar J, Lcsowitz M: School-based developmental facilitation groups for children of divorce: a preventative intervention. Am J Orthopsychiatry 54:613–623, 1984

Rutter M: Psychosocial resilience and protective mechanisms. Am J Orthopsychiatry 57:316–331, 1987

Wallerstein JS: Children of divorce: the psychological tasks of the child. Am J Orthopsychiatry 53:230–243, 1983

Wallerstein JS: Children of divorce: preliminary report of a ten-year follow-up of older children and adolescents. J Am Acad Child Psychiatry 24:545–553, 1985a

Wallerstein JS: The overburdened child: some long-term consequences of divorce. Soc Work 30:116–123, 1985b

Wallerstein JS: Father-child relationships after divorce: child support and educational opportunity. Fam Law Q 20:109–128, 1986a

Wallerstein JS: Women after divorce: preliminary report from a ten-year follow-up. Am J Orthopsychiatry 56:65–77, 1986b

Wallerstein JS: Children of divorce: report of a ten-year follow-up of early latency-age children. Am J Orthopsychiatry 57:199–211, 1987

Wallerstein JS, Blakeslee S: Second Chances: Men, Women and Children a Decade After Divorce. New York, Ticknor & Fields, 1989

Wallerstein JS, Kelly JB: Surviving the Breakup: How Children and Parents Cope With Divorce. New York, Basic Books, 1980

CHAPTER 10

Prevention of the Psychiatric and Cognitive Consequences of Communication Disorders

Dennis P. Cantwell, M.D.
Lorian Baker, Ph.D.

This chapter will discuss children who have communication disorders (disorders of speech and/or language development). The nomenclature, epidemiology, and demographics of subtypes of communication disorders in children will be reviewed. Evidence will be presented suggesting that communication disorders have a major effect on two important areas of development: psychiatric status and educational achievement. Possible preventive interventions with this group of children will be outlined, and, finally, the results of an empirical study designed to test the preventive intervention maneuver will be presented.

CONCEPTUALIZATION OF THE PERSON/ENVIRONMENT SYSTEM

CHILDHOOD SPEECH AND LANGUAGE DISORDERS

Definitions

In the present work we distinguish between speech disorders and language disorders (although we recognize that they most commonly co-occur). Speech disorders are disorders involving the physical production of the sounds used for communication (Cantwell and Baker 1987a). Speech disorders may involve articulation, fluency, voice, and/or rate of speech. Language disorders are disorders involving the understanding or production of an abstract system of symbols to represent meanings. Language disorders may involve comprehension, expression, and/or communicative use of language.

Various terminology has been used for speech and language disorders, and there is still limited agreement among professionals regarding this nosology. Terms for speech disorders include apraxia, articulation disorder, dysarthria, phonological disorder, aphonia, and stuttering. Terms for language disorders include childhood aphasia, dysphasia, retarded language, receptive aphasia, word deafness, verbal apraxia, and delayed language. In addition, certain etiological labels referring to other disorders (such as cleft palate, hearing impairment, or mental retardation) have also been used to refer to different types of speech and language disorders.

Prevalence

The literature on the prevalence of childhood speech and/or language disorders shows a wide range of results. In particular, prevalence estimates for childhood speech disorders range from a low of 2.8% (Wallin 1916) to a high of 33% (Mills and Streit 1942); prevalence estimates for childhood language disorders range from a low of 1% (Herbert and Wedell 1970) to a high of 9.8% (Stewart et al. 1979).

These differences in prevalence estimates are due primarily to differences in terminology and definitions of speech and language disorders. Differences in establishing cutoffs for normal speech and language acquisition and differences in the samples of children studied are also responsible for some of the variability in prevalence estimates. Because of these vast differences in the methodologies of epidemiological studies, comparisons across studies are confusing.

Even when the different studies have used standardized testing on large samples of children approximately the same age, the results can be vastly different. For example, three similar studies done in the United States, Canada, and Britain, respectively, have each produced prevalence estimates for any speech or language disorder ranging from less than 1% to 33%. Drillien and Drummond (1983), Stewart et al. (1979), and Williams et al. (1980) all used standardized speech and language screening tests on large epidemiological samples of preschool-age children to examine the prevalence of disorders in the areas of speech articulation, receptive language, and language comprehension. Unfortunately, it is not clear what criteria were used by these authors to define a failure on the screening tests.

Despite the lack of precision in the various epidemiological studies of speech and language disorders, there are four relatively clear conclusions that may be drawn from the prevalence literature. First, speech disorders are more common than language disorders. Second, articulation disorders are more common than other types of speech disorders. Third, disorders involving language expression are more common than disorders involving language comprehension. Fourth, almost all types of speech and language disorders are more common in younger children than in older children, and they are more common in boys than in girls.

CHILDREN WITH SPEECH AND LANGUAGE DISORDERS

There is considerable evidence across the epidemiological studies that the children most likely to have speech and language disorders are young boys with certain demographic and family features. A young age is one of the key features associated with speech and language disorders. Studies of preschool-age children tend to report higher prevalence rates for speech and language disorders than studies of school–age children. Similarly, studies of elementary school–age children tend to report higher prevalence rates for speech and language disorders than studies of high school–age children.

In studies that have examined age-stratified samples of children, the trend is more clear. For example, Mills and Streit (1942) found a 33% prevalence rate for speech disorders among children in grades 1 through 3 as compared to only a 10% prevalence rate among children in grades 1 through 6. Similarly, Milisen (1971) reported a prevalence rate of 12–15% for speech disorders among children in kindergarten through grade 4 as compared to a prevalence rate of only 5% among children in grades 4 and up. Hull et al. (1971) found extreme articulation deviance in 9.7% of first graders, 4.6% of second graders, and 0.5% of twelfth graders. Gillespie and Cooper (1973) found a 7.9% prevalence rate for speech disorders among children in grade 7 as compared to only a 3% prevalence rate among children in grade 12.

The age distribution of language disorders in children is less clear than is the age distribution of speech disorders. The apparent higher prevalence of language disorders in younger children may be an artifact of the tendency to label older children with language disorders as "learning disordered" rather than "language disordered" (Snyder 1984; Baker and Cantwell 1989a).

The epidemiological studies show a clear trend for speech and language disorders being more prevalent in males than in females. Speech disorders have been reported in the following ratios: 1.5 boys for every girl (Gillespie and Cooper 1973); 1.7 boys for every girl (Blanton 1916); 1.9 boys for every girl (White House Conference 1931); 3.3 boys for every girl (Mills and Streit 1942); 4.0 boys for every girl (Hier and Kaplan 1980); and 4.3 boys for every girl (Morley 1952). Stuttering has been

190 / PREVENTING MENTAL HEALTH DISTURBANCES IN CHILDHOOD

reported in 3.8 boys for every girl (Hier and Kaplan 1980); in 4.0 boys for every girl (Silverman 1986); and in 5.3 boys for every girl (Mills and Streit 1942). Disorders involving language have been found in 2.5 boys for every girl (Drillien and Drummond 1983); in 12.8% of boys versus only 8.8% of girls (Beitchman et al. 1983); in 14% of boys versus only 8% of girls (Williams et al. 1980); in 3.0 boys for every girl (Hermansen et al. 1985); and in 4.0 boys for every girl (Satz and Zaide 1983).

There is some evidence that certain family and demographic features (in addition to age and sex) may predict the children most at risk for speech and language disorders. The role of family history in stuttering has now been well documented (Andrews and Harris 1964; Kidd 1983), and there is considerable clinical evidence of such a role in other speech and language disorders (Byrne et al. 1974; DeFries and Plomin 1983; Hier and Rosenberger 1980; Ingram 1959). In addition, there is some suggestion that family structure and socioeconomic class (i.e., large family size, lower socioeconomic class) are weakly associated with speech and language disorders (Butler et al. 1973; Calnan and Richardson 1976; Drillien and Drummond 1983; Morley 1972; Johnson et al. 1977; Randall et al. 1974).

Why These Children May Be at Risk for Psychiatric Disorders

There are a number of reasons why children with speech and language disorders may be at risk for psychiatric disorders (Cantwell and Baker 1977; Baker and Cantwell 1982). These reasons fall into two major groups: first, that psychiatric disorders and speech and language disorders seem to share a number of background factors; and, second, that speech and language disorders may result in certain social and/or cognitive difficulties that may produce a psychiatric disorder.

There are several background factors that are shared by speech and language disorders and psychiatric disorders and that may, in fact, be common etiological mechanisms for all three types of disorder. These factors include large family size, lower IQ, environmental deprivation, hearing impairment, and organic brain disorder.

As mentioned above, there is some evidence that speech and language disorders are associated with certain family factors, including large family size. Speech and language disorders are associated with mental retardation (Brindle and Dunster 1984; Miller and Chapman 1984; Weiss and Lillywhite 1981), extreme deprivation or abuse (Allen and Oliver 1982; Blager and Martin 1976; Elmer 1977; Richardson and McLaughlin 1981; Rutter 1972), hearing impairment (Bloodstein 1979; Butler and Nober 1982; Gottlieb and Williams 1987), and organic brain disorder (Nichamin 1972; Rutter et al. 1970). Similarly, there is evidence of increased prevalence of psychiatric disorders in children from larger families (Jones et al. 1980; Rutter et al. 1970; Rutter and Giller 1982), children with extreme environmental stress (Garmezy and Rutter 1985), children with hearing impairment (Freeman 1977), and children with various types of organic brain disorders (Rutter et al. 1970; Shaffer 1985).

Those speech- and language-disordered children who do not have any of the psychiatric risk factors mentioned above are still likely to have psychiatric disorders as a result of the social and/or cognitive difficulties that arise from speech and language disorders. Children with speech and language disorders are likely to have social difficulties with peer relationships as a result of deficits in the areas of self-image, play, humor, and general social skills.

The self-image of speech- and language-disordered children may be damaged when they are teased by peers for "talking baby talk" (in the case of children with speech disorders) or for failing to understand instructions in school or team sports (in the case of children with language comprehension disorders). Impairment in establishing friendships with other children also results when language-disordered children are unable to participate in make-believe play with peers. Such group games are a very important part of the development of social relationships for young children.

Another aspect of social relationships involves using and understanding humor. Because children's humor is based on, first, phonological ambiguity and, then, lexical and syntactic ambiguity (Shultz and Horibe 1974), speech- and language-impaired children will be at a considerable disadvantage.

A final area in which speech- and language-disordered children are at a disadvantage socially involves social skills. Social skills are closely tied to language development because they encompass such skills as knowing how and when to use slang, knowing how and when to use polite or formal forms of language, knowing how and when to take turns, and knowing how and when to use questions instead of commands.

In addition to these impairments in social functioning, speech- and language-disordered children may also suffer from impairments in cognitive functioning that may lead to the development of psychiatric disorders. For example, there is some evidence that language-disordered children suffer from limitations in the development of concepts and symbolism (Blank 1974; Inhelder 1976; Johnston and Ramstad 1983; Savich 1984). Such limitations impair the speech- or language-disordered child's understanding of how the world operates and may thus predispose him or her more to psychiatric problems.

A final area of difficulty for speech- and language-disordered children is in general learning and school achievement. (The possible reasons for these difficulties are discussed below.) It is possible that these learning disorders are another factor placing the speech- or language-disordered child at risk for psychiatric problems. For example, there is evidence from epidemiological studies (Rutter et al. 1970) that learning disorders, and particularly reading disorders, are associated with psychiatric disorders in general, and with conduct disorders in particular.

Why These Children May Be at Risk for Learning Disorder

As stated above, there are data suggesting that language-disordered children may suffer from certain additional limitations in the development of concepts and symbolism. If this is the case, then it is reasonable to expect that such limitations would impair the speech- or language-disordered child's ability to learn in the school setting.

However, even if it is not the case that speech- and language-disordered children suffer from such additional limitations, the limitations that these children do have in language development are sufficient to produce considerable problems in learning. Indeed, the public school definition of learning disorder as specified in U.S. Public Law 94-142 (1975) more or less defines learning disorder as a disorder in language development: "[Learning-disordered children are] those children who have a disorder in one or more of the basic psychological processes involved in *understanding or in using language* [italics added], spoken or written, which disorder may manifest itself in an imperfect ability to listen, think, speak, read, write, spell, or do mathematical calculations" (Sect. /1, Par. 15).

Typically, the language-disordered child has difficulty in understanding or using vocabulary (in particular, in recognizing the multiple meanings that a word may carry, in word retrieval or "word-finding," and with specific types of words such as abstract nouns) or linguistic units (e.g., singular versus plural, verb tenses such as past, present, and future, or degrees of adjectives) (Snyder 1984; Wiig and Semel 1973, 1980). The language-disordered child also has difficulty with understanding or using word-ordering rules (or syntax), vague or ambiguous linguistic structures, social or dialectal variations, and story-telling rules (Fey and Leonard 1983; Snyder 1984).

Considering these deficits, it is not difficult to picture that the language-disordered child will have trouble understanding the teacher's instructions, will have trouble responding to the teacher's questions, and finally, will have trouble translating between auditory and written language. Similarly, there is evidence that children with articulation disorders may also suffer from subtle deficits in aspects of language processing that could clearly result in learning difficulties (Johnson et al. 1977; Deputy et al. 1982).

In fact, there are some authors who have argued that the core of "learning disabilities" is, in fact, a language disability (Wallach and Goldsmith 1977). Close examination of the clinical features of developmental language disorder reveals permutations of these features present in almost all subtypes of specific learning disorders (Baker and Cantwell 1989b). More detailed discussions of the features of these disorders may be found in other publications (Baker and Cantwell 1985a, 1985b; Cantwell and Baker 1987a; Chalfant and Scheffelin 1969).

RESEARCH EVIDENCE SUPPORTING THE CONCEPTUALIZATION OF RISK

ASSOCIATION BETWEEN SPEECH AND LANGUAGE DISORDERS AND PSYCHIATRIC DISORDERS

The literature on the relationship between speech and language disorders and psychiatric disorders has been reviewed in other publications (Cantwell and Baker 1977, 1987a; Baker and Cantwell 1985c). There are a substantial number of articles dealing with this topic. However, much of the literature (particularly the earlier work) suffers from methodological flaws, including the following:

1. Limited sample size (e.g., often only single-case reports)
2. Lack of operational diagnostic criteria for defining the speech and language disorders
3. Lack of operational diagnostic criteria for defining the psychiatric disorders (e.g., use of vaguely defined diagnostic terms such as "developmental conflict," "infantile oral gratification," and/or "unresolved underlying conflicts")
4. Invalid psychiatric methodology (e.g., projective psychological tests such as the Thematic Apperception Test or Rorschach)
5. No prevalence rates reported for the psychiatric problems (e.g., group mean scores only being reported)
6. Inappropriate source of sampling (e.g., samples from psychiatric or psychological clinics, or the juvenile justice system)

Nonetheless, there have been several studies that have used more rigorous methodology such as parent questionnaires, parent interviews, teacher ratings, child interviews, behavioral observations, and combinations of these methods. The general finding of such studies is that children with communication disorders have high rates of both behavioral and emotional symptomatology and of diagnosed psychiatric disorders. Behavioral problems (particularly overactivity and oppositional behaviors) are apparently found in the majority of speech- and language-disordered children. Emotional problems (including "neurosis," anxiety, and shyness or withdrawal) are also reported in many of the studies.

Two studies (Beitchman et al. 1983; Richman and Stevenson 1977) have used control groups of age-matched children without communication disorders. The studies found that the speech- and language-disordered children had significantly more psychiatric symptomatology. Several studies have followed children with speech and language disorders over time (Aram et al. 1984; de Ajuriaguerra et al. 1976; Fundudis et al. 1980; Griffiths 1969; King et al. 1982; Paul and Cohen 1984; Sheridan and Peckham 1975). These studies found that these children tended to have behavioral and emotional problems long after their speech or language problems were identified. Our own research (Baker and Cantwell 1982; Cantwell and Baker 1985, 1987b), discussed in more detail below, has compared children with different types of speech and language disorders. We found that different types of speech and language disorders have different rates of psychiatric illness, and, in particular, disorders involving only areas of speech production are associated with lower rates of psychiatric illness.

ASSOCIATION BETWEEN SPEECH AND LANGUAGE DISORDERS AND LEARNING DISORDERS

Because the majority of childhood speech and language disorders are diagnosed during the preschool period, the learning status of the children with these disorders, when the children are first identified, cannot readily be evaluated. As a result, the learning difficulties that these children experience have received less attention than might be expected. Nonetheless, there have been several follow-up studies that have considered the educational achievement of speech- and language-disordered children once they reach school age. Detailed discussions of this literature may be found in other publications (Cantwell and Baker 1987a; Baker and Cantwell 1985c; Baker and Cantwell 1989a). Much of the literature on the learning status of these children suffers from a lack of objective methodology. In particular, learning status is commonly defined by class placement or by parent or teacher reports rather than by objective achievement testing data.

The general finding from this literature is that children with various types of language disorders are at risk for learning difficulties. Studies following children with language disorders over time (Aram and Nation 1980; de Ajuriaguerra et al. 1976; Fundudis et al. 1980; Griffiths 1969; Richman et al. 1982; Sheridan and Peckham 1975, 1978; Stark et al. 1984; Wolpaw et al. 1979) have consistently found educational difficulties, for even as long as 10–15 years after initial diagnosis (Aram et al. 1984;

Cooper et al. 1979; King et al. 1982). However, as early as in the first grade, children with language disorders manifest reading difficulties on screening tests (Levi et al. 1982).

Less is known about the educational status of children with disorders involving only speech production. Our previous literature reviews (Baker and Cantwell 1985c; Cantwell and Baker 1987a) noted contradictory findings regarding the educational performance of children with functional articulation disorders or speech fluency (stuttering) problems. Similarly, the literature does not provide sufficient data to determine which speech- and language-disordered children are most at risk for learning problems, or which types of learning problems are most likely to occur.

POSSIBLE PREVENTIVE INTERVENTIONS

Because speech and language disorders are most commonly developmental in nature, there are many points in the person-environment system where access is possible for a clinical preventive intervention. Children with communication disorders often show abnormalities right from the time they begin to speak. Theoretically, the earlier these children are detected and the earlier intervention is started, the greater the likelihood that prevention of other problems can be accomplished.

Ideally, such intervention should occur in the preschool years so that children with communication disorders may enter the school system unimpeded by difficulties in speech and/or language that may affect their academic development. In fact, in a number of cases children are not brought for intervention until after they have entered the school system. By that time they may already have secondary academic problems. In such cases intervention would have to take place using multiple modalities. One intervention would be directed toward the basic underlying communication disorder; a second intervention would deal with the academic difficulties. In addition, if psychiatric disorders were also present, they would require additional intervention. Thus, the nature of the interventions could be individual speech and language therapy, placement in a language disorder class, placement in a learning disorder class with individual speech and language therapy, and appropriate psychiatric intervention when indicated.

EMPIRICAL STUDY

DESCRIPTION

Our empirical study was designed to answer a number of questions, including the following:

1. Do children with speech and language disorders have higher rates of clinically significant psychiatric disorders than children in the general population?
2. Do children with speech and language disorders have higher rates of certain specific subtypes of psychiatric disorder than children in the general population?
3. Do children with communication disorders have higher rates of specific developmental disorders, particularly developmental disorders of learning?
4. Which speech- and language-disordered children are most at risk for psychiatric disorder?
5. Are there any specific associations between subtypes of speech and language disorders and subtypes of psychiatric disorder?
6. What role do factors such as the child's age and gender and the presence of various biological factors, family factors, and other psychosocial factors play in the development and maintenance of psychiatric and learning disorders?
7. If intervention is aimed primarily at treating the speech and language disorders, what is the impact on (a) the speech or language disorder, (b) the psychiatric disorder, and (c) the learning disorder? (This question addressed the issue of preventive intervention.)

These questions were investigated with a representative sample of communication-disordered children who were psychiatrically unselected. These subjects consisted of 600 children taken from new evaluations who were consecutive referrals to a community speech and hearing clinic in the greater Los Angeles area. The clinic offered no service other than speech and language services (i.e., no psychiatric or educational services).

The sample of 600 children ranged in age from 1½ to 18 years, and two-thirds of the sample were male. The majority of the sample were preschool-age children: The mean age was 5 years, 5 months, and 60% of the children were less than 6 years old. The socioeconomic class distribution of the children in the sample was quite broad, approximating the socioeconomic class and ethnic distribution of the San Fernando Valley area of Los Angeles. Further demographic features of the sample are presented elsewhere (Cantwell and Baker 1985).

Two hundred three of these children had a pure speech disorder, and 45 had a pure language disorder; however, the great bulk of the children (352) had both speech and language problems.

Operational definitions were devised for the various types of speech, language, psychiatric, and learning disorders under investigation. Methods of known reliability and validity were used to make the diagnoses of both communication disorder and the various types of psychiatric and developmental disorders. Psychiatric diagnosis was made on the basis of a semistructured parent interview, a semistructured child interview, and parent behavior and teacher behavior rating scales. In addition, the developmental neurological examination was performed on each child above the age of 5, and systematic intelligence and academic testing was administered.

RESULTS

Below, the results of the study are summarized. These results are discussed further in other publications (Baker and Cantwell 1982, 1987a, 1987b; Cantwell and Baker 1984, 1985, 1987b).

Prevalence of Psychiatric Illness

Approximately 50% of the sample had a definable Axis I DSM-III psychiatric diagnosis at the time they first presented with a speech or language disorder. This illness rate is considerably higher than that of the general population. The fact that this sample was a clinical sample of children referred for speech and language evaluation raises the question of whether one would find similar rates of clinical psychopathology in speech- and language-disordered children selected from the general population rather than from a community speech and hearing clinic. The available data, such as that of Beitchman et al. (1983), Stevenson and Richman (1976), and Richman et al. (1982), show rates of psychopathology in epidemiologically derived samples strikingly similar to the rate in this study.

Prevalence of Specific Types of Psychiatric Disorders

Generally, the types of psychiatric disorders found in our sample were the same types of psychiatric disorders found in children in the general population without communication disorders. However, the prevalence of pervasive developmental disorders (17%) was somewhat elevated over the prevalence in the general population (estimated to be about 5 per 10,000). However, because disturbance of communication is a cardinal feature of these disorders, it is not surprising that there was an elevated prevalence in the sample. The prevalence rates for the specific types of psychiatric disorders found are reported by Cantwell and Baker (1985).

Prevalence of Developmental Disorders

There was a high rate of Axis II DSM-III developmental disorders in the 600 children. Twenty-one percent of the sample had some Axis II diagnosis, with the most common diagnosis being some type of developmental learning disorder. This number represents approximately 25% of the school-age children in the sample.

These data demonstrate a strong association between the presence of a communication disorder and the presence of psychiatric and learning disorders. However, not all the children in the group had demonstrable psychopathology or demonstrable learning disorders.

Risk Factors for Psychiatric Disorder

The data on the factors associated with psychiatric disorders in the above sample of children are presented in Baker and Cantwell (1987a). In order to identify the factors associated with psychiatric illness, those children with some Axis I psychiatric disorder were compared to those children without any Axis I psychiatric diagnosis. The comparison included background, developmental, linguistic, biological, and psychosocial factors.

There were few background factors that significantly distinguished the ill from the well children. As expected, the psychiatrically ill children were less likely to come from homes with intact marriages. However, the rate of broken homes among these children was still not high (30%). Male sex was not positively associated with an Axis I psychiatric disorder diagnosis. However, psychiatric illness was associated with a somewhat greater age: The psychiatrically ill children were approximately 1½ years older than the well children. It was expected that the psychiatrically ill group would be substantially older, providing more opportunity for a transactional effect between the child and the environment to take place. That is, the longer a child has a speech or language disorder, the longer he or she has to cope with that disorder at home, in school, and with peers. However, this expectation was not borne out by the data. Rather, more preschool-age children had an Axis I diagnosis than grade school–age children. The small number of children in the adolescent age range had an intermediate rate of psychiatric disorder between that of the younger group and that of the school-age group. Thus, these data do not support the hypothesis that the longer the communication disorder is present, the greater the likelihood of a psychiatric disorder.

Theoretically, one might postulate that certain developmental factors are associated with psychiatric disorder in children with speech and language disorders. One such factor could be mental retardation (a common cause of speech and language disorders that is often associated with psychiatric disorder). The psychiatrically ill and the psychiatrically well groups of children did not differ in the prevalence of mental retardation diagnosis, although mean performance IQ in the well group was 108.2 versus 101.9 in the psychiatrically ill group. Although this difference was statistically significant, both the ill group and the well group were well within the average range. Thus, the data do not support the hypothesis that either intellectual retardation or a clinical diagnosis of mental retardation plays a major role in development of psychiatric disorder among children with communication disorders.

A second viable hypothesis is that the speech or language disorder could lead to a learning disorder that in turn is associated with a high rate of psychiatric disorder. Because we know that children with learning disorders do have high rates of psychiatric disorder, particularly disruptive behavior disorders, this hypothesis is a plausible line of thinking. The data showed that children with an Axis I psychiatric disorder were approximately twice as likely to have any Axis II developmental disorder diagnosis. In particular, these children had high rates of learning disorder (10% versus 4% in the sample who were psychiatrically well). Thus, these findings are compatible with the possibility that a communication disorder plus a learning disorder provides "cumulative risk" toward the development of a clinical psychiatric disorder.

Linguistic factors seem to have played a significant role in adding to the vulnerability of the children with psychiatric disorder. Children with language disorder were much more likely to have an Axis I clinical psychiatric disorder. Moreover, abnormalities in language expression, in language comprehension, and in language processing were strongly associated with the presence of an Axis I psychiatric disorder. (It should be pointed out, however, that children with pure speech disorder do have higher rates of psychiatric disorder than children in the general population, and that the severity of delay in articulation is positively correlated with the likelihood of an Axis I psychiatric diagnosis.) However, children with any single type of language involvement, be it in the expressive, receptive, or processing area, are even more likely to have clinical psychiatric disorders than children with only abnormalities in speech. These data suggest that the communication disorders per se play a strong direct etiological role in the development of Axis I and Axis II disorders in language-disordered children.

Among the biological factors that might be related to the presence of psychiatric disorder in children with communication disorders are brain damage or brain dysfunction, chronic respiratory difficulties, deafness, and problems associated with hearing (particularly chronic otitis media). Indeed, comparisons revealed that a greater percentage of children with psychiatric illness had histories of chronic respiratory problems. Chronic otitis media may be associated with delayed speech and language development and intermittent hearing problems, and there are other studies (e.g., Hagerman and Falkenstein 1987) that suggest an association of chronic otitis media with attentional and behavioral difficulties, auditory processing, and attentional problems. In the present study neither brain dysfunction nor hearing impairment was significantly associated with psychiatric illness.

Although the psychiatrically ill group did have higher rates of psychosocial stress, it is possible that some of the psychosocial stressors were a by-product of the child's psychiatric disorder. Thus, the direction of effect between stress and psychiatric disorder cannot be determined.

Family illness and family discord were associated quite strongly with the presence of psychiatric disorder, as is true with children in the general population. However, parental mental illness did not significantly distinguish the psychiatrically ill group from the psychiatrically well group, although more children in the well group tended to have two parents who were psychiatrically well (Cantwell and Baker 1984).

Subtypes of Speech and Language Disorders

The sample of 600 children consisted of three large subgroups: a pure speech disorder group ($n = 203$), a speech and language disorder group ($n = 352$), and a pure language disorder group ($n = 45$). There were quite striking differences among the groups in the prevalence of psychiatric and developmental disorders. These data are presented in detail in Cantwell and Baker (1987b).

Briefly, 31% of the children with a pure speech disorder had an Axis I psychiatric diagnosis, and 9% had a developmental disorder (Axis II) diagnosis. The comparable figures for the speech and language disorder group were 58% and 27%, respectively, and for the pure language disorder group, 73% and 31%, respectively. Thus, the children with language involvement were much more likely to have both psychiatric and developmental learning disorders. The three groups also differed in sex distribution, in medical disorders (more common in the speech and language disorder group), and in age (the children in the speech and language disorder group being slightly younger; those in the pure language disorder group being older).

Verbal IQ, not surprisingly, was lowest in the speech and language disorder group, highest in the pure speech disorder group, and intermediate in the pure language disorder group. Performance IQ followed a similar pattern: It was not significantly different between the pure speech disorder group and the pure language disorder group. Thus, the children in the speech and language disorder group were much younger at the time of initial evaluation and had lower mean, verbal, and performance IQs. The pure speech disorder group had much lower prevalence rates of developmental disorders, with learning disorders being significantly more common in the pure language disorder group than in the other two groups.

The presence of any medical disorder was also more common in the speech and language disorder group than in the other two groups. In particular, perinatal problems were much more common in the speech and language disorder group. These data give some clues to identifying those children who are most vulnerable to the development of psychiatric and learning disorders.

When the situation was looked at the other way around—that is, by subdividing the population into the two large groups of psychiatric disorders (i.e., disruptive behavior disorders and emotional disorders)—surprisingly few differences were found in background and demographic factors. The one major difference was that the disruptive behavior disorder group were much more likely to be male, as is true of children with disruptive disorders in the general population. The disruptive behavior disorder group were also more likely to have an Axis II diagnosis, particularly that of a developmental learning disorder. Developmental learning disorders are more likely to be correlated with disruptive behavior disorders in the general population as well. The type of speech and language diagnosis did not distinguish the behavioral group from the emotional group.

Follow-Up Data on Development and Maintenance of Disorders and the Role of Intervention

The data reviewed above from the initial study strongly suggest that children with communication disorders are an at-risk group for psychiatric and learning disorders. They also identify some of the characteristics that may make children vulnerable to development of psychiatric and learning disorders. All of the findings taken together suggest that speech and language factors play a rather direct etiological role in the development of psychiatric and learning disorders. Because there were very few factors of any type (demographic, psychosocial, family, etc.) that were as strongly correlated with the presence and type of psychiatric disorder as were the linguistic factors, it appears likely that a preventive intervention aimed at the underlying communication disorder might be effective in ameliorating a psychiatric or learning disorder that was present initially and/or preventing the development of a psychiatric or learning disorder in those children who did not have one at the time of initial evaluation.

All of the children in the study received speech and language therapy. In addition, many were in special language disorder classes within the public school setting. Conversely, very few of the children received any type of psychiatric intervention.

The follow-up data on 300 of the children have been published in Baker and Cantwell (1987b). The key findings and their relevance to the intervention issue are presented below.

Speech and language therapy appeared to be reasonably effective. Overall, none of the children had normal speech and language initially, whereas 26% tested normally at follow-up. Thirty-eight percent of the children had a speech disorder initially, and 17% had one at follow-up. Fifty-five percent of the children had a speech and language disorder initially, and 48% at follow-up. Seven percent of the children had a pure language disorder initially, and 9% at follow-up.

However, the change data show that the effect of the speech and language therapy on the underlying communication disorder was not that significant. For language comprehension, expressive language, auditory processing, and language usage, the results were discouraging. In 10% of the cases language comprehension became normal, but in another 10% of the cases language comprehension became abnormal. In 52% of the cases language comprehension remained normal, and in 28% of the cases it remained abnormal. With regard to expressive language, in 11% of the cases it became abnormal, but in 14% of the cases it became normal. Further, in 43% of the cases it remained abnormal. With regard to auditory processing deficits, the situation was quite poor. In only 2% of the cases did auditory processing become normal; in 33% of the cases it became abnormal, and in 28% of the cases it remained abnormal. Language usage became abnormal in 20% of the cases and became normal in only 4% of the cases. It remained abnormal in 2% of the cases. Thus, the speech and language therapy seemed to have little effect on language functioning, with auditory processing and language usage actually worsening over time and expressive and receptive language remaining rather stable.

The major impact of the speech and language therapy was on speech functioning, which did show significant change for the better. However, language abnormalities are most strongly associated with both psychiatric disorder and learning disorder, and those areas were relatively untouched.

Considering these findings, it is not surprising that the percentage of children with Axis I psychiatric diagnoses actually increased with time (60% ill at follow-up versus 44% initially). Again, these change data suggest that children are likely to get worse. In fact, 24% became ill, while only 8% became well, and 36% remained ill.

With developmental disorders as a whole, 17% of the cases had disorders present initially that remained present; in 28% of the cases developmental disorders appeared for the first time over the period of follow-up; in only 3% of the cases did the disorders disappear. When learning disabilities per se were looked at, none of the children who had learning disabilities initially lost their learning problems. Thus, 6% of the cases had learning disabilities throughout the initial and follow-up studies. Further, in 26% of the cases learning disabilities appeared for the first time. The data for children who were school age initially were even worse than those for the preschool-age children. None of the preschool-age children had learning disorders initially. But as these children entered the grade school–age range, 21% of them developed learning disorders. In those children who were already of school age at the time of initial evaluation, 24% had learning disabilities that remained present, and none of these children lost their disabilities; further, learning disabilities appeared for the first time in 38% of the sample.

The presence of an Axis II disorder, particularly a developmental learning disorder, was strongly associated with the development of psychiatric disorder over time. Thus, it can be seen that speech and language intervention, which was geared toward the underlying communication disorder, had very little impact on the major areas of language functioning—that is, language comprehension, expressive language, auditory processing, and language usage—that were strongly associated with the presence of Axis I psychiatric disorders. Thus, the first goal of the preventive intervention—that is, significant change in linguistic functioning—did not occur. Not surprisingly, there was no impact then on either Axis I psychiatric disorders or Axis II developmental learning disorders.

CONCLUSIONS

Both the data and the review of the literature presented above show a number of areas in which further research is sorely needed. These areas include the continuity and natural history of communication disorders in children, the continuity and natural history of psychiatric disorders in children with communication disorders, the impact of communication disorders on the educational status of these children, and the correlation (if any) between speech and language improvement and improvement in psychiatric disorders and learning disorders. We need to know much more about whether speech and language therapy has any significant impact on major areas of linguistic functioning and whether psychotherapy or other types of appropriate psychiatric intervention ameliorate the psychopathology and/or language pathology of these children.

There have been few outcome studies dealing with childhood communication disorders that have used control groups, and very few of these studies have examined psychiatric or educational status. The chief finding of follow-up studies in children with speech and language disorders is that there generally tends to be improvement over time, with speech disorders being more likely to improve than language disorders. However, the effectiveness of speech and language therapy, and the effect of this therapy on psychiatric and learning problems, need to be assessed by a properly controlled preventive intervention study. Such a study should include the following:

1. There must be a random assignment of patients with the same type of speech and/or language disorder of the same severity to different therapeutic types of intervention—speech and language intervention alone, psychiatric intervention alone, the combination of psychiatric intervention and speech and language intervention, the combination of speech and language intervention and educational intervention, educational intervention alone, etc.
2. The therapeutic groups must be matched on speech and language diagnosis, psychiatric diagnosis, and educational diagnosis, but also on severity and type of diagnosis as well as on relevant background factors that may alter outcome.
3. Any intervention procedures that are employed must be standardized and monitored.

There are several studies of learning disorders that suggest that the prognosis is rather poor (Kroll 1984). Moreover, there is little evidence that one type of treatment for reading disorders is any better or any worse than another type. Indeed, some interventions have not been clearly demonstrated to be any better than no intervention at all. It is a sad fact that with the exception of some behavior modification literature and psychopharmacological literature, essentially the same thing can be said for the study of intervention of psychiatric disorders in childhood.

Our data and other data available in the literature suggest that of the large group of children with communication disorders, those who have language difficulty rather than pure speech problems, and those who have problems involving comprehension, production, and processing of language, are at the greatest risk for the development of psychiatric disorders and learning disorders. Therapeutic efforts should be concentrated on these children when resources are limited.

The data here suggest that the type of speech and language therapy has very little impact in the language area and only affects a minority of the children in their speech functioning. There is no evidence to suggest that speech and language therapy *alone* will affect the outcome of any associated psychiatric disorders or learning disorders. Thus, the results from a controlled intervention study should have a major impact on determining the most optimal interventions to use in the future with this very commonly found group of children.

REFERENCES

Allen RE, Oliver JM: The effects of child maltreatment on language development. Child Abuse Negl 6:299–305, 1982

Andrews G, Harris M: The Syndrome of Stuttering. Spastics Society of Medical Education & Information. London, Heinemann, 1964

Aram DM, Nation JE: Preschool language disorders and subsequent language and academic difficulties. J Commun Dis 13:159–170, 1980

Aram DM, Ekelman B, Nation JE: Preschoolers with language disorders: 10 years later. J Speech Hear Res 27:232–244, 1984

Baker L, Cantwell DP: Language acquisition, cognitive development and emotional disorder in childhood, in Children's Language, Vol 3. Edited by Nelson KE. Hillsdale, NJ, Erlbaum, 1982, pp 286–321

Baker L, Cantwell DP: Developmental arithmetic disorder, in Comprehensive Textbook of Psychiatry, 4th Edition. Edited by Kaplan H, Sadock B. Baltimore, MD, Williams & Wilkins, 1985a, pp 1697–1699

Baker L, Cantwell DP: Developmental language disorder, in Comprehensive Textbook of Psychiatry, 4th Edition. Edited by Kaplan H, Sadock B. Baltimore, MD, Williams & Wilkins, 1985b, pp 1700–1704

Baker L, Cantwell DP: Psychiatric and learning disorders in children with speech and language disorders: a critical review. Adv Learn Behav Disabil 4:1–28, 1985c

Baker L, Cantwell DP: Factors associated with the development of psychiatric illness in children with early speech/language problems. J Autism Dev Dis 17:499–510, 1987a

Baker L, Cantwell DP: A prospective psychiatric follow-up of children with speech/ language disorders. J Am Acad Child Adolesc Psychiatry 26:546–553, 1987b

Baker L, Cantwell DP: Association between emotional/behavioral disorders and learning disorders in a sample of speech/language impaired children. Adv Learn Behav Dis 6:27–46, 1989a

Baker L, Cantwell DP: Specific language/learning disorders, in Handbook of Child Psychopathology, 2nd Edition. Edited by Ollendick T, Herson M. New York, Plenum, 1989b, pp 93–104

Beitchman JH, Patel PG, Ferguson B, et al: A survey of speech and language disorders among five-year-old kindergarten children. Unpublished manuscript, University of Ottawa, Ontario, 1983

Blager F, Martin HP: Speech and language of abused children, in The Abused Child. Edited by Martin HP, Kempe CH. Cambridge, MA, Ballinger, 1976, pp 83–92

Blank M: Cognitive functions of language in the preschool years. Dev Psychol 10:229–245, 1974

Blanton S: A survey of speech defects. J Educ Psychol 7:581–592, 1916

Bloodstein O: Speech Pathology: An Introduction. Boston, MA, Houghton Mifflin, 1979

Brindle BR, Dunster JR: Prevalence of communication disorders in an institutionalized mentally retarded population. Hum Commun Canada 8:72–80, 1984

Butler KG, Nober LW (eds): Language Disorders of Hearing Impaired Children (special issue). Top Lang Dis, Vol 2, No 3, 1982

Butler NR, Peckman C, Sheridan M: Speech defects in children aged 7 years: a national study. Br Med J 1:253–257, 1973

Byrne BM, Willerman L, Ashmore LL: Severe and moderate language impairment: evidence for distinctive etiologies. Behav Genet 44:331–345, 1974

Calnan M, Richardson K: Speech problems in a national survey: assessment and prevalences. Child Care Health Dev 2:181–202, 1976

Cantwell DP, Baker L: Psychiatric disorder in children with speech and language retardation: a critical review. Arch Gen Psychiatry 34:583–591, 1977

Cantwell DP, Baker L: Parental mental illness and psychiatric disorders in "at-risk" children. J Clin Psychiatry 45:503–507, 1984

Cantwell DP, Baker L: Psychiatric and learning disorders in children with speech and language disorders: a descriptive analysis. Adv Learn Behav Disabil 4:29–47, 1985

Cantwell DP, Baker L: Developmental Speech and Language Disorders. New York, Guilford, 1987a

Cantwell DP, Baker L: Prevalence and type of psychiatric disorder and developmental disorders in three speech and language groups. J Commun Dis 20:151–160, 1987b

Chalfant JC, Scheffelin MA: Central Processing Dysfunctions in Children. National Institute of Neurological Diseases and Stroke Monograph No 22. Washington, DC, U.S. Government Printing Office, 1969

Cooper J, Moodley M, Reynell J: The developmental language programme results from a five year study. Br J Dis Commun 14:57–69, 1979

de Ajuriaguerra J, Jaeggi A, Guignard F, et al: The development and prognosis of dysphasia in children, in Normal and Deficient Child Language. Edited by Morehead D, Morehead A. Baltimore, MD, University Park Press, 1976, pp 345–385

DeFries JC, Plomin R: Adoption designs for the study of complex behavioral characters, in Genetic Aspects of Speech and Language Disorders. Edited by Ludlow CL, Cooper JA. New York, Academic, 1983, pp 121–138

Deputy PN, Nakasone H, Tosi O: Analysis of pauses occurring in the speech of children with consistent misarticulations. J Commun Dis 15:43–54, 1982

Drillien C, Drummond M: Developmental screening and the child with special needs. Clin Dev Med 86:1–284, 1983

Elmer E: A follow-up study of traumatized children. Pediatrics 59:273–279, 1977

Fey ME, Leonard LB: Pragmatic skills of children with specific language impairment, in Pragmatic Assessment and Intervention Issues in Language. Edited by Gallagher TM, Prutting CA. San Diego, CA, College-Hill Press, 1983, pp 65–82

Freeman RD: Psychosocial problems associated with childhood hearing impairment, in Hearing and Hearing Impairment. Edited by Bradford LJ, Hardy WG. New York, Grune & Stratton, 1977, pp 405–415

Fundudis T, Kolvin I, Garside R: A follow-up of speech retarded children, in Language and Language Disorders in Childhood. Edited by Hersov L, Berger M, Nicol A. New York, Pergamon Press, 1980, pp 97–114

Garmezy N, Rutter M: Acute reactions to stress, in Child and Adolescent Psychiatry: Modern Approaches, 2nd Edition. Edited by Rutter M, Hersov L. Oxford, UK, Blackwell, 1985, pp 152–176

Gillespie SK, Cooper EB: Prevalence of speech problems in junior and senior high schools. J Speech Hear Res 16:739–743, 1973

Gottlieb MI, Williams JE (eds): Textbook of Developmental Pediatrics. New York, Plenum, 1987

Griffiths CPS: A follow-up study of children with disorders of speech. Br J Dis Commun 4:46–56, 1969

Hagerman RJ, Falkenstein AR: An association between recurrent otitis media in infancy and later hyperactivity. Clin Pediatr 26:253–257, 1987

Herbert GW, Wedell K: Communication handicaps of children with specific language deficiency. Paper presented to the annual conference of the British Psychological Society, Southampton, UK, April 1970

Hermansen A, Jensen HR, Ibsen KK: On children with defective speech. Int J Rehabil Res 8:203–207, 1985

Hier DB, Kaplan J: Are sex differences in cerebral organization clinically significant? Behav Brain Sci 3:238–239, 1980

Hier DB, Rosenberger PB: Focal left temporal lesions and delayed speech acquisition. Dev Behav Pediatr 1:54–57, 1980

Hull FM, Mielke PW Jr, Timmons RJ, et al: The national speech and hearing survey: preliminary results. ASHA 13:501–509, 1971

Ingram TTS: Specific developmental disorders of speech in childhood. Brain 82:450–467, 1959

Inhelder B: Observations on the operational and figurative aspects of thought in dysphasic children, in Normal and Deficient Child Language. Edited by Morehead D, Morehead A. Baltimore, MD, University Park Press, 1976, pp 335–343

Johnson AF, Shelton RL, Arndt WB, et al: Factor analyses of measures of articulation, language, auditory processing, reading, spelling and maxillofacial structure. J Speech Hear Res 20:319–324, 1977

Johnston J, Ramstad V: Cognitive development in pre-adolescent language impaired children. Br J Dis Commun 18:49–55, 1983

Jones MB, Offord DR, Abrams N: Brothers and sisters and antisocial behaviour. Br J Psychiatry 136:139–145, 1980

Kidd KK: Recent progress on the genetics of stuttering, in Genetic Aspects of

Speech and Language Disorders. Edited by Ludlow CL, Cooper JA. New York, Academic, 1983, pp 197–213

King R, Jones C, Lasky E: In retrospect: a 15 year follow-up of speech-language-disordered children. Lang Speech Hear Serv Schools 13:24–32, 1982

Kroll LG: LD's—What happens when they are no longer children? Acad Ther 20:133–148, 1984

Levi G, Capozzi F, Fabrizi A, et al: Language disorders and prognosis for reading disabilities in developmental age. Percept Motor Skills 54(3):119–122, 1982

Milisen R: The incidence of speech disorders, in Handbook of Speech Pathology and Audiology. Edited by Travis L. Englewood Cliffs, NJ, Prentice-Hall, 1971, pp 619–633

Miller JF, Chapman RS: Disorders of communication: investigating the development of language of mentally retarded children. Am J Ment Defic 88:536–545, 1984

Mills A, Streit H: Report of a speech survey: Holyoke, Massachusetts. J Speech Dis 7:161–167, 1942

Morley D: A ten-year survey of speech disorders among university students. J Speech Hear Dis 17:25–31, 1952

Morley ME: The Development and Disorders of Speech in Childhood. Baltimore, MD, Williams & Wilkins, 1972

Nichamin S: Recognizing minimal brain dysfunction in the infant and toddler. Clin Pediatr 11:255–257, 1972

Paul R, Cohen DJ: Outcomes of severe disorders of language acquisition. J Autism Dev Dis 14:405–421, 1984

Randall D, Reynell J, Curwen M: A study of language development in a sample of three-year-old children. Br J Dis Commun 9:3–16, 1974

Richardson C, McLaughlin TF: An examination of environmental deprivation and its influence on language development. Correc Soc Psychiatry J Behav Tech Meth Ther 27(2):93–94, 1981

Richman N, Stevenson J: Language delay in 3-year-olds: family and social factors. Acta Paediatr Belg 30:213–219, 1977

Richman N, Stevenson J, Graham PJ: Pre-School to School—A Behavioural Study. London, Academic Press, 1982

Rutter M: The effects of language delay on development, in The Child With Delayed Speech. Edited by Rutter M, Martin JAM. London, Heinemann, 1972, pp 176–188

Rutter M, Giller H: Juvenile Delinquency. Harmondsworth, Middlesex, UK, Penguin, 1982

Rutter M, Graham P, Yule WA: Neuropsychiatric Study in Childhood. Lavenham, Suffolk, UK, Lavenham Press, 1970

Satz P, Zaide J: Sex differences: clues or myths on genetic aspects of speech and language disorders, in Genetic Aspects of Speech and Language Disorders. Edited by Ludlow CL, Cooper JA. New York, Academic, 1983, pp 85–105

Savich PA: Anticipatory imagery ability in normal and language-disabled children. J Speech Hear Res 27:494–501, 1984

Shaffer D: Brain damage, in Child and Adolescent Psychiatry: Modern Approaches, 2nd Edition. Edited by Rutter M, Hersov L. Oxford, UK, Blackwell, 1985, pp 129–151

Sheridan MD, Peckham CS: Follow-up at 11 years of children who had marked speech defects at 7 years. Child Care Health Dev 113:157–166, 1975

Sheridan MD, Peckham CS: Follow-up to 16 years of school children who had marked speech defects at 7 years. Child Care Health Dev 4:145–157, 1978

Shultz TR, Horibe F: Development of the appreciation of verbal jokes. Dev Psychol 10:13–20, 1974

Silverman E: The female stutterer, in The Atypical Stutterer. Edited by St. Louis KO. Orlando, FL, Academic, 1986, pp 35–63

Snyder LS: Developmental language disorders: elementary school age, in Language Disorders in Children. Edited by Holland A. San Diego, CA, College-Hill Press, 1984, pp 129–158

Stark RE, Bernstein LE, Condino R, et al: Four-year follow-up study of language-impaired children. Ann Dyslexia 34:49–68, 1984

Stevenson J, Richman N: The prevalence of language delay in a population of three-year old children and its association with general retardation. Dev Med Child Neurol 18:431–441, 1976

Stewart JM, Martin ME, Brady GM: Communicative disorders at a health-care center. J Commun Dis 12:349–359, 1979

U.S. Public Law 94-142, The Education of the Handicapped Act, 1975

Wallach GP, Goldsmith SC: Language based learning disabilities: reading is language too. J Learn Disabil 10:178–183, 1977

Wallin JEW: A census of speech defectives among 89,057 public school pupils—a preliminary report. School Soc 3(58):213–216, 1916

Weiss C, Lillywhite H: Communicative Disorders: Prevention and Early Intervention. St. Louis, MO, CV Mosby, 1981

White House Conference on Child Health and Protection: Special Education. New York, Century, 1931

Wiig E, Semel E: Comprehension of linguistic concepts requiring logical operations by learning disabled children. J Speech Hear Res 16:627–636, 1973

Wiig E, Semel E: Language Assessment and Intervention for the Learning Disabled. Columbus, OH, Charles E Merrill, 1980

Williams DM, Darbyshire JD, Vaghy DA: An epidemiological study of speech and hearing disorders. J Otolaryngol [Suppl] 7:5–24, 1980

Wolpaw T, Nation J, Aram D: Developmental language disorders: a follow-up study. Ill Speech Hear J 12:14–18, 1979

CHAPTER 11

Mental Health Disturbances in Children Exposed to Disaster: Preventive Intervention Strategies

Robert S. Pynoos, M.D., M.P.H.
Kathi Nader, M.S.W.

Disasters are ubiquitous, affecting all 50 states, from major urban areas to remote rural communities. Since the inception of the 1974 Disaster Relief Act (Public Law 93-288; see U.S. Government 1976), 798 major federal disasters and 3,092 federal emergencies, which are slightly less severe, have been declared in the United States (D. Dannels, Federal Emergency Management Agency, September 21, 1987, personal communication). In addition to these recognized disasters, 38% of the requests from states for disaster assistance since 1974 were denied by the federal government (Rubin et al. 1986).

The cost in human life is significant. More than 8,000 deaths annually in the United States are attributed to natural and man-made disasters; estimates suggest that there are 50 injuries for every death (Logue et al. 1981a). Even when loss of life is minimal, serious economic losses often result from destruction of homes and businesses.

A disaster is one of the few life stresses for which early access to affected children and their families is authorized as a public health measure. SECTION 413 of the Disaster Relief Act mandates such assistance to states and local agencies within the disaster area "to help preclude possible damaging physical or psychological effects" (U.S. Government 1976).

This chapter is a revised and expanded version of a paper commissioned by the American Academy of Child and Adolescent Psychiatry Prevention Project.

Thus, disasters provide an uncommon opportunity for mental health professionals to employ preventive strategies.

In this chapter issues related to the effects of disaster on children, including psychiatric morbidity, mediating factors, child intrinsic factors, the impact on child development, and methods of prevention, will be explored.

CASE EXAMPLES

EARTHQUAKE

Seven-year-old Richard was entering his father's warehouse when the side of the building and part of the roof collapsed on top of him. When his father arrived at the site he was frustrated by the need to wait for the proper equipment before his son could be rescued. He stood by, helplessly listening to his son's cries for help.

Richard suffered a broken arm and lacerations. While he was in the hospital, nurses were concerned he would hurt himself further during his observably agitated sleep. He reported dreams of falling objects, of being closed in and suffocating, and of harm coming to family members and his not being able to see them again. When a volunteer accidently dropped her basket of toys, making a loud crashing noise, Richard started screaming and was difficult to comfort.

After his return home Richard was chronically tense and anxious, startled easily, and talked little to his parents. He had difficulty getting to sleep and cried in his sleep. He was irritable and aggressive with his siblings and peers. Richard would pause upon entering any building as though to make certain that nothing was about to happen, and he refused to go into older buildings. In the first months after the earthquake he ran for cover whenever a large truck passed outside and the building shook. He was afraid to be away from his family. Although his parents were warned that he may fear closed spaces after his experience, instead he reenacted his experience by lying down and squeezing himself into tight spots several times per week.

In addition to his anger over bureaucratic delays in obtaining insurance money to repair the damages to his business, Richard's father remained depressed about his inability to protect or immediately act in assisting his injured son. As a result the father acted irritable and increased his drinking. He seemed to avoid Richard.

FLOOD

David, aged 11, was taken with his father to search for his older brother who had been playing with friends when the flood occurred. Both were upset by the sight of the dead and bloated body of a boy David's age. Months afterward, his father said that David was no longer the outgoing, friendly boy that he used to be; he was quiet and withdrawn, tense, nervous, and cautious. He seemed to prefer to stay inside. His hands trembled, and he was afraid to go to sleep at night. He had nightmares of the drowned boy calling to him to follow. David became anxious whenever it started raining, and he refused to be alone. He became very involved with learning to be an expert swimmer.

PSYCHIATRIC MORBIDITY

Standard criteria for posttraumatic stress disorder (PTSD) (American Psychiatric Association 1987), standardized psychiatric instruments, and systematic research methodology have permitted investigators to clarify some long-standing issues regarding postdisaster psychiatric morbidity. In the following discussion we refer to adult studies that have best delineated the range of disaster reactions, the role of exposure, and the process of coping and recovery. These studies also indicate the level of adult stress that children are exposed to after a disaster, a factor that may influence child morbidity. We extrapolate from studies of children exposed to violence because these studies also provide insight about children's responses to life threat.

PRIMACY OF EXPOSURE

Degree of exposure is the key variable in determining initial posttraumatic stress reactions (Wilkinson 1985). Considerations of exposure and personal impact have focused on proximity to the impact zone, life threat, physical injury, witnessing of injury or death, injury or death of a significant other, property damage, and financial loss. In the Buffalo Creek Dam flood study (Gleser et al. 1981), researchers using a stressor scale found that subsequent psychiatric morbidity was significantly associated with the degree of exposure. Shore et al. (1986) demonstrated that the onset of psychiatric disorders after the Mount St. Helens volcanic eruption followed a dose-response exposure pattern.

Two years after the Beverly Hills Club fire, Green et al. (1985a) found degree of exposure to be the principal factor explaining chronicity of psychiatric impairment. Some investigators have found that specific experiences, especially witnessing the grotesque or hearing cries of distress, are associated with psychiatric morbidity (Green et al. 1985b). Rescue workers, especially body handlers, not directly exposed to the actual disaster but exposed to the mutilation and death of others have also exhibited increased morbidity (Jones 1985).

Even without a clear model of PTSD in children, early studies suggested the primacy of exposure in children's disaster reactions (Bloch et al. 1956; Gleser et al. 1981; Burke et al. 1982). Children did not seem to be as affected by residential property damage as adults, although individual children reported distress at the loss of personal possessions. A phenomenological construct of PTSD in children has slowly emerged (Anthony 1986). In a recent study of community violence, Pynoos et al. (1987a) systematically confirmed that the degree of exposure to life threat in school-age children had a dose-response relationship with severity of PTSD that continued to be present at the 14-month follow-up.

PERIMETER OF DANGER

Three systematic studies of adults found a perimeter of danger or impact beyond which there was no measurable change in psychiatric morbidity (Shore et al. 1986; Green et al. 1983; Dohrenwend et al. 1981). The perimeter of impact may be difficult to determine in technological disasters, especially those involving "invisible contaminants" (Berezofsky 1987), because the danger zone and measurable life or health threat may not be well established. For children exposed to violent life threat, a perimeter was also demonstrated beyond which there was no appreciable increase in acute PTSD without the presence of mediating factors (Pynoos et al. 1987a). For the same group of children, 14 months later, the impact zone was measurably smaller, restricted only to the area of direct danger—the school playground on which the sniper had opened fire.

TYPES OF PSYCHIATRIC MORBIDITY

Systematic studies have found an increase in some psychiatric disorders but not in others. Shore et al. (1986) demonstrated a dose-response onset of three disorders (cited in order of frequency) following exposure to the Mount St. Helens volcanic eruption: (1) PTSD, (2) single-episode depression, and (3) generalized anxiety disorder. A significant rate of comorbidity existed. Increased morbidity could not be attributed to mediating factors such as age, education, income, employment, or state of physical health.

In a study of Cambodian adolescent refugees exposed to massive trauma, Kinzie et al. (1986) reported the onset of disorders that were similar to those found by Shore et al. (1986). Fifty percent of the children were diagnosed with PTSD, 12% with major depressive disorder, 37% with intermittent depressive disorder, and 18% with generalized anxiety disorder. Kinzie et al. also found a significant rate of comorbidity.

Pynoos and Nader's (1987) 14-month follow-up study of children exposed to a sniper incident suggests a distribution of psychiatric disorders similar to that reported by Kinzie et al. (1986). In this school-age sample, separation anxiety disorders were more frequent than generalized anxiety disorders.

Clinical studies of children exposed to severe traumas have also documented a high frequency of PTSD symptoms. For example, Terr (1979) reported that 5 to 15 months after being kidnapped and facing life threat, an entire group of 25 children had developed moderate to severe PTSD.

Using more systematic data collection, we have been able to correlate different exposure factors with the relative frequency of specific forms of morbidity. The experience of life threat and the witnessing of injury and death are highly correlated with the onset and persistence of PTSD; loss of a significant other is correlated with the onset of a single depressive episode or adjustment reaction; worry about or sudden separation from a significant other is correlated with persistent anxiety regarding the safety of significant others (Pynoos et al. 1987a). While these factors may sometimes operate independently, at other times there may be an interplay between them. Grief, for example, may increase PTSD, while life threat may increase the risk of a depressive episode (Pynoos and Nader 1987).

Adams and Adams (1984) demonstrated that adult stress reactions in the Mount St. Helens community increased after exposure to the disaster. Examination revealed a substantial increase in stress-induced disorders, mental illness, alcohol abuse, family stress, aggression with related adjustment problems, and domestic and other violence. Adams and Adams also noted an increase in juvenile arrests in the acute postdisaster period.

Some studies have found an increase in somatic complaints, especially in school-age children, reflected in greater demands on school and camp nursing services (Pynoos et al. 1987a; Kliman 1976). After disasters children have reported, for example, increased headaches, nausea, cuts and scrapes, and minor infections. Even when there is no destruction of property, for example, after community violence, school absences may increase dramatically for several weeks (Pynoos et al. 1987a). After a disaster, exposed children may have a slightly increased absentee rate for several years (McFarlane 1987).

Terr (1979) found that 33% of a group of children showed deterioration in school performance during the first posttrauma year. Using the Child Global Assessment Scale, Kinzie et al. (1986) demonstrated that severely traumatized children have a significant degree of functional impairment. However, well-controlled data on school performance are needed.

MORBIDITY

Prevalence

The prevalence of psychiatric morbidity varies greatly with variations in a disaster's overall impact on the community, the type and severity of exposure, and the percentage of the population affected. After Mount St. Helens erupted, psychiatric disorders appeared in 20% of the women and 11% of the men (Shore et al. 1986). Disorders appeared in up to 75% of those individuals exposed to the Buffalo Creek Dam disaster (Gleser et al. 1981).

No comparable prevalence data for children have been collected after major disasters. However, after traumas, severely exposed children have been reported to exhibit high prevalence rates of posttraumatic stress symptoms (Pynoos et al. 1987a). After finding a significantly higher rate of PTSD in children than in adults 1 year following severe burns, Andreasen (1985) proposed that children were more vulnerable to PTSD than adults.

Course

With the completion of more systematic studies, the concept of a delayed onset disorder is losing favor because investigators have not found sufficient evidence for it. Instead, most of the evidence indicates that initial exposure predicts later symptomatology. Summarizing the adult literature, Figley (1986) concluded: "The disorder was detectable soon after exposure to the traumatic event or catastrophe . . . and delayed reactions are rare." Shore et al. (1986) verified this statement when they found that the rate of onset was highest during the first year and dropped sharply in subsequent years. They also found that 3 years after the disaster, PTSD symptoms tended to persist, while depression and anxiety disorders had abated.

Similar to the adult studies, more recent studies of school-age and adolescent children have found no apparent delay in the onset of PTSD symptoms, and that an early onset is strongly predictive of later course (Terr 1979; Pynoos and Nader 1987; Pynoos et al. 1987a; Nader and Pynoos 1988). Judging the onset of PTSD in preschool-age children is difficult because of the limits inherent in the instruments available and in the child's self-report and cognitive maturity.

MEDIATING FACTORS

SITUATIONAL VARIABLES

Appraisal of Threat

Because of the unique dangers they face, certain segments of the population may experience additional stress after a disaster. For example, pregnant women showed a significant level of anxiety after the Three Mile Island nuclear reactor accident because they perceived danger to their unborn children (Bromet 1980). Children who had been in Mexico City during the destructive 1985 earthquake were often more frightened than their peers following the 1988 Whittier-Narrows (California) earthquake. Mothers who were in the San Fernando Valley earthquake of 1971 were more anxious after the Whittier-Narrows earthquake, and their children's behavior reflected this anxiety.

Very young children may gain partial protection from the traumatic impact because they do not understand the extent of the danger. However, their appraisal of threat depends, partially, on the accompanying adult's or sibling's actions and attitude, especially in situations of potential danger, such as air raid warnings (Freud and Burlingham 1943; Mercier and Despert 1943). Still, there are many horrifying and catastrophic situations in which adults cannot be expected to appear unalarmed. In fact, children can be confused, disturbed, and potentially put in greater jeopardy by adults who minimize the obvious threat (Pynoos and Nader 1986).

Human Accountability

The psychological aftereffects of man-made disasters may be more chronic than those of natural disasters. Several investigators have noted that post-traumatic stress reactions are more persistent after an event for which human beings are perceived to be responsible (Frederick 1980). The highest rates of PTSD for children have been reported after acts of violence (Terr 1979; Kinzie et al. 1986; Pynoos et al. 1987a). For adults, Grinker and Spiegel (1943) attributed this phenomenon partly to the debilitating effect of prolonged or unexpressed revenge fantasies, an effect also observed in children by Pynoos and Eth (1986).

Separation From a Significant Other

Worry about the safety of a significant other during a disaster may be an additional source of extreme stress for children and their families. Mothers have been noted to exhibit an intense concern with the whereabouts and safety of their children, which results in continued anxiety afterward (McFarlane 1987). Adolescents who were worried about a younger sibling have reported greater postdisaster distress and more somatic complaints than their peers (Dohrenwend et al. 1981). After the sinking of the Andrea Doria, psychiatric morbidity occurred in children only when they were separated from parents (Friedman and Linn 1957).

For all family members, worry about a significant other may persist, leading to chronic preoccupation about the person's whereabouts or safety, to emotional detachment, and to impairment of daily functioning

(Pynoos and Nader 1988b). This point is illustrated in the following vignette: An 8-year-old boy's 6-year-old sister was at a friend's house in the area where a tornado struck. After the tornado, phone lines were down and his family had been unable to verify the girl's safety for several hours while hearing media reports of extensive property damage and loss of life. After his safe reunion with his sister, the boy continued to be anxious whenever his sister was out of his sight. He demanded to know where she was and would sometimes make her return home from playing with friends. He awakened a few times each night to check on his sister to be sure that she had not been stolen or harmed.

Several investigators have found that separation from parents or siblings immediately after a disaster can further exacerbate the stress reaction, especially for the preschool- and school-age child (McFarlane and Raphael 1984; Pynoos and Nader 1988b). For example, there was a measurable increase in duration of symptoms for children who were sent away to stay with relatives after the Australian Ash Wednesday fire (McFarlane 1987).

Guilt

Guilt is an associated feature of PTSD that is not well examined in children. There are major developmental difficulties in assessing guilt in children of varying ages. However, there is preliminary evidence from the study of violent events that when children report guilt, it increases the severity of children's posttraumatic stress reactions independent of exposure (Pynoos et al. 1987a). School-age children reported "feeling bad" at being unable to provide aid, being safe when others were harmed, or believing their actions endangered others (Pynoos and Nader 1988b). Particular experiences—for example, hearing a wounded person's cry for help or watching someone bleed to death—may create an intense level of empathic arousal in children that remains undiminished if no effective intervention occurs (Hoffman 1979). In a longitudinal study of children exposed to a sniper attack, both immediately following the attack and 1 year later, children who reported guilt had greater numbers of posttraumatic stress symptoms than those who did not report guilt. Guilt sometimes explained the persistent posttraumatic stress reactions of children who were not directly exposed to the violence (Nades and Pynoos 1988).

Multiple Adversities

Multiple adversities, which result from an event such as a disaster, may have more than an additive effect in increasing psychiatric morbidity (Rutter 1985). One disaster alone can lead to the experience of severe life threat, death of a significant other, loss of residence and relocation, involuntary unemployment of a parent, and change in the family's financial state. This additive effect may be responsible for the high rate of comorbidity in severely affected children and adults after major disasters and massive traumas.

INTERVENING VARIABLES

Recovery of the Community

Disasters disrupt community cohesion and function (Erickson 1976). Some evidence suggests that the inefficiency of postdisaster organizational efforts directly and independently influences the persistence of psychological problems (Quarantelli 1985). On the other hand, the influence of the social group can be positive and reparative (Quarantelli 1985). Fear of recurrence affects everyone in the community regardless of his or her degree of exposure to the event (Pynoos et al. 1987a). This widespread fear is sometimes fueled by myth, rumor, lack of information, and misinterpretation.

Cultural Factors

Cultural or ethnic differences may have little influence on the emergence of acute PTSD. Given similar exposure, however, they may influence the behavioral responses of children. Kinzie et al. (1986) found no increase in substance abuse or delinquency among adolescent Cambodians, even though they had a high prevalence of PTSD years after enduring massive trauma and family loss. This finding contrasts with the increased delinquency and substance abuse generally found among bereaved adolescent groups (Krupnick 1984). Additional studies are needed to assess the relevance of cultural factors among different subpopulations experiencing different types of disasters.

Family

Parental and family functioning is a major mediating factor in children's psychiatric morbidity (Rutter 1985). Parental distress, parental disagreement about appropriate action during the disaster, and change in parenting function after the disaster influence children's reactions and recovery (Bloch et al. 1956; Handford et al. 1986). Four parental responses have been found to be significantly associated with the persistence of symptoms in children: (a) parents' excessive dependence on children for support (Silber et al. 1958), (b) overprotectiveness (McFarlane 1987), (c) a prohibitive attitude toward temporary regressive behavior or toward open expression and communication about the experience (Bloch et al. 1956), and (d) preexisting parental psychopathology (Bloch et al. 1956).

Family members often experience similar exposure to a disaster and share the loss of a family member or property damage. Gleser et al. (1981) found a high symptom correlation between parents and children, and McFarlane et al. (1987) had a similar finding between mothers and their school-age children. When children's exposure exceeds that of other family members, their symptomatic behavior may disrupt normal family functioning (Terr 1979).

Every study in which children have been interviewed regarding their PTSD and grief reactions has found a significant discordance between parent and child reports (Bloch et al. 1956; McFarlane 1987; Weissman 1987). Initially, children experience core symptoms quite privately, and parents and teachers may not notice behavioral changes. When the children's distress is not fully appreciated, they may not receive adequate emotional support. They may become more withdrawn or isolated (Kinzie et al. 1986) or may face disturbing parental demands to act unaffected.

Kinzie et al. (1986) have documented the powerful influence that family relationships have in constructively mediating the effects of massive psychic trauma. Cambodian adolescent refugees who, after relocating, lived with family members or relatives, had a significantly lower rate of psychiatric morbidity than those who lived in adoptive settings.

Family Bereavement

Even though there has been a trend toward decreasing disaster mortality in the United States, disasters still account for significant loss of life (Logue et al. 1981b). There is some evidence that the sudden, unexpected death of a parent or sibling is associated with a higher risk of pathological or persistent grief and psychiatric morbidity in both children (Pynoos and Nader 1987) and adults (Lundlin 1984). As Rutter (1985) notes, loss sets in motion a number of changes in the child's life that can result in chronically unsatisfactory family circumstances and thus increase the risk of psychiatric morbidity.

School-age children appear to be confused, frightened, and disturbed by their normal grief reactions after traumatic loss (Pynoos et al. 1987b). Because they may not be adequately understood, children's grief reactions are often overlooked by other family members, who are preoccupied with their own mourning (Bowlby 1980). Whereas adults commonly share their grief experiences with others and seek reassurance, many children report that they do not receive sufficient emotional support from family, teachers, and friends (Pynoos and Nader, in press).

Influence on Peer Relationships

Temporary dislocation and permanent relocation of residence can interrupt peer friendships, which are an important source of social support, especially for adolescents. In addition, posttraumatic irritability, inhibition, or aggression can strain sibling and peer relationships. After 7-year-old Richard's experience in the earthquake (see case example above), when he played with other children they often complained that he had become a bully. He insisted on having some control of what happened during the play. He was easily offended and responded with verbal aggression. Posttrauma changes in personality also affect interpersonal relations. For example, after a hostage-taking in which all of a 16-year-old girl's family members were killed, teenage friends complained that the formerly popular and social girl had become serious and no longer carefree. The girl was openly judgmental of her peers when they seemed unappreciative of their family members.

Posttraumatic stress reactions in children, especially those who have not reached adolescence, may include a reduction of interest in and enjoyment of normal activities, a tendency to stay inside more or nearer to protective adults, and feelings of estrangement from others. These symptoms can result in isolation and, consequently, disruption of the social, cognitive, and emotional developmental tasks accomplished through play and interpersonal interaction.

Influence of the School Milieu

Garmezy (1986) has commented on the importance of the role of the teacher as an external support figure for stressed children. Teachers themselves may be severely affected, and children may respond to the teachers' distress as they do to parental distress. For example, children were shown to reflect their teachers' emotional responses to news of President Kennedy's assassination (Kliman 1968). Teachers' and staff members' posttrauma behaviors may affect children. For example, after a woman committed suicide in front of elementary school children, one staff member would not allow pictures of guns or toy guns on campus. She required one child to turn his T-shirt inside out because it pictured a gun on it.

Because children spend much of their week in school, they may be just as likely to experience a disaster there as at home. How the school reacts in the immediate situation as well as in the aftermath and recovery periods may substantially affect children's recovery. The anxiety in students and teachers precipitated by a disaster can result in more general classroom changes in behavior and disruption of the educational process. In addition, the milieu of schools may vary in tolerating postdisaster reactions, depending upon the attitude of the principal and other administrators.

CHILD INTRINSIC FACTORS

Some children seem relatively resilient to a stressor, while others respond more significantly than their degree of exposure explains. Preexisting psychopathology, especially anxiety and depressive disorders, and previous loss or trauma have been associated with more severe and prolonged postdisaster symptoms (Lacey 1972; Pynoos et al. 1987b). The disaster may remind the child of a previous traumatic event and renew his or her reactions (Pynoos and Nader, in press).

Predisposition to Arousal Behavior

Frequently, after a traumatic event, children exhibit sleep disturbances, hypervigilance, and exaggerated startle reactions (Pynoos and Nader 1988a, in press; Newman 1976; Burke et al. 1982; Davis 1983). Children may be more likely to experience neurophysiological changes than adults, such as stage 4 sleep phenomena (Fisher et al. 1973). There is some evidence that persistence of increased states of arousal helps to reinforce other PTSD symptoms (Kramer et al. 1984; Kolb 1987). For example, sleep disturbance has been correlated with difficulties in attention and academic performance (Pynoos et al. 1987a). Children's propensity to arousal behavior may vary according to genetic, constitutional, and environmental factors.

Coping

Whereas effective coping reduces distress, maladaptive coping responses, such as drug abuse, may exacerbate it or become problems themselves (Silver and Wortman 1980). There is, as yet, no acceptable taxonomy of childhood coping (Garmezy 1986). Influenced by their phase of development and prior experience, children vary widely in their attempts to interpret the event and their symptoms, to regulate their emotions, and to search for meaning, information, and assistance. We have observed that some sensitive children suffered more empathic arousal than their peers at the distress of others.

Similar to adults, children prominently manifest avoidant behaviors and anxiety associated with specific traumatic reminders. Some children appear to overgeneralize the auditory and visual aspects of a traumatic reminder, especially incident-specific stimuli (Bloch et al. 1956), while others display accurate cognitive discrimination. The way in which children process these reminders and manage the renewed anxiety may significantly affect their recovery.

Children vary in their acceptance of their postdisaster reactions. They may interpret their reactions as an indication that something is wrong with them, and may feel that other children are not similarly affected. Along with their caretakers, children may unrealistically expect their recovery time to be shorter. These expectations can intensify distress and prevent them from seeking needed support (Silver and Wortman 1980; Kaltreider et al. 1979).

Further studies are necessary to investigate the factors influencing more constructive postdisaster child behaviors—for instance, increased academic motivation, increased courage, or more empathic responses to others (Pynoos and Nades 1988b). In turn, these behaviors may have varying influence on aspects of child development.

AGE

Several studies have reported differences among age groups after catastrophic events. Carey-Trefzer (1949) observed that younger children were more likely to reflect adults' reactions to war conditions. Neurotic reactions occurred for them only if they were personally endangered. The older the child, the more the sight of destruction aroused anxiety. Similarly, Gleser et al. (1981) found that school-age children exposed to a flood exhibited more severe psychiatric impairment than preschool-age children: Psychiatric Evaluation Form (PEF) Overall Severity and Depression scores increased with age, while Belligerence scores were higher for teenagers, and Anxiety scores were higher for the oldest group, ages 16–20.

While some studies have found no differences within age groups (for elementary school children, see Pynoos et al. 1987a; for adolescents, see Kinzie et al. 1986), age-related findings may sometimes reflect the differences in the traumatic situation and the children's appraisal of threat. After the Three Mile Island nuclear accident, Handford et al. (1986) found that children under the age of 8 did not appear to recognize the potential danger resulting from the accident.

Anthony (1986) has noted that after a disaster, individuals feel significantly less secure and more vulnerable, and exhibit increased attachment behavior. In elementary school–age children this often manifests as a continued fear of recurrence, new incident-specific fears, and regressive behavior. Children may become afraid of specific places, concrete items, and human behaviors that specifically remind them of the incident. They may also exhibit more generalized fear of being vulnerable; for instance, they may become afraid of strangers, being in the dark, being alone, being in their own room or in the bathroom, or going to bed. Regressive behaviors commonly observed in children following a disaster include enuresis, abandonment of previously learned skills, and increased dependency, including clinging, a need to stay near home, and asking to sleep with parents (Burke et al. 1982; Newman 1976).

IMPACT ON CHILD DEVELOPMENT

While there has been some discussion of the influence of children's levels of maturity on their initial reactions and assimilation of traumatic events

(Eth and Pynoos 1985; Cohen 1986), there is little systematic data available concerning the effects of disaster or other traumatic experiences on child development. Studies are needed that examine the differential outcome of substantial numbers of children who have experienced a stress at different ages. While there is no conclusive evidence for an interaction between trauma and developmental stage, posttraumatic stress phenomena may influence a number of characteristics that affect the developmental process, including cognitive functioning, initiative, personality style, self-esteem, outlook, and impulse control. Intrusive, reexperiencing phenomena can affect cognitive functioning by altering attention either toward or away from concrete or symbolic traumatic reminders. Without resulting in a phobic disorder, traumatic avoidant behavior can lead to inhibitions or altered interests. Children's imaginative play can become constricted and less enjoyable with the repetition of disaster-related themes in play (Bloch et al. 1956; Terr 1979).

Several researchers have reported prominent personality changes even in very young children (Terr 1979; Gislason and Call 1982), ranging from reduced impulse control to increased inhibition, from attraction to danger to a debilitating sense of fear, from emotional withdrawal to exhibitionism. Researchers have described changes in self-image that accompany the onset of adult PTSD (Kaltreider et al. 1979). How children's sense of self-efficacy, self-confidence, or self-esteem is influenced remains unknown. Without adequate predisaster data it is difficult to assess the degree of change and to determine whether there is an actual discontinuity in personality development or merely an exaggeration of preexisting traits.

Silver and Wortman (1980) concluded that although the change may go unnoticed, one of the most devastating effects of trauma on adults is the tendency for them to permanently change their views of the world. Childhood trauma studies have consistently found a marked change in orientation toward the future, including a sense of foreshortened future, negative expectations, and altered attitudes toward marriage, having children, and career (Terr 1979; Pynoos and Eth 1984). Children may anticipate that the experience of a trauma will affect their adult behavior. A study of concentration camp survivors demonstrated the influence of trauma on later parental behavior (Danieli 1985).

PREVENTIVE INTERVENTION STRATEGIES

After disasters, opportunities exist to implement the principles of preventive psychiatry in outreach intervention strategies (Lystad 1984). These strategies focus on strengthening individual and family coping capacities, as well as decreasing adverse influences on recovery. They include fostering the continued adaptation of resilient children, as well as assisting those children with severe stress reactions.

Preventive interventions may be implemented before, during, or after a disaster, and may focus on the individual(s), the agent (event), or the environment. Degree of exposure and personal impact primarily determine the variability of response. Interventions specifically geared to these varying effects should take precedence over less-focused solutions.

BEFORE A DISASTER

If exposure to life threat, injury, loss, property destruction, and community disruption is the primary risk factor for psychiatric morbidity, then the first goal of prevention should be to minimize exposure. Prevention requires formulation and implementation of instrumental social policy, for example, improved building standards to reduce earthquake injuries, loss, and property damage. Psychiatry can assume an important role in this area of public policy.

In the United States predisaster training is commonly conducted in schools where there is a high risk of natural disaster. The goals of the training are severalfold: (1) to instruct in the storing of appropriate home emergency supplies; (2) to familiarize with certain types of natural disasters (for example, in Los Angeles County schools a traveling van is used to simulate an earthquake); and (3) to teach methods of physical self-protection during and after a disaster. Although these programs typically acknowledge that children will be frightened, little effort is made to prepare the children for the broad range of emotional reactions commonly experienced. In schools in other countries, intervention programs have been implemented to enhance coping with a wide spectrum of potential situations, including disasters (Ayalon 1979; Klingman 1978). No evaluation studies of preparedness or stress inoculation efforts have been reported.

Before a disaster it is important to prepare parents and teachers to act decisively and effectively despite personally feeling overwhelmed by a crisis. Responding in a systematic way and appearing to be in control of the situation will help to reduce children's stress (Klingman 1978).

DURING A DISASTER

Evacuation

Input by mental health professionals into the preparation of evacuation protocols can address—for schools, medical teams, and the media—both adaptation-enhancing and stress-producing factors during a disaster. Early warning and prompt evacuation are recommended. Evidence from the Buffalo Creek Dam flood suggests that those evacuated prior to the destruction suffered significantly less psychiatric morbidity and chronic functional impairment. Familiarity with evacuation plans, including parents' understanding of evacuation procedures at their children's schools, can be an important factor in allaying anxiety during and after a disaster. Inopportune or abrupt separation of young children from parents, siblings, and other trusted adults carries its own risk for postdisaster distress.

Emergency Medical Relief

Emergency medical relief is intended to ensure prompt, coordinated care of large numbers of injured persons. Inefficiencies can add to the medical morbidity of injured children and substantially increase their immediate psychological stress. This may occur, for example, when casualties are evacuated to various hospitals throughout the region. The authors have provided consultation in the aftermath of two school emergencies, one in which a bomb exploded, and another in which an insecticide pollutant contaminated classrooms. In each case, injured or sick children were transported by ambulance or helicopter to several outlying hospitals. No records indicated which children were sent to which hospital. Consequently, parents could not locate their children for extended periods— in one case for hours, in another for more than a day. After a traumatic incident it is common for children to fear repeated disaster or danger to themselves or to significant others. Prolonged separation can increase and intensify these fearful preoccupations and the concomitant stress. After the school bombing incident, the prolonged separation and worry became focal points of parents' and children's subsequent anxiety.

Secondary Exposure

Children need protection from unnecessary exposure to the injured, mutilated, and dead. Involving children and adolescents in disaster rescue work compounds their exposure, introducing secondary risk of psychiatric morbidity. After the disaster, inappropriate media coverage, such as exhibiting corpses or mutilated bodies, may also have a harmful effect.

Media

The media has the capacity to play a greater role in informing and educating the public about the mental health aspects of disaster reactions, coping strategies, parenting, and available services. After the Mexico City earthquake a group of psychiatrists organized a major outreach program in collaboration with the media (Palacios et al. 1986). Too often, however, media efforts have not been consistent with good mental health practices.

Need exists for a library of accessible and well-evaluated multimedia messages, including materials designed for children. Studies are needed to evaluate the best methods of public education.

AFTER THE DISASTER

Psychological first aid provides prompt relief from acute distress both for direct victims and for those awaiting word on the condition of a family member. Clinical studies have recommended first-aid techniques applicable to specific developmental stages (Pynoos and Nader 1988b; Farberow and Gordon 1981). For example, from preschool to second grade, first aid would include repeated concrete clarifications, consistent caretaking, and help in verbalizing fears, feelings, and complaints. Older children might be cautioned about risk-taking and an increased post-traumatic tendency toward impulsive behavior (Eth and Pynoos 1985; Terr 1981). Systematic research is needed on the use of age-appropriate techniques, and on early intervention at key sites, such as temporary relocation centers, homes, disaster relief offices, and schools.

In working with families and children at risk for psychiatric morbidity, prevention goals include (1) ameliorating traumatic stress reactions and facilitating grief work, (2) preventing interferences with child development and the resulting maladjustments, and (3) promoting competence in effectively adapting to the crisis situation. Successful preventive intervention requires access to children who are identifiably at risk, treatment of populations undergoing normative reactions to extreme stress, and prevention of the onset of disorders, or reduction of their duration and progression.

Family

The family is the key setting in which feelings of vulnerability can be mitigated and a sense of security restored. The goals for family work are (1) to give children the experience of being supported, (2) to establish a sense of physical security, (3) to validate children's affective responses rather than dismissing them, and (4) to assist children in dealing with traumatic reminders by accepting their renewed anxiety and providing helpful reassurances. Family members often need support, guidance, and sometimes therapeutic intervention to reduce their own levels of stress before they can effectively help their children. They need information about the wide range of children's disaster responses, the effect of traumatic reminders, the presence of arousal behavior, realistic expectations regarding recovery, and the need to encourage open communication with their children.

Much remains unknown. Research is particularly needed about (1) enhancing parenting ability following trauma and loss; (2) managing children's new, incident-specific fears, regressive behaviors, and arousal states; and (3) facilitating children's grief work.

School-Based Mental Health Intervention

Some school districts have instituted psychological crisis teams that can respond immediately to emergencies or community disasters. Using classroom consultations, an entire school can be screened and children prioritized according to varying levels of risk. Early case findings should be followed by therapeutic consultations.

The school is the optimal site because (1) it is most convenient to children and parents, and (2) the stigmatization that accompanies use of mental health facilities is obviated. The school is an ideal locus to involve parents, teachers, and children in preventively oriented trauma response programs. Crabbs (1981), Blom (1986), and Pynoos and Nader (1988b) have provided guidelines for such programs. Elements of such programs include consultation with school administrators, training of teachers, and education of parents and children. Identifying and addressing the most common rumors, misconceptions, and fears has helped to minimize anxiety in all members of the school community and to limit interference with everyday activities.

Classroom drawing exercises and engaging children, over time, in symbolic reconstruction in play have proved to be effective methods of initial intervention (Pynoos and Nader 1988b). The usefulness of these classroom interventions in reducing children's fear of recurrence was demonstrated in the aftermath of an Italian earthquake. Redramatizing the earthquake's destructive force and then reconstructing their village in play proved to be an important two-step process in reducing the children's cognitive preoccupations (Galante and Foa 1986). Special procedures are needed to reintegrate hospitalized or severely traumatized children into the classroom, to deal with bereaved children, and to monitor school behavior and performance.

Intervention With Individual Children

Children who have had severe exposure to life threat and witnessing of injury or death may require direct forms of individual intervention in order to avert more serious psychiatric morbidity. While only preliminary investigations are available into the appropriate therapeutic techniques for children, investigators of adult PTSD have found that the optimum time for intervention is in the acute period when the intrusive phenomena are most apparent and the associated affect most available (Kaltreider et al. 1979). Incident-specific traumatic reminders are most easily identifiable during the acute phase after the disaster.

Clinically, school-age children and adolescents have participated in the same kind of acute debriefing that has been a hallmark of adult trauma work (Pynoos and Eth 1986; Frederick 1985). The goal is to assist children to explore thoroughly their subjective experiences and to help them to understand the meaning of their responses. The consultation serves to bolster the child's observing ego and reality-testing functions, thereby dispelling cognitive confusions and encouraging active coping (Caplan 1981). In so doing, a child is assisted to identify traumatic reminders that elicit psychophysiologic reactions, intrusive imagery, and intense affective responses. The specific aim is to increase a child's sense of being able to anticipate or, at least, manage the recurrence of these reminders. Managing what are usually unavoidable daily reminders may be the key to enhancing the child's sense of mastery of a disaster experience. Enabling the child to share these traumatic reminders with his or her parents increases the likelihood that the child will receive essential parental support and understanding. Perhaps the best gauge of the effectiveness of acute individual intervention may be the child's improved capacity to participate in solving problems secondary to the crisis, e.g., to prevent unnecessary separations from siblings or to arrange contacts with peers.

Posttraumatic stress reactions are expectable and understandable psychological phenomena that result from traumatic exposure. By using their authority, mental health professionals can legitimize children's feelings and reactions and assist these children to maintain their self-esteem. Children can also be prepared to anticipate and cope with the transient return of unresolved feelings over time.

Although trauma debriefing and consultation have proven helpful, many severely exposed children will require more extended therapeutic interventions. There is an immediate need for investigation of brief, focal psychotherapy with traumatized children (Pynoos and Eth 1984). Adult studies provide evidence that such therapy can be effective in the treatment of PTSD (Kaltreider et al. 1979). These methods need to be modified to reflect developmental considerations and to be tested for efficacy.

Modifying arousal behavior may be an important aspect of an overall treatment plan. Laboratory and preliminary clinical data in adults indicate that this neurophysiological response can be attenuated by pharmacological intervention (Kolb 1987). A pilot investigation of persistent arousal behavior in children exposed to gunfire incidents is being conducted at UCLA. Preliminary data suggest that abnormalities in acoustic startle response and stage 4 sleep phenomena are present and can be arrested by the use of clonidine. In a study of acute PTSD in children, arousal behavior (especially sleep disturbance) was associated with interference with attention and learning (Pynoos et al. 1987a). Early alleviation of this symptom may decrease chronicity and reduce functional impairment in severely exposed children.

CONCLUSIONS

We are presently in the midst of a growing knowledge base emerging from solid research studies of the psychiatric impact of disasters. These newer studies are leading to more data-based strategies of intervention for exposed populations. The study of children's reactions is an area of particular concern, requiring more systematic investigation.

The involvement of child psychiatrists in this area provides a new dimension for psychiatrists concerned with school mental health, preventive and community psychiatry, child development, and child psychopathology. Given the high frequency of disasters, it is important for child psychiatrists to be aware of their roles and functions in the planning and delivery of appropriate preventive mental health disaster services.

REFERENCES

Adams PR, Adams GR: Mount Saint Helens's ashfall. Am Psychol 39:252–260, 1984

American Psychiatric Association: Diagnostic and Statistical Manual of Mental Disorders, 3rd Edition, Revised. Washington, DC, American Psychiatric Association, 1987

Andreasen NC: Posttraumatic stress disorder, in Comprehensive Textbook of Psychiatry, 4th Edition Vol 1. Edited by Kaplan HI, Sadock BJ. Baltimore, MD, Williams & Wilkins, 1985, pp 918–924

Anthony EJ: The response to overwhelming stress: some introductory comments. J Am Acad Child Psychiatry 25:299–305, 1986

Ayalon O: Community oriented preparation for emergency. Death Educ 3:227–244, 1979

Berezofsky EE: Post-Traumatic Stress Disorder and the Technological Disaster. Washington, DC, Bureau of National Affairs, 1987

Bloch D, Silber E, Perry S: Some factors in the emotional reaction of children to disaster. Am J Psychiatry 113:416–422, 1956

Blom GE: A school disaster—intervention and research aspects. J Am Acad Child Psychiatry 25:336–345, 1986

Bowlby J: Attachment and Loss, Vol III. New York, Basic Books, 1980

Bromet E: Three Mile Island: mental health findings. National Institute of Mental Health Contract Report No. 287-79-0048(SM). Washington, DC, U.S. Government Printing Office, 1980

Burke JD Jr, Borus JF, Burners B, et al: Changes in children's behavior after a natural disaster. Am J Psychiatry 139:1010–1014, 1982

Caplan G: Mastery of stress: psychological aspects. Am J Psychiatry 138:413–420, 1981

Carey-Trefzer CJ: The results of a clinical study of war-damaged children who attended the child guidance clinic, the Hospital for Sick Children, Great Ormond Street, London. J Ment Sci 95:535–559, 1949

Cohen RE: Developmental phases of children's reactions following natural disasters. J Emerg Disaster Med 1(4):89–95, 1986

Crabbs M: School mental health services following an environmental disaster. J School Health 51:165–167, 1981

Danieli Y: The treatment and prevention of long-term effects and intergenerational transmission of victimization: a lesson from holocaust survivors and their children, in Trauma and Its Wake. Edited by Figley C. New York, Brunner/Mazel, 1985, pp 295–313

Davis M: Neurobiological perspectives on anxiety. Psychopharmacol Bull 19:457–465, 1983

Dohrenwend BP, Dohrenwend BS, Warheit GJ, et al: Stress in the community: a report to the President's Commission on the accident at Three Mile Island. Ann NY Acad Sci 365:159–174, 1981

Erickson KT: Loss of communality at Buffalo Creek. Am J Psychiatry 133:302–305, 1976

Eth S, Pynoos R: Developmental perspectives on psychic trauma in children, in Trauma and Its Wake. Edited by Figley C. New York, Brunner/Mazel, 1985, pp 36–52

Farberow NL, Gordon NS: Manual for child health workers in major disasters (DHHS Publ No ADM-81-1070). Washington, DC, National Institute of Mental Health, 1981

Figley CR: Introduction, in Trauma and Its Wake, Vol 2. Edited by Figley C. New York, Brunner/Mazel, 1986, pp xvii–xxix

Fisher C, Byrne J, Edwards A, et al: A psychophysiological study of nightmares and night terrors. J Nerv Ment Dis 157:75–98, 1973

Frederick CJ: Effects of natural versus human-induced violence upon victims. Eval Change (special issue), 1980, pp 71–75

Frederick CJ: Children traumatized by catastrophic situations, in Post-Traumatic Stress Disorder in Children. Edited by Eth S, Pynoos R. Washington, DC, American Psychiatric Press, 1985, pp 71–99

Freud A, Burlingham D: War and Children. New York, Medical War Books, 1943

Friedman P, Linn I: Some psychiatric notes on the Andrea Doria disaster. Am J Psychiatry 114:426–432, 1957

Galante R, Foa D: An epidemiological study of psychic trauma and treatment effectiveness for children after a natural disaster. J Am Acad Child Psychiatry 25:357–363, 1986

Garmezy N: Children under severe stress. Critique and commentary. J Am Acad Child Psychiatry 25:384–392, 1986

Gislason IL, Call J: Dog bite in infancy: trauma and personality development. J Am Acad Child Psychiatry 2:203–207, 1982

Gleser GC, Green BL, Winget C: Prolonged Psychosocial Effects of Disaster: A Study of Buffalo Creek. New York, Academic, 1981

Green BL, Grace MC, Lindy JD, et al: Levels of functional impairment following a civilian disaster: the Beverly Hills Supper Club fire. J Consult Clin Psychol 50:573–580, 1983

Green BL, Grace MC, Gleser GC: Long-term impairment following the Beverly Hills Supper Club fire. J Consult Clin Psychol 53:672–678, 1985a

Green BL, Lindy JD, Grace MC: Post-traumatic stress disorder: toward DSM IV. J Nerv Ment Dis 173:406–411, 1985b

Grinker RR, Spiegel JP: War Neuroses in North Africa: The Tunisian Campaign. New York, Josiah Macy, Jr Foundation, September 1943

Handford HA, Mayes SD, Mattison RE, et al: Child and parent reaction to the Three Mile Island nuclear accident. J Am Acad Child Psychiatry 25:346–356, 1986

Hoffman M: Development of moral thought, feeling and behavior. Am Psychol 34:958–966, 1979

Jones DR: Secondary disaster victims: the emotional effects of recovering and identifying human remains. Am J Psychiatry 142:303–307, 1985

Kaltreider NB, Wallace A, Horowitz MJ: A field study of the stress response syndrome: young women after hysterectomy. JAMA 242:1499–1503, 1979

Kinzie JD, Sack WH, Angell RH, et al: The psychiatric effects of massive trauma on Cambodian children: I. The children. J Am Acad Child Psychiatry 25:370–376, 1986

Kliman A: The Corning flood project: psychological first aid following a natural disaster, in Emergency and Disaster Management. Edited by Parad HJ, Resnik HLP, Parad LG. Bowie, MD, Charles Press Publishers, 1976, pp 325–335

Kliman G: Psychological Emergencies of Childhood. New York, Grune & Stratton, 1968

Klingman A: Children in stress: anticipatory guidance in the framework of the educational system. Pers Guid J 57:22–26, 1978

Kolb LC: A neuropsychological hypothesis explaining posttraumatic stress disorders. Am J Psychiatry 144:989–995, 1987

Kramer M, Schoen LS, Kinney L: The dream experience in dream-disturbed Vietnam veterans, in Post-Traumatic Stress Disorder: Psychological and Biological Sequelae. Edited by van der Kolk B. Washington, DC, American Psychiatric Press, 1984, pp 81–95

Krupnick JL: Bereavement during childhood and adolescence, in Bereavement: Reactions, Consequences, and Care. Edited by Osterweis M, Solomon F, Green M. Washington, DC, National Academy Press, 1984, pp 99–141

Lacey G: Observations on Aberfan. J Psychosom Res 16:257–260, 1972

Logue JN, Melick ME, Hansen H: Research issues and directions in the epidemiology of health effects of disasters. Epidemiol Rev 3:140–162, 1981a

Logue JN, Melick ME, Struening EL: A study of health and mental health status following a major natural disaster. Res Commun Ment Health 2:217–274, 1981b

Lundlin T: Morbidity following sudden and unexpected bereavement. Br J Psychiatry 144:84–88, 1984

Lystad M: Children's response to disaster: family implications. Int J Fam Psychiatry 5:41–60, 1984

McFarlane AC: Posttraumatic phenomena in a longitudinal study of children following a natural disaster. J Am Acad Child Adolesc Psychiatry 26:764–769, 1987

McFarlane AC, Raphael B: Ash Wednesday: the effects of a fire. Aust N Z J Psychiatry 18:341–351, 1984

McFarlane AC, Policansky SK, Irwin C: A longitudinal study of the psychological morbidity in children due to a natural disaster. J Psychol Med 17:727–738, 1987

Mercier MH, Despert JL: Psychological effects of the war on French children. Psychosom Med 5:266–272, 1943

Nader K, Pynoos R: Childhood PTSD reactions: a longitudinal study. Paper presented at the annual meeting of the American Academy of Child and Adolescent Psychiatry, Seattle, WA, October 1988

Newman CF: Children of disaster: clinical observations at Buffalo Creek. Am J Psychiatry 133:312–316, 1976

Palacios A, Cueli J, Camacho J, et al: The traumatic effect of mass communication in the Mexico City earthquake: crisis intervention and preventive measures. Int J Psychoanal 13:279–294, 1986

Pynoos RS, Eth S: The child as witness to homicide. J Soc Issues 40:87–108, 1984

Pynoos RS, Eth S: Witness to violence: the child interview. J Am Acad Child Psychiatry 25:306–319, 1986

Pynoos RS, Nader K: Proximity to violence and later accuracy of recall. Paper presented at the Symposium on the Making of Memory, American Psychiatric Association, Washington, DC, May 1986

Pynoos RS, Nader K: Preliminary results of a follow-up study of childhood bereavement and post-traumatic stress disorder. Paper presented at the annual meeting of the American Psychiatric Association, Washington, DC, October 1987

Pynoos RS, Nader K: Children who witness the sexual assaults of their mothers. J Am Acad Child Adolesc Psychiatry 27:567–572, 1988a

Pynoos RS, Nader K: Psychological first aid and treatment approach to children exposed to community violence: research implications. J Traumat Stress 1:445–473, 1988b

Pynoos RS, Nader K: Children exposed to violence. Psychiatr Ann (in press)

Pynoos RS, Frederick C, Nader K, et al: Life threat and posttraumatic stress in school-age children. Arch Gen Psychiatry 44:1057–1063, 1987a

Pynoos RS, Nader K, Frederick C, et al: Grief reactions in school age children following a sniper attack at school. Isr J Psychiatry Relat Sci 24:53–63, 1987b

Quarantelli EL: An assessment of conflicting news on mental health: the consequences of traumatic events, in Trauma and Its Wake. Edited by Figley C. New York, Brunner/Mazel, 1985, pp 173–215

Rubin CB, Yezer ZM, Hussain Q, et al: Summary of major natural disaster incidents in the United States, 1965–85 (Special Publ 17). Washington, DC, Natural Hazards Research & Applications Information Center, George Washington University, 1986

Rutter M: Resilience in the face of adversity: protective factors and resistance to psychiatric disorder. Br J Psychiatry 147:598–611, 1985

Shore J, Tatum E, Vollmer W: Psychiatric reactions to disaster: the Mt. St. Helens experience. Am J Psychiatry 140:1543–1550, 1983

Silber E, Perry S, Bloch D: Patterns of parent-child interaction in a disaster. Psychiatry 21:159–167, 1958

Silver RL, Wortman CB: Coping with undesirable life events, in Human Helplessness. Edited by Garber J, Seligman MEP. New York, Academic, 1980, pp 279–341

Terr L: Children of Chowchilla: study of psychic trauma. Psychoanal Study Child 34:547–623, 1979

Terr L: Psychic trauma in children: observations following the Chowchilla school bus kidnapping. Am J Psychiatry 138:14–19, 1981

U.S. Government: Rules and regulations for the Disaster Relief Act, PL 93-288, Section 413. Fed Register, November 6, 1976

Weissman, MM: Assessing psychiatric disorders in children: discrepancies between mothers' and children's reports. Arch Gen Psychiatry 44:747–753, 1987

Wilkinson CB: Aftermath of a disaster: the collapse of the Hyatt Regency Hotel skywalks. Am J Psychiatry 140:1134–1139, 1985

CHAPTER 12

Preventing Mental Health Disturbances By Preventing and Treating Child Abuse

Richard D. Krugman, M.D.

THE PROBLEM

The major premise of this chapter is that many of the mental and emotional problems afflicting children and adults are the direct or indirect sequelae of child maltreatment. Therefore, if these psychiatric problems are to be prevented, attention must be paid to the recognition, assessment, and treatment of abused and neglected children.

The prevention of mental health disturbances in childhood and the prevention of physical and sexual abuse of children are integrally related. However, that is not necessarily a conclusion one would reach reading the American Psychiatric Association's *Diagnostic and Statistical Manual of Mental Disorders* (1980), or the Office of Technology Assessment's background paper entitled *Children's Mental Health: Problems and Services* (U.S. Congress 1986), or if one came in casual contact with most of the child psychiatrists I have been around in Colorado and New York. Raise the issue of child abuse to these colleagues a decade ago and they would get a vacant, faraway look in their eyes and would not respond. Raise it now and they get a concerned, thoughtful look, and say, ". . . Yes," or "It's such a difficult area, isn't it? Fortunately, I see so few of these cases."

A decade ago psychiatric residents never saw child abuse and neglect. Today, psychiatric residents recognize the problem. However, because in many programs they are prohibited from taking cases in which court appearances are likely, they still do not see it! Unfortunately, these residents are inadequately supervised by faculty members who have never seen child abuse and neglect themselves.

What is wrong with this picture? The lack of attention paid to the problem of child abuse and neglect by most academic psychiatrists is appalling. The lack of communication between workers in the field of child abuse and neglect and the psychiatric community is worse. It is like two ships passing in the night, each unaware of the other's presence.

A personal experience illustrates the problem. A young, female pediatric resident was having emotional difficulties. She was seeing her third psychiatrist in 10 years. As we talked, I asked whether her therapy had been helpful. "No," she replied. She reported (after I had directly asked her) that she had been severely physically and sexually abused repeatedly as a child, and as she was the oldest of many children she felt obliged to stay on to protect her younger siblings. Her physical abuse included beatings with whips and belts, knife attacks, and cigarette burns. She was also repeatedly raped by her alcoholic stepfather and his friends beginning at the age of 6.

I inquired if she had discussed these experiences with her therapists. "No, never," she replied. "Did they ask?" I said. "The first two didn't. The one I'm seeing now knows, but we don't talk about it." Incredible!

During the initial visit to her present therapist, she completed a checklist about her past history:

Question 20: "Have you ever been physically abused?" She checked "Yes."
Question 21: "In the family?" She checked "Yes."
Question 22: "Have you ever been sexually abused?" She checked "Yes."
Question 23: "In the family?" Again, "Yes."

Yet, in 10 months the therapist had never discussed these responses with her. I advised her to fire this therapist and suggested she see a noted psychiatrist who has dedicated the past 30 years to working with abusive adults and adult "survivors." She followed my advice, and she is improving.

This woman was not a unique case. In January 1983, in the 48 hours following the telecast of *Something About Amelia*, a network television movie about incest, our center received calls from 220 adult women who had been incest victims. Two-thirds of these women had never been in therapy; one-third were in therapy but, like my pediatric resident, had never discussed being sexually abused.

These sexually abused women in therapy described their depression, suicidal feelings, and other intense emotions that had been dealt with only at a symptomatic level. Their symptoms became their diagnosis! It is unclear whether the problem is educational (i.e., secondary to inadequate professional training), fiscal (i.e., therapists are reimbursed for treating symptoms having a DSM-III code number, but because the sequelae of child maltreatment have no code number, there is no reimbursement), due to some other mechanism, or some combination of the above. What is clear is the mass denial of the extent of the problem.

Most data relating early childhood abuse to later emotional problems are retrospective. Nonetheless, previously abused children are disproportionately represented in greater numbers in detention centers and prisons, special education programs, and teenage pregnancy and substance abuse programs. Prior abuse and neglect make one far more likely to be depressed, suicidal, a runaway, an abused spouse, a mother of a failure-to-thrive infant, or an active or passive participant in the abuse of one's own child.

After studying cohorts of juvenile delinquents and murderers, Lewis and her colleagues concluded that child abuse is a major factor in the development of these individuals' antisocial behavior (Lewis et al. 1979a, 1979b, 1987). Prospective follow-up studies of emotionally neglected (failure-to-thrive) infants show that a disproportionate number develop behavioral, developmental, and/or psychiatric problems (Haynes et al. 1984; Korstansson and Fallstrous 1987; Hufton and Oates 1977). Sexually abused children present many symptoms: abdominal pain, recurrent urinary tract infections, enuresis, encopresis, unusual fears, sleep disturbances, genital or anal trauma or infection, and prostitution and sexual acting-out behavior. Most significantly, perpetration to others and such adult problems as marital difficulties, sexual dysfunction, relationship problems, depression, and eating disorders have all been associated with childhood sexual abuse (Krugman 1986).

Nationally, the public and professional recognition of abuse and neglect is at an all-time high, as measured by reports to child protective services agencies. In 1962, C. H. Kempe estimated there were 447 cases of battered children in the United States. In 1986, 2.25 million reports of abused or neglected children were filed (American Humane Association 1988). According to the estimates of emotionally disturbed children cited in the various commission studies on mental health needs of children, 3 to 9.6 million children need mental health services (U.S. Congress 1986). It is clear to those of us working with the millions of abused children and their families that they need some mental health services. Where will they get these services?

Many of these 2.25 million cases of child abuse are substantiated and filed for adjudication in court. Treatment plans are filed that occasionally mandate treatment at a mental health center (for the adults) or a brief course of family therapy. But the children are rarely treated, and most plans call for little more than parental participation in parenting classes. Further, some abused children perceive family therapy as the place "where adults get together and gang up on the kids" (Jones and Alexander 1987, p. 342). The lack of access to treatment has led some judges to question whether any good is achieved by adjudicating these cases when therapists are not available to treat the families.

The lack of mental health treatment services for victims and abusers would appear to be related to the following factors: (1) Community mental health centers have been overwhelmed by the service needs of the deinstitutionalized, adult chronically mentally ill. (2) There has been a dramatic increase in recognition of sexual abuse and the treatment needs of these abusers. (3) Too few mental health professionals have received training in how to treat abused children, or understand the complexity of the problem. These complexities include differing approaches to (a) the child victim and family involved in intrafamilial abuse versus cases of extrafamilial abuse, and (b) the child's abuser if in or out of the family, or if an adult or adolescent perpetrator. It would be presumptuous of a pediatrician to tell psychiatrists how to treat children, because adequate guidance is available in the literature (Jones and Alexander 1987). However, it is not presumptuous for a pediatrician to plead with psychiatrists and other mental health professionals to develop the will to treat these children.

ROLES FOR MENTAL HEALTH WORKERS

Opportunities exist for mental health workers to involve themselves in four aspects of child abuse and neglect work.

RECOGNITION

The nature of abuse and neglect of children requires first and foremost that mental health professionals accept the existence of the problem, for should they fail to do so, they are not likely to recognize or include it in their differential diagnosis. Abused children are helpless and often coerced into secrecy. One result is that their symptoms are nonspecific. If the therapist does not consider the possibility of abuse, the symptom can be viewed as the problem, and a treatment applied to the symptom will not deal with the underlying abuse.

Many mental health professionals have difficulty asking parents or children if they have been abused. A successful approach in many centers around the country has been to view abuse as a diagnosis in the same way as any other diagnosis is considered; of course, as noted previously, because there is no DSM-III category for abuse, this approach requires some effort. Recent public opinion polls have indicated that 95% of the American public is aware of the existence of child abuse and neglect and wants something done about it (National Committee for the Prevention of Child Abuse 1988). Therefore, mental health professionals do not need to worry that by raising the issue they will be frightening or exposing parents to a problem parents do not understand. Rather, the approach can be a calm discussion indicating that the child's symptoms are consistent with several entities, one of which is abuse, and parents can be asked if they have considered that possibility. For some parents this question may stimulate a need to follow up on vague concerns they had about unusual occurrences at, for example, the babysitter's or at day care.

The parent who brings the child to a mental health therapist may or may not be the individual who has abused the child or even knows that the child has been abused. With large numbers of children in institutional or other types of day care or school settings, the risk of physical, sexual, or emotional abuse to children in out-of-home settings is considerable. The failure to recognize and evaluate abuse as a possibility has led to malpractice suits brought by parents in cases in which the mental health professional did not raise the possibility of abuse and the children were returned to out-of-home abusive environments and molested for months longer or killed. Mental health professionals must be aware that many of the problems that they deal with (e.g., suicide, reactive depression, adjustment reactions, conduct disorders) may have abuse and neglect as the key etiological factors. The literature describing the symptomatology of abused children should be included in the education of all mental health professionals.

TREATMENT

Although abusive behavior has been recognized to be an extremely complex problem that is clearly influenced by many social factors, several common characteristics have been observed in abusive parents: (1) a history of abuse in the abuser's early life; (2) lack of empathy for the child; (3) excessively high expectations of the child by the abusive adult; and (4) an impaired parent-child attachment (Steele 1987).

These four common characteristics come together in the adult to form the first of four features needed for abuse to occur: (1) a propensity to physically attack a child; (2) a crisis that puts extra stress on the adult; (3) behavior of the child that triggers the assault (most often inconsolable crying or loss of bowel or bladder control); and (4) a lack of lifelines or sources of help for the caregiver because either he or she is unable to reach out or the facilities are not available. To a greater or lesser degree, the propensity to abuse probably is inherent in most, if not all, parents.

For some abusers the cycle begins in their childhood in what has been called the "World of Abnormal Rearing" (WAR) (Helfer 1987, p. 70); for others, abuse may only be expressed when the abuser is under the influence of drugs and/or alcohol. This formulation has been adapted to sexual abuse by Finkelhor (1985), who lists four preconditions to the occurrence of sexual abuse: (1) the motivation to sexually abuse children; (2) lack or bypassing of internal inhibitors; (3) lack or bypassing of external inhibitors; and (4) erosion of resistance by the child.

In Finkelhor's model, the motivation to sexually abuse has three components: emotional congruence, sexual arousal, and blockage (from peer sexual relationships). Any or all of these factors may be present in most if not all adults at any given time. Internal inhibitors (e.g., moral standards, taboos, laws) can be bypassed if the potential abuser is taking drugs or is under the influence of alcohol. The most common external inhibitor is the presence of a protective adult or spouse to protect the child. If none is present or the spouse is ill, absent, or emotionally unable to protect, sexual abuse still may not occur because of the child's resistance.

Although resistance is not well understood, experience suggests an association with self-esteem—the lower the self-esteem, the lower the resistance. Individual and cultural/societal factors influence each of these four preconditions. The complexity of the problem mitigates against a simple solution to treatment or prevention. Recognition of these factors, including the stresses and unrealistic expectations, can only occur if the mental health professional takes an adequate clinical history. In many cases the types of information that are required are not readily available to the solo practitioner, and reliance on other professionals (e.g., teachers, social workers, law enforcement persons) may be required to obtain adequate details.

Treatment of the physically abusive family involves specialized mental health professionals and self-help support groups, as well as social interventions to reduce crises and stress in families. Interventions may be aimed at a single individual in the family, or at the extended family network that provides care for the child (Jones and Alexander 1987). Issues that often come up in treatment include the emotional unavailability of one or both parents, a history of early attachment problems, and diminished empathy.

Before embarking on the treatment process, a clear assessment of the family unit, as well as of each of the individuals within it, is needed that includes attention to the safety of the child in the family environment, and the development of a treatment plan that will ensure that child's safety while treatment is in progress. The Kempe National Center has tried consistently to take a "child's eye view" when assessing and treating a family for abuse in order to understand and appreciate a child's predicament and the pressures brought to bear in abusive situations (Jones 1986).

The treatment process has several phases. The first phase deals with an elucidation of the child's perception of the family. The second phase focuses on acknowledgment of the abuse by the adults, including the following: (a) the fact that the abuse has occurred; (b) its impact on the child; (c) the family's inability to provide adequate protection for the child; and (d) the degree and extent of the parental unavailability that the abuse has revealed. In some families there is extensive denial that the abuse took place; many therapists do not think it is possible to treat families in which such strong denial continues to exist. The acknowledgment phase may take some time. The authority of the court is often useful during this phase. A study from Florida showed that the outcome of a group of families who were ordered by the court to undergo therapy was better than the outcome of those who volunteered to accept treatment (Wolfe et al. 1980).

The third phase of treatment deals with trying to repair the emotional unavailability of the adults to the child by helping them develop sensitivity and empathy. This process also takes time. Issues arise that are related primarily to the child, e.g., responsibility for the abuse, disclosure of the abuse, the child's fear of recurrent abuse, and the child's guilt over what has occurred since the disclosure. Some adults may use their own prior victimization as a means of excusing their abusive behavior. Other adults may have difficulty confronting some of the troublesome aspects of their marital relationships.

The fourth and last phase of the treatment process is resolution, which optimally may mean reunification of the family, but may possibly involve relinquishment and/or potential termination of the parent-child relationship. This latter outcome may be viewed by many therapists as a failure, but from the child's view, this solution may be the most successful outcome. A societal need exists to recognize that for some children a "no-fault divorce" from their parents is the best possible outcome. This phase involves the courts and requires that mental health professionals be actively involved and willing to assist the juvenile court and family court systems.

Difficult families exist, and when a family is deemed untreatable, quick termination of parental rights is needed. One study (Kempe 1987) showed that approximately 10% of families with the following characteristics were untreatable: sadistic parents, some mentally handicapped parents, psychotic and borderline parents, alcohol and substance abusers who do not respond to treatment, violent and aggressive psychopathic individuals, and those families in which there have been prior violent deaths secondary to physical abuse. Jones and Alexander (1987) add the following untreatable cases in the area of child sexual abuse: those cases involving sadistic individuals, individuals who use violent force to coerce and silence their victims, or recidivist sex offenders; those cases in which there is active abusive involvement by both parents; and those cases in which the child has been exploited for a long period of time and the perpetrator continues to deny the abuse while remaining in contact with the child. Not all families with these characteristics are always untreatable, but they present more difficulties and are more commonly represented in termination cases when they come to trial.

Regrettably, most treatment efforts have occurred in model settings and have not been replicated. However, some excellent programs have been described for physically abusive and neglected families (Fraiberg 1980; Provence 1983) and sexually abusive families (Giarretto 1981). Successful programs have been characterized by (a) a multidisciplinary approach to treatment, (b) intervention enduring for 2 or more years, and (c) court involvement to ensure a good outcome (Wolfe et al. 1980). When sexual abuse is being treated, civil juvenile (protective), civil family (divorce), and criminal courts may be involved in the same case. Maintaining progress in therapy coincident with all this court activity may be difficult.

PREVENTION

The third area for involvement by mental health professionals is prevention. Prevention of physical and sexual abuse of children is possible, provided the problem is recognized. Sgroi (1975) noted that the "recognition of sexual molestation in a child is entirely dependent on the individual's inherent willingness to entertain the possibility that the condition may exist" (p. 18).

Numerous studies indicate that serious physical abuse of children can be prevented. Children at risk can be identified during the pre- and perinatal periods. Providing a home visitor—either a public health nurse (Olds et al. 1986) or a lay person (Gray et al. 1977)—will prevent severe physical abuse of children. In addition, children can learn sexual abuse prevention skills and change behaviorally following their training (Fryer et al. 1987).

Our experience at the KEEPSAFE project at the Kempe National Center indicates that a therapeutic preschool environment for physically and sexually abused children between ages 3 and 5 can help reverse developmental delays. Fourteen of the 28 children who have graduated from the preschool over the past 3 years have attained regular, "mainstream" kindergarten and have not required special education (Kempe 1987, p. 370). Prevention efforts can be either primary (e.g., giving the family or the child the education and skills that will keep them from ever abusing or being abused) or secondary (e.g., treating an abused child to prevent repetition of the cycle, or treating adults to keep them from abusing again). For preventive programs to succeed, mental health professionals need to be involved in a multidisciplinary community effort to deal with the problem.

AVOIDING CONTRIBUTING TO THE PROBLEM (PROFESSIONAL ABUSE)

Fourth, the mental health professional, like all professionals, needs to be part of the solution. Each year individuals in all professions are identified who are themselves abusive (physically, sexually, or emotionally) to children. Such instances should not be surprising as there is no reliable screening test or profile by which an abuser can be identified. We should not expect the percentage of adults in the helping professions who are abusers to be dissimilar from that of the general population. When a physician, a mental health professional, a teacher, or other professional who works with children is found to be physically, sexually, or emotionally abusing children, it becomes incumbent upon us as a profession to monitor our own representatives. While the number of our colleagues who are abusers is small, their impact is significant, because each may come in contact with many children during his or her career.

Finally, there are some community- and broad-based policy issues that require the participation and support of mental health professionals:

1. We need to implement and replicate programs that have been demonstrated to be effective. A reordering of priorities and significant political action will be required. Almost a decade after home visitation has been shown to be an effective means of preventing physical abuse of children, it is a travesty that such programs are not routine for all children.
2. Professional and public awareness should focus on the complexity of the problem. Abuse requires an adult or adolescent with the motivation to abuse who then overcomes individual and societal internal and external inhibitors, as well as the resistance of the child (Finkelhor 1985). Many sexual abuse prevention programs focus on enhancing the resistance of the child. Although some of these programs have been shown to be effective, we cannot expect young children to bear the responsibility for protecting themselves alone.
3. We must recognize that providing early and effective treatment for the child victim is one of the most effective measures we can take to prevent the intergenerational transmission of abuse and neglect. Because it does not appear imminent that psychiatry as a profession or

mental health as a system is ready to provide such treatment, we should explore alternative modes. Certain preschools, Headstart programs, elementary school classrooms, and day care centers should be designated as therapeutic so that children who are being abused at home can have a few safe hours each day. Simultaneously, we need to guard against placing children, especially those who are abused at home, in classrooms staffed by abusive teachers. In this way a few psychiatrists could oversee many treatment sites and multiply the therapeutic effect.

4. We must be aware that no one professional can alone recognize and treat abused children and their families. Multidisciplinary approaches to the recognition, treatment, and prevention of the problem are crucial (Krugman 1984). Those programs that have achieved some measure of success rely on the collaboration of physicians, social workers, law enforcement personnel, district and county attorneys, judges, mental health professionals, educators, and members of lay self-help groups. This multidisciplinary approach is like a chain that can pull a family out of their morass.

5. Funding for prevention should be sought. The proliferation of children's trust funds in 46 states is a good start. The use of victim assistance dollars to pay for treatment for child victims of crime is another. The funding effort will require political action as well as a reordering of priorities at the local, state, and national levels.

6. One needs to maintain perspective and constantly evaluate outcomes. This will take a commitment heretofore sadly lacking among many professionals in mental health and child protection. There are no true longitudinal follow-up studies of outcomes for the millions of children known to be abused and neglected.

Over the past decades the absence of a commitment by the mental health field to the problems of child abuse and neglect has been painfully obvious. This absence has contributed to the erosion of the child protective service system—from the therapeutic intervention designed to help families of the 1970s to an investigational "machine" identifying hundreds of thousands of abused children and abusive adults but helping too few of them. Unless the system evaluates its efforts, it may collapse under the weight of its processes.

The time to get involved is now.

REFERENCES

American Humane Association: Highlights of Official Child Abuse and Neglect Reporting, Annual Report. Denver, CO, American Humane Association, 1988

American Psychiatric Association: Diagnostic and Statistical Manual of Mental Disorders, 3rd Edition. Washington, DC, American Psychiatric Association, 1980

Finkelhor D: Child Sexual Abuse: New Theory and Research. New York, Free Press, 1985

Fraiberg S (ed): Clinical Studies in Infant Mental Health: The First Year of Life. New York, Basic Books, 1980

Fryer GE, Kraizer SK, Miyoshi T: Measuring children's retention of skills to resist stranger abduction: use of the simulation technique. Child Abuse Negl 11:181–186, 1987

Giarretto H: A comprehensive child sexual abuse treatment program, in Sexually Abused Children and Their Families. Edited by Mrazek PB, Kempe CH. Oxford, UK, Pergamon, 1981, pp 179–198

Gray JD, Cutler CA, Dean JG, et al: Prediction and prevention of child abuse and neglect. Child Abuse Negl 1:45–58, 1977

Haynes CF, Cutler CA, Gray JD, et al: Hospitalized care of non-organic failure to thrive. Child Abuse Negl 8:229–242, 1984

Helfer RE: The developmental basis of child abuse and neglect: an epidemiologic approach, in The Battered Child, 4th Edition. Edited by Helfer RE, Kempe RS. Chicago, IL, University of Chicago Press, 1987, pp 60–80

Hufton LW, Oates RK: Non-organic failure to thrive: a long term follow-up. Pediatrics 59:73–77, 1977

Jones DPH: Individual psychotherapy for the sexually abused child. Child Abuse Negl 10:377–385, 1986

Jones DPH, Alexander H: Treating the abusive family within the family care system, in The Battered Child, 4th Edition. Edited by Helfer RE, Kempe RS. Chicago, IL, University of Chicago Press, 1987, pp 339–359

Kempe CH: The battered child syndrome. JAMA 181:17–24, 1962

Kempe RS: A developmental approach to the treatment of abused children, in The Battered Child, 4th Edition. Edited by Helfer RE, Kempe RS. Chicago, IL, University of Chicago Press, 1987, pp 360–381

Korstansson B, Fallstrous SP: Growth at the age of 4 years subsequent to early failure to thrive. Child Abuse Neglect 11:35–40, 1987

Krugman RD: The multidisciplinary treatment of abusive and neglectful families. Pediatr Ann 13:761–764, 1984

Krugman RD: Recognition of sexual abuse in children. Pediatr Rev 8:25–30, 1986

Lewis DO, Shanok SS, Pincus JH: Juvenile male sexual assaulters. Am J Psychiatry 136:1194–1196, 1979a

Lewis DO, Shanok SS, Pincus JH, et al: Violent juvenile delinquents. J Am Acad Child Psychiatry 18:307–319, 1979b

Lewis DO, Pincus JH, Lovely R, et al: Biopsychosocial characteristics of matched samples of delinquents and nondelinquents. J Am Acad Child Adolesc Psychiatry 26:744–752, 1987

National Committee for the Prevention of Child Abuse: Memorandum. Chicago, IL, 1988

Olds DL, Henderson CR, Chamberlin R, et al: Preventing child abuse and neglect: a randomized trial of nurse home visitation. Pediatrics 78:65–78, 1986

Provence S (ed): Infants and Parents (Clinical Case Reports). New York, International Universities Press, 1983

Sgroi S: Sexual molestation of children: the last frontier of child abuse. Children Today 44 (May):18–21, 1975

Steele BS: Psychodynamic factors in child abuse, in The Battered Child, 4th Edition. Edited by Helfer RE, Kempe RS. Chicago, IL, University of Chicago Press, 1987, pp 81–114

U.S. Congress, Office of Technology Assessment: Children's mental health: problems and services—a background paper (Publ No OTA-BP-H-33). Washington, DC, U.S. Government Printing Office, 1986

Wolfe DA, Aragona J, Kaufman K, et al: The importance of adjudication in the treatment of child abusers: some preliminary findings. Child Abuse Negl 4:127–135, 1980

Index